Studies in
THE APOSTOLIC FATHERS
AND THEIR BACKGROUND

STUDIES IN
THE APOSTOLIC FATHERS
AND THEIR BACKGROUND

L. W. BARNARD

SCHOCKEN BOOKS · NEW YORK 1966

Published in U.S.A. in 1966
by Schocken Books Inc.
67 Park Avenue, New York, N.Y. 10016

Copyright © BASIL BLACKWELL 1966

Library of Congress Catalog Card No. 62-24902

BR
67
.B36

CANISIUS COLLEGE LIBRARY
BUFFALO, N. Y.

PRINTED IN GREAT BRITAIN

PREFACE

This book contains a series of studies of the Apostolic Fathers and their background. The reader will notice that several of these studies revolve around the Epistle of Barnabas. This is due not only to the special interests of the writer but to a growing conviction that this Epistle has been undervalued as a source for the understanding of both Judaism and Christianity during an eventful period of their histories.

Thanks are due to the Editors of the following journals for permission to use material from articles: New Testament Studies 7, pp. 31–45, 10, pp. 251–60; Vigiliae Christianae 15, pp. 8–22, 17, pp. 193–206; Church Quarterly Review 160, pp. 320–34, 163, pp. 421–30, 165, pp. 277–89; Scottish Journal of Theology 13, pp. 45–59; Studia Evangelica 3, pp. 306–13; Zeitschrift für die Neutestamentliche Wissenschaft 56, pp. 130–37. In some instances this material has been rewritten and considerably expanded for the purposes of this book. I am also grateful to Miss E. Balfour Barrow for typing a somewhat untidy manuscript.

L.W.B.

All Saints Rectory,
Winchester.

Erratum

Library of Congress Catalog Card No. should read: *66-24902*

CONTENTS

	PAGE
PREFACE	v
ABBREVIATIONS	ix
1 Introduction	1
2 St. Clement of Rome and the Persecution of Domitian	5
3 The Background of St. Ignatius of Antioch	19
4 The Problem of St. Polycarp's Epistle to the Philippians	31
5 Judaism in Egypt A.D. 70–135	41
6 St. Stephen and Early Alexandrian Christianity	57
7 Is the Epistle of Barnabas a Paschal Homily?	73
8 The Dead Sea Scrolls, Barnabas, the *Didache* and the Later History of the 'Two Ways'	87
9 The Use of Testimonies in the Early Church and in the Epistle of Barnabas	109
10 Hadrian and Christianity	137
11 Hermas, the Church and Judaism	151
12 The Enigma of the Epistle to Diognetus	165
INDEX	175

ABBREVIATIONS

A.C.	*Apostolic Constitutions*
A.C.O.	*Apostolic Church Order*
A.C.W.	*Ancient Christian Writers* (KLEIST)
ATR	Anglican Theological Review
BJRL	Bulletin of the John Rylands Library, Manchester
CP	Classical Philology
CQR	Church Quarterly Review
D.C.B.	*Dictionary of Christian Biography*
E.R.E.	*Encyclopaedia of Religion and Ethics*
G.J.V.	*Geschichte des jüdischen Volkes im Zeitalter Jesu Christi* (SCHÜRER)
H.D.B.	*Hastings' Dictionary of the Bible*
HTR	Harvard Theological Review
JEA	Journal of Egyptian Archaeology
JBL	Journal of Biblical Literature
JEH	Journal of Ecclesiastical History
JRS	Journal of Roman Studies
JTS	Journal of Theological Studies
Migne P.G. (L.)	Migne Patrologia Graeca (Latina)
P.W.K.	*Pauly-Wissowa-Kroll Realencyclopädie*
RB	Revue Biblique
RHE	Revue d'histoire ecclésiastique
RHR	Revue de l'histoire des religions
RTAM	Recherches de théologie ancienne et mediévale
VC	Vigiliae Christianae
VT	Vetus Testamentum

INTRODUCTION

The Apostolic Fathers is the name given to a group of Christian writers who, it was alleged, had possessed either a historical connexion with the Apostles (ἀποστολικός) or had set forth doctrinal teaching in accord with that of the Apostles.

Originally there were five authors whose works were first edited by J. B. Cotelier (Paris 1672) [1]—Barnabas, Clement of Rome, Ignatius, Polycarp and Hermas. Later there was added to this corpus Papias, the Epistle to Diognetus and, after its publication in 1883, the *Didache*. More recently [2] an attempt has been made to restrict the group to what is described as 'the pastoral literature of the primitive Church', viz., 1 Clement, the seven Epistles of Ignatius, the Letter of Polycarp and the Quadratus fragment, on the grounds that only these authors had been in contact with men of the apostolic age and had taught close to the spirit and language of the New Testament. However this restriction appears to be somewhat unjustified, as Papias had heard John the Apostle [3] and the authors of both Barnabas and the *Didache*, whom I believe belong to the early decades of the second century, used catechetical and liturgical material close to that found in the New Testament. Moreover the *Grundschrift* of Hermas belongs to the sub-apostolic age and to a Church where leading Apostles had laboured. Accordingly we shall adhere to the traditional classification and count eight writers as 'Apostolic Fathers'.

When we examine these writings closely the claim that the writers had *direct* historical association with Our Lord's Apostles, as distinct from those who had known the Apostles, is open to doubt in the case of Clement, Ignatius and Polycarp and cannot be maintained at all in the case of the other writers, with the exception of Papias. The question of their doctrinal affinity with the New Testament writings is a vaguer yardstick to use. In general Reformed theologians, under the influence of Reformation and Barthian theology, have returned a negative verdict on this question. The Apostolic Fathers represent, in their eyes, a degeneration from the purity of the Pauline doctrine of Justification by Faith alone and are, at the most, a side-track

[1] On his title page Cotelier describes the authors as 'S.S. Patrum qui temporibus Apostolicis floruerunt opera'. The next editor, L. T. Ittig (Leipzig 1699), adopts as his title Patres Apostolici, and from then on it became common.
[2] J. A. Fischer, Critical text and translation (Munich 1956).
[3] Iren. *adv. haer.* v. 33.4 = *Fr.* i. 4; cf. *Fr.* xiii. 2.

from the main lines which Christian doctrine took. However this somewhat cavalier treatment does less than justice to these writers. It is true that none of them is a systematic theologian possessed of an incisive style of writing reflecting the processes of logical thought. In this sense they present a contrast to the reasoning of St. Paul in the Epistle to the Romans and the interpretation of the Person of Christ in the Fourth Gospel. Moreover they lack the clear grasp of doctrine which the later Fathers exhibit in their formularies. Yet we should do the Apostolic Fathers an injustice if we judged them solely by the higher flights of St. Paul's mind or by the theology of St. Athanasius, St. Augustine or the Continental Reformers. They witness rather to the predominating problems which the sub-Apostolic Church faced in its day to day existence. They show that the real need of this period was the strengthening of the moral, corporate and devotional life of Christian communities scattered throughout the Graeco-Roman world which, in certain cases, were threatened with persecution or with the revival of a militant Judaism. If these writers lack theological precision, as they undoubtedly do, this is amply compensated by the sense of personal responsibility and Christian love which pervades their pages. The gentleness and serenity of Clement; the fiery zeal of Ignatius to share the martyrdom of Christ in a literal way; the constancy of Polycarp under persecution testify, as the great scholar J. B. Lightfoot avers,[1] to the influence of the Christian religion on divers types of character. And it is no different with the other writers. The moral earnestness of the authors of the *Shepherd of Hermas* and the *Didache* shines through their pages; and even in the Epistles of Barnabas and to Diognetus, where exegetical and polemic arguments are to the forefront, a genuine Christian faith and pastoral concern is evident.

The doctrinal norm of the Apostolic Fathers was the Old Testament which they regarded, when correctly interpreted, as a Christian book possessing an absolute authority in the Church. For this reason the formula ὡς γέγραπται almost always introduces an Old Testament quotation,[2] usually from the prophets who, it was believed, had foretold every detail of Our Lord's ministry and work. But it is not to be supposed that the dominance of the Old Testament in this period implies any disrespect for the Apostles and the Christian writings belonging to the apostolic age. Polycarp[3] states that the

---

[1] *St. Clement of Rome*, Vol. I, p. 7.
[2] The only exception to this is Barn. iv. 14. The passage in Polyc. *ad Phil.* xii. 1, only extant in Latin, prefaces a composite quotation from Ps. iv. 4, Eph. iv. 26 with the words: Modo, ut his scripturis dictum est. But we cannot be sure if this correctly translates the original.
[3] Polyc. *ad Phil.* vi. 3.

Christian standard is Christ and the Apostles who brought the Gospel, together with the prophets who foretold the coming of the Saviour. The other writers, in varying degrees, echo this judgement. We have to remember that the New Testament Canon, as we know it, was only just coming into existence when the Apostolic Fathers wrote and for the most part they were dependent on the tradition which had been handed down in their communities—a tradition which they freely adapted and used. Apart from the direct use of certain apostolic writings—and the Pauline epistles were especially favoured—these writers had inherited a body of Christian facts and doctrines which had long been in use in the Church's catechetical, homiletic and paraenetic teaching and liturgical worship; and in addition collections of *verba Christi*, which had been brought together in the earliest period of the Church, were known to them.[1] It would also appear that they were familiar with an authoritative outline or pattern of teaching (τύπος διδαχῆς)[2] which, at a later date, came to be codified in formal creeds. The hellenistic synagogue was another formative influence especially in the development of catechesis, homiletics and liturgy.

The treatment of the great themes of Christian doctrine in the Apostolic Fathers is speculative in the extreme. But the pre-existence of Jesus and his work in creation and redemption is generally taken for granted and, in particular, the theory that the divine element in Christ was pre-existent Spirit was widely held.[3] Of a more formal trinitarian theology there is no trace although the three-fold formula, Father, Son and Spirit was well known. Variety of interpretation, within a broadly accepted framework of facts, even within the confines of a single area, was a characteristic of the first and second century Church.

When full weight is given to these facts the Apostolic Fathers will be seen to stand firmly in the tradition of the Church and to be the necessary link between the apostolic age and the period of the Apologists.[4] They represent no degeneration from the purity of Pauline doctrine but instead an earnest attempt to sustain various Christian communities in the faith. If these writings fail to satisfy us intellectually that is because we look at them through the medium of eighteen or nineteen centuries of Christian history. In their own

[1] Ign. *ad Smyrn.* iii. 2; Polyc. *ad Phil.* ii. 3, vii. 2; Papias fragment (in Eus. *H.E.* iii. 39); Barn. iv. 14. Cf. also Justin 1 *Apol.* xiv–xvii.
[2] Rom. vi. 17; cf. Ign. *ad Eph.* xviii. 2; *ad Trall.* ix. 1–2; *ad Smyrn.* i. 1–2, Polyc. *ad Phil.* ii. 1; Barn. v. 5–6.
[3] J. N. D. Kelly, *Early Christian Doctrines*, p. 95.
[4] What Methodius says of Justin Martyr could have been said of the Apostolic Fathers: that they were men 'remote from the apostles neither in time nor in virtue'. (*de res.* ii. 18. 9).

day they endeavoured, not unsuccessfully, to express a real Christian experience which, however overlaid with an interpretation of the Old Testament alien to our ways of thought, cannot but command our respect. The judgement of Professor C. C. Richardson cannot be bettered: 'What marks these writings, taken as a whole, is their literary simplicity, their earnest religious conviction, and their independence of Hellenistic philosophy and rhetoric. They are closer to the New Testament in their artlessness, and while they may lack something of its spiritual depth, they reveal an intense concern for its basic message.'[1]

[1] Library of Christian Classics: *Early Christian Fathers*, p. 16.

II

ST. CLEMENT OF ROME AND THE PERSECUTION OF DOMITIAN

Christian writers and Roman historians have tended to approach the problem of the Persecutions of the Church from different angles. In general the first have sought to interpret the evidence provided by Christian sources and only then have turned to the non-Christian sources for confirmation or otherwise of their deductions. The second, specializing in Roman history rather than that of the Church, have tended to look for the tendentious element in the Christian tradition and, in consequence, have usually adopted a cautious attitude towards the so-called persecutions. Thus, in face of the universal Christian tradition that Domitian was a second Nero, B. W. Henderson [1] could state that his persecution, if it occurred at all, was very short and of no lasting significance. H. M. Last [2] believed that with Nero the curtain fell until it rose again on Pliny's Bithynian scene when the whole atmosphere was changed. E. T. Merrill [3] described the Christian tradition as springing from the vague notion that Domitian had for a short time been a persecutor.

What are the facts? Is there sufficient ambiguity in the Christian sources to justify the cautious view of the eminent Roman historians cited above? This question cannot be divorced from a consideration of the known facts of Domitian's reign. He was born in Rome on October 24th, A.D. 51 the second son of Vespasian and Flavia Domitilla; he lost his mother and only sister in early life, and when his father and brother became embroiled in the great Jewish War in A.D. 66 Domitian was barely fifteen years old. On his father's accession to the Imperial purple in A.D. 69 the youth received the praetorship which he held from January 1st, A.D. 70. During this period there began to appear traits in his character which were later to take on a more sinister aspect. He robbed L. Aemilianus of his wife Longina and, after living with her for some time, finally married her. Such were the complaints against him that they served to hasten his father's return to Rome from the Jewish War. Domitian was now kept in the background, as far as the direct government of the coun-

---

[1] *Five Roman Emperors*, p. 45.
[2] JRS, p. 90.
[3] *Essays in Early Christian History*, p. 173. See also the discussion by J. Moreau, 'A propos de la persécution de Domitien' in La Nouvelle Clio 5 (1953), pp. 121–9.

try was concerned, although he received further distinctions. On the death of Vespasian in A.D. 79 Titus became Emperor and Domitian, though openly spoken of as *consors imperii*, was wisely kept in an inferior position.

History presents no universal pattern which can be predicted in advance; neither is it wholly determined by social and economic causes which can be calculated by students of those branches of learning. The impact of human personalities and 'the changes and chances of this fleeting world' have a decisive effect in shaping and moulding the texture of history for good or evil, as was the case in 1940 when the advent of Sir Winston Churchill rejuvenated the English nation and put backbone into its determination to resist a mortal enemy. On September 13th, A.D. 81 the Emperor Titus died from fever and the unstable Domitian was at once acclaimed Emperor with the title *Imperator Caesar Domitianus Augustus*. His reign —which lasted until A.D. 96 when the hated Emperor met his death at the hands of his friends, his freedmen and his wife—was marked by capable administration and no small ability in the art of war. But administrative and military prowess is of little avail if the administrator or commander is a tyrant, for then constitutional safeguards can be swept aside at will and tyranny introduced by the back door. So it was with Domitian. His jealousy had already become evident early in his reign when he recalled Agricola from Britain soon after his victory, which had left that country in a pacified state. It was however after A.D. 85 that the Emperor became more and more of a tyrant and less and less of a constitutional ruler. It is significant that in A.D. 85–86 he allowed himself to be called *dominus ac deus*. Now many of the more republican of the senators were condemned and a conspiracy against the Emperor discovered and crushed. The year A.D. 89 brought triumph over the Dacians and Germans with the recognition of Domitian as victor. Yet parallel with these military successes the arrest and condemnation of distinguished persons and the confiscation of their property continued unabated. In A.D. 91 a Vestal Virgin, charged with having broken her vows, was, by order of Domitian, buried alive. This year also saw the unveiling of the great equestrian statue of the Emperor in the Forum of Rome which is celebrated by Statius in his *Siluae* i. 1. The hounding of the nobility continued as Domitian's character deteriorated; he became obsessed with the idea that anyone of note was his enemy—and in A.D. 93 the great Agricola fell victim. There followed a reign of terror almost unsurpassed in Roman history for its capriciousness and mental torture: 'His poverty made him grasping and his fears made him savage.'[1] Everyone went in fear of his life. No

---

[1] Inopia rapax, meta saevus (Suet. *Domit*. iii. 2).

one could tell if the next assault would fall on him or his family. One here, one there, was struck down from malice, jealousy or caprice and Roman life was harrowed with an agony of suspense. The reign of terror only ended with Domitian's death on September 18th, A.D. 96, when the world breathed again and Romans began to wonder how Nerva, his successor, would act towards them.

The characters of Nero and Domitian were quite different. Nero made a fierce, wholesale and reckless assault and enlisted the passions of the multitudes on his side; Domitian, on the other hand, was stealthy and treacherous, striking down his victims one by one. In some respects the last part of Domitian's reign resembles that of Stalin in Russia. The latter's victims were carefully selected, subjected to brain torture, and then arraigned on 'trumped-up' charges which generally ended in a confession of guilt. Then they were shot without mercy or pity. In some respects this kind of 'persecution' is more terrible to endure than a frontal assault, for psychological factors play a major role in it. These considerations need to be born in mind when considering whether Domitian was a 'persecutor' of the Christian Church. As they look back over the years those who lived through the terror of Stalin's Russia may well regard that as a more dreadful time than the Russo-German war of 1942–5, when at least everyone knew that no quarter would be given on either side and that wholesale massacres would occur.

The Christian tradition about the so called 'persecution' of Domitian first appears in the *Apology* of Melito, Bishop of Sardis, which he addressed to Marcus Aurelius some seventy years after Domitian's death: 'Alone of all the Emperors, Nero and Domitian, misled by certain malicious persons, saw fit to slander our faith.' (Eus.*E.H.* iv. 26). This tells us little, as it is clearly influenced by Melito's theory that the bad Emperors were persecutors while the good Emperors were favourable to the Christian religion. More to the point is a statement by Melito's contemporary, Hegesippus, which is recorded by Eusebius:

'There were yet living the family of our Lord, the grandchildren of Jude, called the brother of our Lord, according to the flesh. These were reported as being of the family of David, and were brought to Domitian by the Evocatus (i.e. the prefect of Judaea). For this Emperor was as much alarmed at the appearance of Christ as Herod. He put the question, whether they were of David's race, and they confessed that they were. *He then asked them what property they had, or how much money they owned.* And both of them answered, that they had between them only nine thousand denarii, and this they had not in silver, but in the value of a piece of land, containing only thirty-nine acres . . . When asked, also, respecting Christ and his Kingdom, what was its nature, and when and where it was to appear, they replied, that it was not a temporal nor an earthly Kingdom, but celestial and angelic; . . . *Upon which Domitian despising them made no reply; but treating them with contempt as simpletons, commanded them to be dismissed, and by a decree ordered the persecution to cease.*' (Eus.*E.H.* iii. 20, italics mine).

The significance of this statement of Hegesippus lies in the words which I have italicized. It appears that it was not Christianity as a doctrinal system which Domitian wished to persecute but persons of eminence whom he might suspect of undermining his authority. The grandsons of Jude were peasants and of no account—so the persecution ceased. A further point is that the Emperor would not tolerate Christians who might incite the conquered Jewish population to acts of rebellion.

This account falls into line with what we know, from Roman sources, of the character of the Emperor. Christians no more than others would escape if Domitian thought they were a threat to his position. But it is unlikely, without firm evidence to the contrary, that he would have instituted a wholesale persecution of Christians simply because of their faith. Domitian was suspicious of people rather than of their beliefs.

Later Christian tradition did not understand this and has painted the Emperor in the darkest hues. Tertullian describes Domitian as resembling Nero in savagery but having his wits about him and soon giving up the persecution which he had initiated (*Apol.* v; cf. Eus.*E.H.* iii. 20). Eusebius states that Domitian at length established himself as the successor of Nero, in his hatred and hostility to God: 'He was the second that raised a persecution against us, although his father Vespasian had attempted nothing to our prejudice.' (Eus.*E.H.* iii. 17.) Eusebius states that even pagan historians record this persecution and its martyrdoms in their histories (*E.H.* iii. 18). In subsequent writers the persecution of Domitian is portrayed with increasingly vivid details; even that of Nero falls into the background.[1] While the tendentious element in these accounts is obvious we must allow for the fact that a reign of terror, in which the victims were killed one by one, would take on darker hues to those who looked back on it over a period of years. Tradition after all does not arise out of nothing.

We now turn to the contemporary Christian literary evidence for the persecution of Domitian which is found in the First Epistle

[1] J. B. Lightfoot has given the relevant passages in *St. Clement of Rome*, Vol. I, pp. 105—15.

of Clement, written to the Church in Corinth which was suffering from some grave internal dissensions. This document is assigned, by near universal assent, to the last decade of the first century and is the earliest writing to issue from the Roman Church after apostolic times. Clement, according to Hermas *Vis.* ii. 4. 3, was a kind of foreign secretary of the Roman Church.[1] Certainly, to judge from his Epistle, he acted on behalf of his Church. The letter itself contains no personal references; the first person plural is used throughout and Clement's name nowhere appears. His personality, at once attractive, modest and reasonable, is absorbed in the Church of which he is leader and spokesman.

It has generally been assumed by Christian commentators that this Epistle contains references to the 'persecution' of Domitian. This was maintained with great erudition by Bishop Lightfoot in his justly famous commentary. Recently however Mr. R. L. P. Milburn (now Dean of Worcester) in an important, though neglected, article [2] has sought to show that 1 Clement contains no allusion whatsoever to persecution at Rome or 'anything of that kind'. A few other scholars, from different angles, have cast doubt on the usual view. Thus Edmundson in his Bampton lectures, *The Church of Rome in the First Century*, argues strongly for a date *c.* A.D. 70 and refers 1 Clem. i. 1 to the outbreak of persecution under Nero.[3] The Roman historian E. T. Merrill went to the other extreme and argued for a date as late as A.D. 140.[4] Both of these dates seem quite impossible in view of the evidence cited below. There appears to be no good reason, on the literary evidence, for doubting the usual date in the last decade of the first century.

Mr. Milburn (and we shall deal mainly with his thesis) places great emphasis on the translation of 1 Clem. i. 1, the opening words of the Epistle, in which Clement apologizes for his delay in writing to the Corinthian Christians:

> 'Owing to the sudden and repeated misfortunes (συμφορὰς) and calamities (περιπτώσεις) which have befallen us, we consider that our attention has been somewhat delayed in turning to the

[1] Clement is a baffling figure. In most lists of the early rulers of the Roman Church he is placed third, after Peter and Paul, being preceded by Linus and Anencletus or Cletus. In the Liberian list he is placed second, as in Augustine (*Ep.* liii). In the Clementine Romances he follows Peter, as with Tertullian (*de praes.* xxxii). Attempts to explain or reconcile these discrepancies are, at the most, conjectures and we must resign ourselves to ignorance as to Clement's order and status.
[2] CQR 139 (Jan.–Mar. 1945), pp. 154–64.
[3] He is rather surprisingly followed by L. E. Elliott-Binns, *The Beginnings of Western Christendom*, p. 102.
[4] *Essays in Early Church History*.

questions disputed among you, beloved, and especially the abominable and unholy sedition, alien and foreign to the elect of God, which a few rash and self-willed persons have made blaze up to such a frenzy that your name, venerable and famous, and worthy as it is of all men's love, has been much slandered.'

Mr. Milburn maintains that περιπτώσεις, translated 'calamities' by Kirsopp Lake and 'reverses' by Bishop Lightfoot, could equally well mean 'accidents'. In this case the word could refer to some troublesome domestic hindrances in the life of the Roman Church which had caused this delay in writing to Corinth. This interpretation is just possible linguistically as, according to Liddell and Scott, περίπτωσις has the meaning 'accident' or 'chance occurrence' in Heliod. vi. 14, Hipp. xxvi. 1 (the last in a medical context). Its meaning, in Classical Greek, is close to συμφορά which in Pindar, Aeschylus (and often in Attic Greek) has the meaning 'misfortune' or 'mishap'. If the reading of Codex Constantinopolitanus (περιστάσεις) is accepted (Latin *impedimenta*) then again this could refer to hindrances or unfavourable circumstances. However these misfortunes or unfavourable circumstances (whatever they were) are described as 'sudden and repeated'. This does not suggest a mere internal, domestic upset within the Roman Church but repeated pressure which has caused the Church grave concern such that its Bishop has been delayed in writing to another Christian community which *is* suffering from grave internal trouble. Moreover if the Church of Rome had been suffering from the kind of thing which had afflicted the Corinthian church what kind of advice or help could it have given? Would Clement's message of harmony, unity, order, moderation and reasonableness of conduct have meant much? The primacy of Rome in early times was a moral and spiritual one. In seeking to remove the mote from their brother's eye would they not have forgotten the beam in their own eye? It therefore seems more probable that these sudden and repeated misfortunes and unfavourable circumstances had come upon the Roman Church from outside.

Mr. Milburn then states that apart from this disputed passage Clement contains 'no other allusion to persecution at Rome or anything of the kind'.[1] It would seem that this statement cannot be substantiated by a careful study of the Epistle. In Chapter iv Clement has given O.T. examples of those who were persecuted from the motive of jealousy as illustrations of the troubles at Corinth. He then passes, in Chapters v and vi, to more recent examples of this spirit:

[1] Op. cit., p. 157.

'But, to cease from the examples of old time, let us come to those who contended in the days nearest to us; let us take the noble examples of our own generation. Through jealousy and envy the greatest and most righteous pillars of the Church were persecuted and contended unto death. Let us set before our eyes the good apostles: Peter, who because of unrighteous jealousy suffered not one or two but many trials, and having thus given his testimony went to the glorious place which was his due. Through jealousy and strife Paul showed the way to the prize of endurance . . . and thus passed from the world and was taken up into the Holy Place —the greatest example of endurance. To these men with their holy lives was gathered a great multitude of the chosen, who were the victims of jealousy and offered among us the fairest example in their endurance under many indignities and tortures.'

The phrases 'days nearest to us', 'our own generation', used immediately after the Old Testament examples quoted in Ch. iv, cannot easily refer to events in the last year or two, as must have been the case if the letter had been written at the end of Nero's reign. On the other hand the words 'our own generation' are unlikely to refer to a period 50 or 60 years in the past as would be the case if Clement had been writing during the reign of Hadrian. The use of bishop and presbyter as interchangeable terms in the Epistle also points to a date not too far advanced into the second century. A reference to some thirty years in the past, when St. Peter and St. Paul and a great multitude died in the Neronian persecution, is certainly not out of keeping with the context.

Clement then passes from the sufferings of Christians in the past, through the jealousy of a tyrant, to the present time. vii. 1 reads:

'We are not only writing these things to you, beloved, for your admonition, but also to remind ourselves; for we are in the same arena (σκάμματι), and the struggle is before us.'

This verse is a *crux interpretum*. Those who deny that 1 Clement contains any allusion to Christians being persecuted in Clement's day must either forget this verse or explain it away. Moreover if, on the theory of Edmundson and Elliott-Binns, the Epistle was written *immediately after* the Neronian persecution it is difficult to see why Clement should have introduced historical stages into his argument —Old Testament examples in Ch. iv; St. Peter, St. Paul and the Neronian martyrs in Chs. v and vi. 1 (the noble examples of our own generation), followed by 'the same struggle is before us' in vii. 1.[1]

[1] This early dating is also precluded by the fact that the Church of Corinth is called ἀρχαία (xlvii. 6).

Furthermore if, in vii. 1, Clement is merely referring to *internal* troubles of the Roman Church, it is difficult to see why he should give, in Chs. v and vi, references to the *external* persecution by Nero. It would therefore appear probable that vii. 1 should be taken as a reference to a struggle in which the Church of Rome, in Clement's day, was engaged—viz., the possibility that its members might be selected for martyrdom at any time—a situation which required much patient endurance.

The word σκάμμα (literally, list) came to refer to a trench and then to an arena surrounded by a trench or dug up and covered with sand. Many examples occur of its symbolic use both in Classical and Christian writers and here it is metaphorically used of the athletic arena in which the contestants struggle. So Clement and the Roman Church remind themselves that persecution is not yet a thing of the past.

The references in 1 Clement could support the view that the Epistle was written just after the reign of Domitian when the Church was not sure how the new Emperor, Nerva, would react.[1] Or it could perhaps be fitted into a lull a year or two before Domitian was assassinated. In any event we shall not go far wrong if we assign its composition somewhere between the years A.D. 94 and 97.

It is perhaps not without significance that the sins of jealousy and envy are constantly emphasized in Chs. i—vii. For Clement this had a double meaning. He can cite examples of jealousy to the Church of Corinth in order to show how this sin can ruin the internal peace of a community; yet he can also refer to the Neronian martyrs as victims of jealousy and envy from without. Then, in Ch. vii, Clement can remind his own Church that they are struggling and contending against a similar jealousy from without, with the suggestion that martyrdom is always a possibility. This, together with the reference in i. 1 to the sudden and repeated misfortunes which had befallen the Roman Church, fits in with the character of Domitian as revealed by the non-Christian literary sources. He did not persecute groups *en masse*. But he carefully selected and struck down his victims one by one, driven on by malice and jealousy and the belief that everyone of note was his enemy. It is essential for the understanding of Clement's references to realize that the Roman Church in his day was not mainly composed of slaves or the lower strata of Roman Society. J. B. Lightfoot, in memorable phrases, describes it thus: 'It is the tendency of religious movements to work their way upwards from beneath, and Christianity was no exception to the general rule. Starting from slaves and dependants it advanced silently step by step

---

[1] Dio states that Nerva forbade the bringing of accusations of *maiestas* or 'Jewish life' (lxviii. 1).

till at length it laid hands on the princes of the imperial house.'[1] This gaining of converts from the higher ranks of Roman society took place in the decades following the Neronian persecution, but progress was broken by the accession of Domitian who in a succession of sharp, sudden, partial assaults, and motivated by malice or jealousy, struck down his luckless victims. It is very unlikely that Christians would have escaped.[2] The universal Christian tradition that this Emperor was a second Nero may not be true in strict historical fact; yet in another sense it is true, for the Christians, no less than others, suffered mental torture as they were left in an agony of suspense in many ways harder to bear than direct persecution. Tradition does not arise out of nothing, as the exponents of *Formgeschichte* sometimes imagine.

We now turn briefly to the vexed question of the identification of the martyrs during Domitian's reign. One of the most celebrated to be struck down was the Emperor's cousin Titus Flavius Clemens whom he held at one time in high favour. Domitian had given him his niece Flavia Domitilla in marriage and had designated their sons as heirs to the Empire. Yet within a year of nominating Flavius Clemens as his colleague in the consulship Domitian put him to death, banished his wife to Pandateria and his daughter to Pontia. No reason is given in Suetonius' account for his demise, although he states that Flavius Clemens was characterized by 'utterly contemptible indolence' (*contemptissimae inertiae*) which may refer to a certain reluctance in the performance of political and civic duties as well as innate idleness. Dio Cassius tells far more; he states[3] explicitly that Flavius Clemens and Domitilla were accused of atheism. This same accusation, he adds, was brought against many others who showed a bias towards Jewish customs. This last statement is significant. Dean Milburn[4] attempted to evade its force by stating that what Domitian feared was an affection of Jewish beliefs and practices by distinguished citizens who could then belittle his claim to be divine. It may be doubted if this explanation will do. Judaism, as distinct from Christianity, was a *religio licita* and the description 'atheism' was out of place in connexion with it. The combination of Jewish

[1] Op. cit., Vol. I, pp. 29–30.
[2] Pliny, in his famous letter to Trajan, says that though many Christians had been tried for their lives in Rome during his recollection, he was ignorant of the procedure followed in such cases. As Pliny was but an infant in the time of Nero, and the other Emperors in his time, save Domitian, were not 'persecutors' we may be certain that these trials occurred in Domitian's reign. This is very significant pagan evidence. Cf. *Ep.* x. 96.
[3] Dio lxvii. 14. This part of Dio's history is contained in the abridgement of Xiphilinus, an 11th century monk of Constantinople.
[4] Op. cit., p. 160.

rites with the charge of atheism, so often levelled against Christians from the time of Nero onwards,[1] points unmistakably to Christianity and not Judaism.[2] As a Christian Flavius Clemens would not patronize vicious amusements or the State Religion. Many civic and political duties, in a period when men went in fear of their lives, might be closed to a practising Christian. The literary evidence, such as it is, is in favour of Flavius Clemens and his wife being Christians—a striking example of how Christianity, by the end of the first century, had gained a footing within the Imperial Family.

[1] Cf. *Mart. Polyc.* ix; Justin, 1 *Apol.* i. 6 and ii. 8; Athenag. *Suppl.* 3, 4, 30; Tert. *Apol.* x ff. See further P. Allard, *Histoire des persécutions pendant les deux premières siècles*, pp. 104–5.

[2] Miss E. M. Smallwood in her informative and fully documented article 'Domitian's Attitude toward the Jews and Judaism' in CP 51 (1956), pp. 1–13 has followed Milburn (to whom she does not refer) in seeking to show that Flavius Clemens and Domitilla were σεβόμενοι or god-fearers living on the fringe of Judaism who followed Jewish customs to a sufficient extent to be subject to attack from Domitian. She sees the case for regarding them as Christians as resting on a flimsy foundation. Her theory appears to rest on the following premises:
  (i) Conversions to Judaism constituted 'atheism' as it involved refusing Domitian the divine honours which he sought.
  (ii) The fact that Flavius Clemens held high public office is an indication that he was not a Christian.
  (iii) Talmudic and Midrashic writers give support to the view that he was a Jew.
  (iv) Indications that the Jewish race was in danger under Domitian are to be found in Josephus' *Antiquities*.
We have no space to elaborate our objections to Miss Smallwood's thesis in detail but the following points may be noted:
  (i) There is no evidence in Classical or Jewish writings that Domitian attacked Jews *by race* or that they suffered any disabilities during his reign. The status of Judaism as a *religio licita* continued unaffected and there are no indications that Jews were forced to commit idolatry. Why then asssume that god-fearers and proselytes were treated differently from circumcised Jews and regarded as 'atheists'? The one instance of 'atheist' applied to the Jews which Miss Smallwood quotes (by Apollonius Molon—Jos. *in Ap.* ii. 148) comes from the 1st century B.C. and is not relevant to Domitian's reign. On the other hand the fact that Christianity was not a *religio licita* and its followers had the charge of 'atheism' commonly levelled against them would appear to support the interpretation which I have given above.
  (ii) is clearly based on an *a priori* assumption as to the social composition of the Roman Church in the last decade of the 1st century.
  (iii) The Jewish traditions cited by Miss Smallwood are garbled and late and, in particular, there is nothing to show that the proselyte Kalonymos is the same person as Flavius Clemens.
  (iv) Josephus' *Antiquities* only deals with events down to 66 A.D. Deductions as to the *Sitz im Leben* of Judaism in Domitian's reign, when Josephus' work was completed, are too subjective to warrant any certainty in the absence of direct references.

It is possible, but cannot be proved, that another of Domitian's victims, Acilius Glabrio, was a Christian. All we are told is that he was put to death because he was accused of the same kind of charges as many of Domitian's victims—and because he fought with wild beasts (Dio lxvii. 14). The context suggests that these charges were 'Jewish practices', although this is not quite certain and it is not explicitly stated that he was charged with 'atheism'.

Archaeology, in the past, has been invoked in support of the view that certain of Domitian's victims were Christians. The publication of P. Styger's great work, *Die römischen Katakomben*, in 1932, and subsequent work (see especially L. Hertling and E. Kirschbaum, *Die römischen Katakomben und ihre Martyrer* (1950)), has, however, cast doubts on the dating of the catacombs, and the evidence is too uncertain to warrant any finality in the matter. In particular the inscriptions of the *gens Acilia*, found in the vault of the Acilii, appear to belong to the mid-second century at the earliest and any connexion with Acilius Glabrio is ruled out. However the literary evidence from Roman and Christian sources,[1] discussed above, is both early and sound and points to the same conclusion, viz., that Domitian was not a wholesale 'persecutor' of the Church in the sense that Nero was; rather he singled out individual Christians who were prominent members of the Church of Rome, among them his kinsmen Flavius Clemens and Domitilla. Domitian's persecution was a succession of short, sharp, assaults—the series of sudden and repeated misfortunes which had prevented Clement, on behalf of his Church, from writing to the Church in Corinth. When he does write he can remind his own flock what the sins of jealousy and envy had wrought in the past and what, through Domitian, they were still capable of doing (vi. 4–vii. 1).

The Idea of the State in Clement's Epistle

The early Christian attitude towards the State was founded on the teaching of Jesus—'Render unto Caesar the things that are Caesar's; and unto God the things that are God's.' Dr. Selwyn in his well-known commentary on 1 Peter [2] has shown that *c.* A.D. 55 there came into being an expanded catechetical 'form' or 'pattern' which was a later version of the earliest baptismal form. This contained a Christian social code which had a section on obedience to the State which

---

[1] Some scholars think that parts of *The Shepherd of Hermas* have been influenced by a recent persecution in which some Christians had denounced their brethren—thus creating the problem of whether these *lapsi* could be later readmitted to communion. In view of the uncertainty as to the dating of the *Shepherd* I have not used its evidence.
[2] Pp. 426 f.

was used by St. Peter and St. Paul in 1 Pet. ii. 13–17, Rom. xiii. 1–7 and later by the writers of 1 Tim. ii. 1–3 and Titus iii. 1–3, 8. The dominating theme of this catechetical teaching was subordination to the earthly power although in 1 Timothy this is replaced by intercession for rulers. Both 1 Peter and Romans are emphatic as to the divine origin and sanction of the State and its function of restraining and punishing crime, although St. Paul develops both points at length and in characteristic Pauline phrases. Both writers are also agreed on the positive function of the State in encouraging well-doing, an element in the catechetical pattern which also appears in Tit. iii. 1, 8 and possibly 1 Tim. ii. 2. Christians owe the civil power an inward loyalty and not merely an external submission, and this applies even in times of bad government. All four New Testament Epistles which contain fragments of this code connect obedience to the State with the *universal* element in Christianity: 'honour *all* men' (1 Peter), 'render to *all* their dues' (Romans), shew meekness 'towards *all* men' (Titus), offer prayers 'for *all* men' (1 Timothy). Dr. Selwyn, after a careful examination of the references to the State in these Epistles, concludes that the brief passage 1 Pet. ii. 13–17 is nearest to the original teaching given to catechumens.

Clement of Rome takes over and develops this traditional Christian teaching which would have come down to him through the tradition of the Roman Church—and in any case he was directly acquainted with 1 Peter and Romans, which contain the relevant passages. Clement, in fact, goes further in his attitude towards the State than anything found in the New Testament. In spite of the persecution of Nero and the sharp assaults of Domitian, Clement can model the discipline of Christians on that of the Roman Legions:

'Let us then serve in our army, brethren, with all earnestness, following his faultless commands. Let us consider those who serve our generals, with what good order, habitual readiness, and submissiveness they perform their commands. Not all are prefects, nor tribunes, nor centurions, nor in charge of fifty men, or the like, but each carries out in his own rank the commands of the Emperor and of the generals.' (xxxvii. 1–3.)

The climax of Clement's teaching is found in the liturgical section, Chs. lix. 3–lxi. 3, which contains a sublime prayer for temporal rulers:

'Grant that we may be obedient to thy almighty and glorious name, and to the rulers and governors upon the earth. Thou, Master, hast given the power of sovereignty to them through thy excellent and inexpressible might, that we may know the glory and honour given to them by thee, and be subject to them, in nothing resisting thy will. And to them, Lord, grant health, peace, concord, firmness that they may administer the government which thou has given them without offence. For thou, heavenly Master, King of eternity, hast given to the sons of men glory and honour and power over the things which are on the earth; do thou, O Lord, direct their counsels according to that which is good and pleasing before thee, that they may administer with piety in peace and gentleness the power given to them by thee, and may find mercy in thine eyes.' (lx. 4–lxi. 2.)

The attitude towards the Roman Government found in 1 Clement is distinguished by its reserve and by its development of traditional Christian teaching concerning submission to the temporal power. Clement nowhere names Nero or Domitian, although his allusions to them are unmistakable. They were bad rulers, in his eyes, animated by jealousy of the Christians; yet that did not invalidate the divine origin of the State. No doubt great caution was needed, as Christianity, in Clement's day, had gained converts within the Imperial household; persecuted and persecutors were at close quarters and it was useless to invite trouble by blatant opposition. A further point is that Corinth, the destination of the letter, was a city exclusively Roman in the first century. It had been refounded as a Roman colony in 44 B.C. with freedmen and Roman citizens as the colonists. These were antipathetic to the Greeks and established close relations with Rome—a loyalty that persisted into the second century of our era.

Names on inscriptions, sculpture, architecture—all was Roman.[1] There was therefore a natural ethnic solidarity between the Roman Church and that of Corinth which would have made it impolitic, even if Clement had so wanted, to criticize Roman law and institutions and their focus in the person of the Emperor. Yet these considerations do not fully explain the attitude towards the State found in Clement's Epistle. As is the case with many of the influential men of history we dare not ignore the human element—the character of Clement himself. He was a man who eschewed violence. He saw no reason why the world should suddenly come to an end because, for the moment, it had a bad and ruthless Emperor who was unrepresentative of the Empire. The harmony and peace which he enjoined on the Corinthian Church was the fruit of his own gentle and forbearing character. Clement had learnt Christ in the hardest school

---

[1] This is well brought out by R. van Cauwelaert in his essay 'L'intervention de Rome à Corinthe vers l'an 96' in RHE April 1945. I owe this reference to W. K. Lowther-Clarke, *The First Epistle of Clement*, p. 19.

of all—the school of uncertainty and insecurity when men's hearts were failing them for fear—and there shines through his pages a serene and sublime faith in God which enabled him to endure manfully all the changes and chances of this fleeting world. In this he is to be distinguished from another Christian writer whose work, at least in its present form, was occasioned by the cruelties of Domitian's reign. For John of Patmos the present age was dying; the Roman State was anti-Christ which was doomed to terrible tortures through which Christians alone would be preserved for bliss. No greater contrast can be imagined than that between the seer of Patmos with his hatred of the Roman Power and his use of sub-Christian ideas of vengeance, and the gentle leader of the Roman Church with his sense of order, sobriety of temper, sweet reasonableness and forgiving spirit in a time of great difficulty.[1] We cannot doubt who is nearer to the mind of Christ.

Clement of Rome, a voice speaking across the ages to the modern world, would tell us not to despair of the State, not to retire into an inner world of the spirit and neglect civic responsibilities and duties, however difficult and dangerous they may be at times. Above all he would remind us that it is no purpose of the Christian Gospel to overthrow by force social and political institutions, however obnoxious and anti-Christian they may be at one period or another. Rather it is the work of Christianity and the Church to provide a ferment, a new power, a new life, which can be a leaven working slowly and silently—now one way, now another—in the hearts and minds of men and so slowly infusing a new spirit into social and political institutions. In our own time nothing is needed more than informed prayer for temporal sovereigns, Christian and non-Christian alike, for rulers in the West and for those behind the Iron and Bamboo curtains; nothing is needed more than the reserve of the great prayer of the Church of Rome contained in 1 Clem. lx–lxi. It was not for nothing that Lightfoot could write: 'When we remember that this prayer issued from the fiery furnace of persecution after the recent experience of a cruel and capricious tyrant like Domitian, it will appear truly sublime—sublime in its utterances, and still more sublime in its silence. Who would have grudged the Church of Rome her primacy, if she had always spoken thus?'[2]

---

[1] The second-century reception of the Apocalypse in Rome accentuates this difference. Lowther-Clarke, op. cit., p. 6, describes Clement's attitude as 'marvellous'.

[2] Op. cit., Vol. I, p. 384.

III

THE BACKGROUND OF ST. IGNATIUS OF ANTIOCH

Ignatius of Antioch is one of the key figures of the Church of the early second century. Unlike the other Apostolic Fathers he lays bare his innermost thoughts and feelings. In the seven genuine Ignatian Epistles, written or dictated while on his last journey to Rome, there is revealed a person passionately devoted to his faith—one who strongly desires martyrdom—yet one who is concerned with the practical details of Church life and order and especially with the problem of heresy and schism. Ignatius cannot wholly be explained in terms of modern psychology although his language sometimes betrays an exuberance and wildness which could be interpreted as neurotic. However we must never forget that Ignatius was a condemned prisoner who was being transported across Asia Minor in the custody of Roman soldiers whom he calls 'ten leopards'[1] 'who become worse for kind treatment' (*ad Rom.* v. 1). Letters quickly dictated [2] in such circumstances are likely to deal with a few main topics and to lack a developed presentation of ideas. The fact that the Ignatian letters strongly resemble one another in subject matter should cause no surprise. Ignatius was not writing in the leisurely manner of the academic scholar. This fact accounts for the reiteration of his views on episcopacy and his horror of separation from the Church. The saint already lives in the supernatural world in his desire to be with Christ and everywhere he sees indications of this world impinging on the everyday world of space and time. The bishops, presbyters and deacons on earth not only resemble—they *are* God and Jesus Christ. Such mysticism, which seems so lofty and exalted in comparison with the struggling conditions of the Church in the early second century, cannot but move us to admiration. Ignatius is one of those Fathers who cannot be fitted into any hard and fast category. He is unique in every sense of the word.

More recent Ignatian studies have sought to illuminate the background of Ignatius' life and theology. H. Schlier in his *Religionsgeschichtliche Untersuchungen zu den Ignatiusbriefen* (1929) and H. W. Bartsch in his *Gnostisches Gut und Gemeindetradition bei Ignatius von*

---

[1] This is the first instance of the word 'leopard' in Greek or Latin literature.

[2] All the letters were probably written within a fortnight. Those to the Ephesians, Magnesians and Trallians may have been written within a day of each other.

Antiochien (1940) studied the Epistles in the light of the all-embracing German religious-historical school (*Religionsgeschichtliche Schule*). According to this school there stands in the background of Ignatius' thought, as behind all early Christian literature, an Iranian-Gnostic myth of a descending and ascending redeemer which was widely known in the ancient world and had many ramifications in different systems. According to Schlier this form of Gnosticism was such a strong influence on Ignatius that it fully explains his theology. Bartsch, on the other hand, holds that Gnostic influence penetrated Ignatius' thought mainly in his idea of the Unity of God. He distinguishes three strands in Ignatius: the early Christian preaching; an indirect Gnosticism mediated through the Johannine theology; and a direct Gnostic influence. We shall discuss these positions later in this chapter—suffice it to say that the major problem which confronts Ignatian studies today is the understanding of the background of the Ignatian Epistles. In this quest more recent studies have moved away from that concentration on the 'rise' of the monarchical episcopate, the ministry and Church order which characterized earlier studies. The publication of V. Corwin's *St. Ignatius and Christianity in Antioch* (1960) illustrates this change of emphasis.

We shall now attempt to isolate three strands in the background of Ignatius which influenced his theology:

(1) The Local Situation

The Epistles were written within a short period as the Saint journeyed through Asia Minor and they discuss burning problems which had arisen in the Churches of the western end of that area. Ignatius, even in his most lofty moments, has his feet firmly rooted in the everyday life and problems of these small Christian communities. It is then not surprising that an older generation of scholars tended to treat the Ignatian Epistles primarily as sources for the Church history of Asia Minor and even spoke of an 'Asia Minor Theology' as distinct from ordinary Gentile Christianity.[1]

Harnack could say that Ignatius' theology is of the same nature as that of Melito and Irenaeus whose predecessor he is.[2] Albert Schweitzer spoke of the 'hellenization of Christianity by Ignatius and the Asia Minor theology'.[3] It may be doubted if these *ad hoc* judgements will do. Ignatius cannot be interpreted as a kind of intermediate figure between the author of the Fourth Gospel and Melito of Sardis or as the supreme example of hellenization. The essence

---
[1] F. Loofs was however an exception. See his *Leitfaden zum Studium der Dogmengeschichte*, 4th ed. (1906), p. 102.
[2] *Dogmengeschichte*, 4th edn., Vol. I, p. 241.
[3] *The Mysticism of Paul the Apostle*, p. 343.

of his thought springs out of his experience as Bishop of Antioch in spite of his concern for the Churches of Asia Minor. He is primarily a witness to a type of Syrian Christianity which was known and practised in Antioch in the early second century, to which he himself had contributed. A recognition of this fact will do much to explain certain elements in his thought which have been much misunderstood.

The city of Antioch had been made a *civitas libera* by Pompey and such it remained until the time of Antoninus Pius, who made it a *colonia*. In ancient times, although it was called 'the Beautiful' (ἡ καλή), the city's moral reputation was never high. Enjoyment of life was the main occupation of its inhabitants and a sense of responsibility only incidental. It is significant that the city was called 'Antioch upon Daphne' after the name of the pleasure gardens, five miles away, whose name has come down through history with an evil connotation. Juvenal flung one of his wittiest jibes at his own decadent Imperial city when he said that the Orontes had flowed into the Tiber (*Sat.* iii. 62). The brilliant civilization of the hellenistic age had failed to redeem the turbulent, fickle and dissolute character of the Syrian. Cicero, it is true, flattered Antioch as a city of most learned men and most liberal studies (*pro Arch.* iii) but the sober verdict of history is different. No Greek region has fewer memorial stones or fewer inscriptions to show.[1]

The population of Antioch was cosmopolitan. A Jewish community had been in existence since the city's foundation and Jews were allowed special privileges by the Seleucid rulers. Moreover in the time of Pompey a powerful corporation of Roman merchants existed, which dominated trade and commerce. Not far to the north the Roman legions were stationed and, as so often happens with military personnel, intermarriage with local girls was not infrequent. New groups of one kind and another were constantly attracted to Antioch, the third city of the Empire, bringing with them their beliefs and ways of life. Yet beneath this cosmopolitanism Antioch's Semitic and oriental character remained dominant.

It was from this cosmopolitan population that the Christian Church drew its members. In the free atmosphere of the Syrian capital the original disciples had first been called Christians (Acts xi. 26)—the designation perhaps coming from the populace who quickly noticed a new phenomenon in their midst. By Ignatius' time

[1] This is well brought out by G. Downey in his monumental study, *A History of Antioch in Syria from Seleucus to the Arab Conquest* (Princeton 1961). But Downey points out that the paucity of the archaeological and epigraphic evidence is compensated by the fullness of the literary sources—especially for the last three centuries before the Arab Conquest.

Christianity[1] had embraced much Semitic and oriental imagery into its theology and liturgy. The Odes of Solomon show this imagery run riot. In Ignatius it is more disciplined. Thus he speaks of 'the evil odour of the doctrine of the Prince of this world' (*ad Eph.* xvii. 1). He regards the Church as the planting of the Father and its members as branches of the Cross (*ad Trall.* xi. 1-2); those who separate themselves from the Church are wicked offshoots which bear deadly fruit (*ad Trall.* xi. 1). In Ignatius we find references to the sounds of the ear. The harp suggests the bishop who is 'attuned to the commandments as a harp to its strings' (*ad Phil.* i. 2) or the presbyters attuned to the bishop; 'by your concord and harmonious love Jesus Christ is being sung' (*ad Eph.* iv. 1). Christians assembled together for worship join in this choir in order to 'receive the key of God in unison, and sing with one voice through Jesus Christ to the Father, that he may both hear you and may recognize, through your good works, that you are members of his Son' (*ad Eph.* iv. 2). Such imagery, which goes beyond anything found in the New Testament, came from Ignatius' Syrian background. Such is also the case with his passionate feeling, his exuberance, his stream of paradoxes and epigrams and his desire for martyrdom. In essence, although his name Egnatus is Latin, he remained an Oriental.

Miss Corwin, in her valuable book, has attempted, on the basis of the evidence of the Ignatian Epistles, to construct a coherent picture of Church life in Antioch in the Saint's time. She believes that Ignatius represented a 'middle party' within the Church which tried to keep a balance between an Essene-Jewish Christian group, who reverenced the Teacher of Righteousness alongside the figure of Jesus, and a Docetic-Christian group who regarded themselves as 'spiritual' and withdrew from the worship of the local congregations. This situation, she argues, accounts for the eirenic emphasis in the Epistles whereby Ignatius seeks to reconcile Christians of different backgrounds within the one Church (*ad Eph.* x. 1-3; *ad Magn.* x. 3) although standing firmly for his own point of view.[2]

While this thesis is interesting as a new attempt to solve an old problem it cannot be said that the author has succeeded in establishing her position. In the first place Ignatius argues against a Docetism and Judaism which is rampant in the Churches of Asia Minor.

[1] The substantive Χριστιανισμός first appears in *ad Magn.* x. 3, *ad Rom.* iii. 3, *ad Phil.* vi. 1; cf. *Mart. Polyc.* x; Clem. Alex. *Strom.* vii. 1. Together with the verb χριστιανίζειν it was no doubt coined as a matter of course once the word χριστιανός had been used. Note the observation of Lightfoot, *Ignatius*, Vol. II, Sect. 1, p. 134: 'In the N.T. the word "Christian" is still more or less a term of reproach; in the age of Ignatius it has become a title of honour.'

[2] Op. cit., pp. 52-65, especially p. 64.

While it is possible, and perhaps likely, that he had met them before in Antioch, this falls short of proof. Even if we grant her suggestion it is still difficult to show that they represent different groups within the Antiochene Church. As we shall see later, Ignatius nowhere states that there are two parties to which he is opposed. Moreover it is not certain that the 'Judaizers' of the Epistles are correctly interpreted as Essene Christians descended from members of the Dead Sea sect who fled from the Qumran monastery when it was overrun in A.D. 68. Miss Corwin instances Ignatius' reference to Jesus Christ as 'our only teacher' in *ad Magn.* ix. 1 as an indication that he is rebutting the claims of Essene Christians that the Teacher of Righteousness had a position beside that of Christ.[1] This seems farfetched. Ignatius is merely saying that Judaizers who wish to follow Moses and the Rabbis, while still remaining Christians, have a divided allegiance: they must choose one or the other. This question was acute in Magnesia and Philadelphia.

(2) JUDAISM AND GNOSTICISM

We now turn to what is a major battle ground in Ignatian studies. Is Ignatius combating two distinct heresies which were rampant in the Churches of Asia Minor—or is he combating only one form of Judaeo-Gnosticism? How far was Ignatius himself influenced by Gnosticism and perhaps incipient Valentinianism? Firstly let us look at the known facts.

Ignatius accuses certain adversaries of Judaism in two Epistles only, viz., those to the Philadelphians and the Magnesians. There can, I think, be little doubt that in *ad Magn.* he accuses the same persons of Judaism and Docetism. Thus in viii. 1 he refers to strange doctrines or old fables in the midst of a chapter warning his readers against Judaism; in ix. 1 he refers by implication to those who keep the sabbath—now superseded by the Lord's Day—as denying the death of Christ; in x. 3 Ignatius says it is monstrous to talk of Jesus Christ and to practise Judaism; in xi he sums up by warning the Magnesians 'not to fall into the snare of vain doctrine, but to be convinced of the birth and passion and resurrection which took place at the time of the procuratorship of Pontius Pilate; for these things were truly (ἀληθῶς) and certainly done by Jesus Christ, our hope, from which God grant that none of you be turned aside'. This is clearly a warning against Docetism. The attempts of C. C. Richardson,[2] Bartsch, Corwin and other scholars to separate two distinct groups of heretics founders on *ad Magn.* viii–xi. It is also significant that nowhere else in the Epistles does Ignatius give any

[1] Op. cit., p. 63.
[2] *The Christianity of Ignatius of Antioch* (1935), pp. 81–85.

indication that he is fighting on two fronts. He uses the same terms when speaking of both tendencies. Thus both Judaism and Docetism are 'not the planting of the Father' (*ad Trall.* xi. 1; *ad Phil.* iii. 1); both alike are warned 'to repent to the Unity of God', 'to repent towards God' (*ad Phil.* viii. 1; *ad Smyrn.* ix. 1); both are called 'heterodoxy' (*ad Magn.* viii. 1; *ad Smyrn.* vi. 2); he tells his readers in identical language that he does not speak because he accuses them of complicity in these errors but because he wishes to warn them (*ad Magn.* xi. 1; *ad Trall.* viii. 1–2). Lightfoot, in his masterly study, gives further examples of identity of language and concludes that these facts furnish a strong presumption that Ignatius is describing the same thing in the two sets of passages.[1] I cannot see how this judgement can easily be set aside.

So much for the facts. What then was the nature of this Judaeo-Docetism which Ignatius combated so vigorously? The Docetic element is quite clear; it was a denial of the physical birth, death and resurrection of Christ, the same tendency as was combated in 1 John i. 1–3, iv. 1–3; 2 John 7. This was one of the earliest Christian heresies, as Jerome noted: 'The blood of Christ was still fresh in Judaea when His body was said to be a phantasm' (*adv. Lucif.* 23). It is the Jewish element in the Ignatian heresy which has been the subject of much dispute. How can Docetism, with its denial of the corporeal reality of Christ's body, be at the same time Jewish? Was there ever such a thing as Judaeo-Docetism?

The recently discovered Gnostic documents from Nag Hammadi in Egypt have now provided firm evidence that Jewish speculation, particularly concerning the Name of God and of angels, did influence incipient Gnostic thought—and that at a time only slightly later than the time of Ignatius. Moreover the belief that Judaism was a monolithic structure, predominantly Pharisaic, from pre-Christian times down to the age of the Mishna and Talmud,[2] has been shaken by the discovery of the Dead Sea Scrolls which have supplied proof that Judaism was far more varied and open to outside influences—especially before A.D. 70.[3] The Qumran documents show, at the very least, hellenistic ideas and terminology invading Judaism on Palestinian soil: e.g. the term 'mystery' now appears in Hebrew documents—in fact one of the first finds published bore the title 'The Book of the Mysteries'. Thus the likelihood that Ignatius is attacking only one position—a form of Judaeo-Docetism or Judaeo-Gnosticism

---

[1] *The Apostolic Fathers*, Part II, Vol. I, p. 361.
[2] The classic position of G. F. Moore, *Judaism in the First Centuries of the Christian Era* (1927).
[3] This is well brought out by W. D. Davies, *Christian Origins and Judaism*, p. 106.

—is reinforced by recent discoveries. On Palestinian soil Judaism could be influenced by Gnostic terminology and ideas. In the Diaspora Gnosticism itself is found in combination with Jewish ideas.

Let us now take another look at the Ignatian heresy. In addition to denying the reality of Jesus' physical body, i.e., Docetism, these heretics held what Ignatius calls 'Judaism': 'But if anyone interpret Judaism to you do not listen to him; for it is better to hear Christianity from the circumcised than Judaism from the uncircumcised. But both of them, unless they speak of Jesus Christ, are to me tombstones and sepulchres of the dead, on whom only the names of men are written' (*ad Phil.* vi. 1). In other words Christianity propounded by Jewish-Christians is better than 'Judaism' propounded by the uncircumcised, i.e., by these Gentile Christians. It is then certain that these heretical teachers were not themselves circumcised and did not require their followers to be circumcised. This Jewish tendency was quite different from that combated by St. Paul. The Gnostic element in their position is illustrated by *ad Magn.* viii. 1: 'Be not led astray by strange doctrines (ἑτεροδοξίαις) or by old fables (μυθεύμασιν τοῖς παλαιοῖς) which are profitless. For if we are living until now according to Judaism, we confess that we have not received grace.' 'Judaism' here embraces a similar tendency to that found in the Pastoral Epistles—the endless fables and genealogies of 1 Tim. i. 4 (cf. iv. 7) and 2 Tim. iv. 4 and the Judaic fables of Titus i. 14. This is a Judaeo-Gnosticism which taught by myths or fables. A further indication of this form of teaching is found in *ad Phil.* viii. 2 where Ignatius refers to men who say 'if I find it not in the charters (ἐν τοῖς ἀρχείοις) in the Gospel I do not believe, and when I said to them that it is in the Scripture, they answered me, "that is exactly the question". But to me the charters are Jesus Christ, the inviolable charter is his cross, and death, and resurrection, and the faith which is through him. . . .' Most scholars agree in identifying the charters with the Old Testament. It therefore follows that these Judaeo-Gnostics had their own interpretation of the Old Testament in which they found support for their Christological position. Ignatius does not so much argue against them as witness to his faith with the passionate outburst—'to me the charters are Jesus Christ', i.e., the Old Testament is fulfilled in Jesus' physical birth, death and resurrection.

It is possible, although it cannot be proved, that Ignatius had come across a form of Judaeo-Gnosticism in Antioch and was therefore well prepared to deal with the heretics who were plaguing the Magnesian and Philadelphian Christian communities. Certainly Antioch was a hotbed of Christian groups and, no doubt, variant interpretations of the faith existed. The later Gnostics were able interpreters of the Scriptures and this feature may have characterized them at an earlier date. 'It is monstrous to talk of Jesus Christ and to practise Judaism' (*ad Magn.* x. 3) may not only be a polemic against Jewish observances but also against an unbridled interpretation of the Old Testament along Gnostic lines.

If Ignatius set his face so firmly against Judaeo-Gnosticism can a case be made for Gnosticism influencing *his* theology in essential matters? Schlier, in his study, has sought to show that Gnostic influence is *the* explanation of the Ignatian theology. In Ignatius' conception of Christ as the descending and ascending redeemer, in the Saint's idea of his martyrdom, in the belief that Christians are πνευματικοί, Gnostic influence, Schlier argues, is predominant. Schlier's book contains a mass of parallels with Iranian thought and with pre-Valentinian forms of Gnosis, but the great difficulty, as with Reitzenstein's work, is the accurate dating of these parallels. It is easy to compile comparative lists but far more difficult to establish definite influence when Ignatius' Epistles are looked at as a whole. His theology, as we have already suggested, is based on a tradition of Syrian Catholicism, as it was known in Antioch in the early second century, which was firmly incarnational and sacramental. But to say this does not rule out the possibility that the terminology which he sometimes uses may not have been influenced by contemporary speculation.

One of Ignatius' key conceptions is that God is Silence (Σιγή) with its corollary that in human silence (particularly of bishops) the real meaning of a person lies. Silence is existence *sui generis* as against what is explicit. The Silence of the Godhead is only broken by the revealing Word of God: '. . . there is one God, who manifested himself through Jesus Christ his son, who is his Word proceeding from silence, who in all respects was well pleasing to him that sent him' (*ad. Magn.* viii. 2). With this may be compared the well known vision of the star in *ad Eph.* xix. 1: 'And the virginity of Mary, and her giving birth were hidden from the Prince of this world, as was also the death of the Lord. Three mysteries of a cry which were wrought in the stillness of God' (ἐν ἡσυχίᾳ θεοῦ). Where did Ignatius obtain this belief that God is not only Father but also Silence and Stillness? Was it the outcome of his own philosophical and theological reflection? To an extent yes. For Ignatius the Being of God could not be fully comprehended and exhausted in the Incarnation. The *Deus absconditus*—the riches and depths of the Divine Nature—remained beyond human grasp. The idea of God as Σιγή expressed this perfectly. What is remarkable is that Ignatius could transfer this conception to the earthly bishop whose real existence—and existence *sui generis*—lies in silence. When Christians see their bishop silent the more reverence should they feel towards him.[1] Silence whether on earth or in heaven had a profound mystical significance for Ignatius.

If we grant that Ignatius' conception of the Divine Being flows from his own mystical experience there yet remains the possibility that he took over *the terminology* of contemporary speculation. In Valentinian speculation Bythos and Sige beget the aeons Nous and Aletheia who in turn beget Logos and Zoe. Irenaeus (i.2.5) and Hippolytus (*adv. haer.* vi. 29) however state that the Valentinians disputed among themselves about the place that Bythos and Sige should occupy in their systems. According to the Valentinian Theodotus (Clem. Alex. *Exc. Theod.* 29) Sige is 'the mother of all the emanations from Bythos', i.e., the parent of all the aeons. Clearly there was considerable speculation, in Valentinian circles, as to the exact status of Sige and the other aeons. The newly discovered Gospel of Truth, which probably represents an earlier stage of Valentinus' thought, speaks of 'the Mind which pronounces the unique Word in Silent Grace'.[2] The association of Σιγή with the Godhead is not however confined to Valentinianism. It is found in Greek cosmological speculation as early as the comic poet Antiphanes [3] and in the Magical Papyri where Silence is a symbol of the living, incorruptible God.[4] It also occurs in Mandaean and Mithraic speculation.[5] It is also interesting that Gregory Nazianzen gives Σιγή a place in the systems of Simon Magus, Cerinthus and others (*Orat.* xxv. 8. 1) while Irenaeus himself states that Valentinus borrowed his theory, with modifications, from earlier Gnostics (*adv. haer.* i. 11. 1).

These examples illustrate the widespread currency of the term in ancient speculation, especially in Gnostic thought, and suggest that Ignatius may be indebted to this background for his use of the term although his thought is, in itself, firmly anti-Docetic and anti-Gnostic. The same may be true of his use of the words 'pleroma' [6] and 'straining' or 'filtering'.[7] But Ignatius, in taking over this early Gnostic vocabulary, gave it a new content by his grasp of the reality of the Incarnation and the centrality of the Work of Christ accomplished on the Cross. Gnosticism was at the most a peripheral influence on the content of his thought.

[1] This is well brought out by H. Chadwick in HTR 43 (1950), pp. 169-72.
[2] Ed. M. Malinine, H-C. Puech and G. Quispel (Zurich 1956), p. 37, ll. 10ff.
[3] Iren. *adv. haer.* ii. 14. 1. Cf. Hipp. *adv. haer.* vi. 22, ἡ ὑμνουμένη ἐκείνη παρὰ τοῖς "Ελλησι σιγή.
[4] Papyri Graecae Magicae iv. 559.
[5] Qolasta 5 and A. Dieterich, *Eine Mithrasliturgie*, p. 6, ll. 21ff.
[6] *ad Eph.* and *ad Trall.* inscriptions.
[7] Used of Christians in *ad Rom.* inscription and *ad Phil.* iii. 1.

(3) THE CHRISTIAN TRADITION

The problem of Ignatius' use of the tradition embodied in the New Testament is a difficult one which has provoked wide disagreement among scholars. Thus Schlier holds that Gnostic influence was so strong that it virtually explains the Ignatian theology; in comparison the earlier Christian tradition was of no great moment. We have already noted that Schlier grossly overestimates the influence of Gnosticism, which was only peripheral. H. W. Bartsch speaks of the ungnosticized deposit of early Christian preaching in Ignatius' theology but the exact unravelling of this deposit is the cause of a wide divergence of opinion. The surest evidence of literary dependence is Ignatius' indebtedness to St. Paul whom he mentions in *ad Eph.* xii. 2 and *ad Rom.* iv. 3. He must have known 1 Corinthians as there are five certain and twelve possible reminiscences of this Epistle in the Ignatian writings. But it is uncertain how far Ignatius penetrated to the depths of the Pauline theology. He knows nothing of the Pauline idea of the salvation wrought by Christ from σάρξ, conceived as the seat of sin, or of the activity of the indwelling Spirit. Moreover, like his contemporary, Clement of Rome, he has no real appreciation of the Pauline 'righteousness by faith' (cf. *ad Rom.* v. 1). St. Paul was one to be admired as a supreme example of Christian living rather than of reflective thought.

Ignatius, like most of the ante-Nicene Fathers, knew St. Matthew's Gospel or the tradition embodied in it.[1] He opposes Judaism, as does the Gospel, but whereas Matthew reflects a thought-world strongly influenced by Pharisaic Judaism, Ignatius has a more subtle and ill-defined background. The Christian tradition which he represents cannot be wholly characterized as Matthaean, or Pauline, or Johannine, but is in essence his own as he knew and lived it in Antioch. For want of a better name we call it Syrian Catholicism. We can illustrate this from a consideration of Ignatius' relationship to the Fourth Gospel.

This has long been a major battleground of Ignatian studies. How far was Ignatius influenced by St. John? Clearly both have much in common—particularly in their eucharistic theology—as has long been recognized. Thus both St. John and Ignatius connect the resurrection and eternal life with the rite (*ad Eph.* xx. 2, *ad Smyrn.* vii. 1, cf. John vi. 54); note especially the use of ἀγαπᾶν in *ad Smyrn.* vii. 1, denoting participation in the eucharist, as well as φιλαδελφία as in John vi. 54 and 1 John iii. 14. The difficulty is that Ignatius has nothing which could be construed as an exact quotation of the

---

[1] C. C. Richardson, op. cit., p. 103, note 105. Matt. was probably the Gospel used in Antioch in Ignatius's time.

Fourth Gospel—unlike his use of 1 Corinthians. Recent studies have shown that this Gospel contains traditions, Palestinian in character, which may have come down from the earliest age of the Church.[1] The best solution of the Ignatian question is to postulate an anticipatory stream of Johannine teaching, perhaps carried by oral tradition, which spread from Jerusalem to Antioch, where it has left its mark on the liturgical usage of the Syrian Church. This usage has the order of Christian initiation as follows: unction or chrismation, baptism, admission to first communion. Elsewhere the order is baptism, unction, first communion. The late T. W. Manson argued forcibly that 1 John v. 7ff., which mentions the three witnesses, the Spirit, the water and the blood, is a reference to the three stages of initiation in the Syrian order [2]—indicating that Johannine teaching was known in Antioch. Another signpost connecting this stream of tradition with Antioch is the enigmatic Q saying Matt. xi. 25–27, Luke x. 21–22, which was called, by an older generation of scholars, 'a bolt from the Johannine heavens'.[3] We can now understand how Ignatius, early in the second century, shows an affinity with Johannine thought while having no direct knowledge of the Fourth Gospel, for from Antioch this earlier stream of Johannine tradition moved to Ephesus where it achieved literary formulation in the Gospel and Epistles attributed to St. John only slightly before the time of Ignatius. This seems to be a more plausible view than that which would regard the Fourth Gospel as *written* in Palestine or Antioch at a very early date,[4] as then we cannot explain why Ignatius does not quote it in view of the affinity of theological ideas between the two writers.

To conclude, Ignatius is essentially a witness to the Christian tradition as it was known and practised in Antioch. His Catholicism reflects a Syrian, rather than an Asia Minor, milieu. Much of his imagery and mysticism comes from this background. On the other hand he knew the essential facts of the Christian tradition as they had been handed down in the Church and expressed in its liturgy.[5] He was acquainted with St. Matthew's Gospel, or the tradition it contains, with St. Paul's first letter to the Corinthians and possibly other of his Epistles. He was influenced by a stream of Johannine teaching which was known in the Church of Antioch. An early form

[1] W. F. Albright in *The Background of the New Testament and its Eschatology* (ed. W. D. Davies and D. Daube), pp. 153–71.
[2] BJRL 30, No. 2 (1947), pp. 3–20; see especially pp. 17–18.
[3] I believe this expression was first used by the late Bishop H. H. Henson.
[4] Recent scholarship has gone too far in this direction as a reaction against the view that St. John's Gospel was purely a hellenistic writing.
[5] Note, however, how he abandons the earlier use of παρουσία of the Second Coming and uses it only of the historical Coming of Jesus.

of Gnosticism may have left its mark on his terminology although it did not touch the essence of his thought.

In this chapter I have done no more than enumerate a few of the questions which beset the student of the Ignatian Epistles. It would seem that further study of the background of these writings will yield a rich reward, since Ignatius is one of the key figures of the second century. This study will be one of exceptional complexity and will require much patient investigation, for Ignatius is one of those unique figures—magnificent in his defiance of the world—whose thought cannot be expressed in tidy formularies. However much he may have been indebted to the influences which played upon him in the final analysis he is *sui generis*.

IV

THE PROBLEM OF ST. POLYCARP'S EPISTLE TO THE PHILIPPIANS

More than a quarter of a century has passed since the publication of Dr. P. N. Harrison's monumental study of St. Polycarp's Epistle to the Philippians.[1] Harrison's work was at once seen to be of fundamental importance and has gained a wide measure of assent from scholars. The thesis which he advanced, with much detailed learning, was that the so-called Epistle of Polycarp was in fact two letters written on different occasions, each presupposing a different milieu, which had become fused together in the course of literary transmission. Ch. xiii (and possibly xiv) was written within a fortnight of St. Ignatius' leaving Philippi when he was still on the way to martyrdom at Rome. It was essentially a covering note to a collection of certain of the Ignatian Epistles [2]—which were apparently already in Polycarp's possession—which he was sending to the Philippians at their own request. Chs. i–xii, on the other hand, formed a separate letter written by Polycarp some twenty or more years later, i.e., c. A.D. 135, to warn the Philippians against the heresy of Marcion which had, by then, arisen in Asia Minor. This theory and dating won the support of Dr. Streeter and Professor F. C. Burkitt [3] and since then has been adopted by a wide circle of front rank scholars.[4] Our concern here is not to argue for the unity of the Epistle but to consider afresh, with more recent studies in mind, some of the problems raised by Harrison's work. We shall seek to show that he was right in his fundamental thesis of the two letters but that he was wrong in dating the second letter (Chs. i–xii) so long after the first.

THE PROBLEM OF CHAPTER XIII

xiii. 2 reads:

[1] *Polycarp's Two Epistles to the Philippians*, 1936.
[2] This would include *ad Smyrn.* and *ad Polyc.* as well as other Epistles. Both Ignatius and Polycarp were aware of the supreme value of the collected letters of St. Paul for the Church; cf. Ign. *ad Eph.* xii. 2; Polyc. *ad Phil.* xi. 3. The *Corpus Paulinum* seems first to have been collected and published at Ephesus; cf. Ign. *ad Rom.* iv. 3. It quickly became a prototype for collections of Christian literature.
[3] Preface to Harrison's book, pp. v and vi.
[4] F. L. Cross, *The Early Christian Fathers*, pp. 19–21; J. A. Kleist, *A.C.W.*, Vol. VI, p. 71; P. Meinhold, *P.W.K.* xxi, 1683–7 *inter alia*. But see the doubts raised by H-Ch. Puech in RHR 119 (1939), pp. 96–102.

'We send you, as you asked, the letters of Ignatius, which were sent to us by him, and others which we had by us. These are subjoined to this letter, and you will be able to benefit greatly from them. For they contain faith, patience, and all the edification which pertains to our Lord. Let us know anything further which you have heard about Ignatius himself and those with him. (*Et de ipso Ignatio et de his, qui cum eo sunt, quod certius agnoveritis, significate*).'

The most natural interpretation of this passage is that Ignatius was still alive at the time of writing. Unfortunately the last vital sentence is only preserved in a Latin translation and this led Bishop Lightfoot[1] to argue that once the Latin is translated back into Greek (περί τῶν σύν αὐτῷ) all reference to the present time disappears. Polycarp could then have been writing soon after the death of Ignatius became known as a fact but before full details had reached him. This was not therefore inconsistent with ix. 2 which explicitly refers to the death of Ignatius and his companions ('they are with the Lord'). Harrison[2] had no difficulty in showing that this explanation was altogether too simple. In the first place there is no mention in Ch. xiii of the martyrdom of Ignatius and nothing to suggest that this had yet happened. When last heard of, Ignatius had eight hundred miles to cover and some six weeks' journey before he would arrive at Rome. Polycarp's enquiry for further information covers any interesting facts which the Philippians may have known about the earlier stages of the journey when they had accompanied Ignatius. Polycarp is taking nothing for granted and wishes to be told whatever news is available. This explanation fits in much better with the background of Ch. xiii than Lightfoot's theory that Polycarp is taking the final completion and sequel to Ignatius' journey as a foregone conclusion yet strangely makes no mention of it.

It would seem that Harrison's theory can be further strengthened. He failed to notice a small but significant fact which in the event is a strong confirmation of his thesis. Eusebius, in his *Ecclesiastical History* iii. 36. 14–15, quotes both Chs. ix and xiii of Polycarp's Epistle in the original Greek with only the connecting link καί ἑξῆς ἐπιφέρει. After recording the deaths of the blessed martyrs Ignatius, Rufus and Zosimus in Ch. ix Eusebius quotes Ch. xiii in full, *but significantly omits the last sentence*, which is now only extant in the Latin quoted above. Why did Eusebius omit this when he had the original Greek before him? The only feasible explanation is that he saw that in the original, Chs. ix and xiii were in dire conflict, the one recording the

[1] *Ignatius and Polycarp*, Vol. I, pp. 572–3.
[2] Op. cit., pp. 133–40.

death of Ignatius and the other presupposing he was still alive. Accordingly, as befitted one who assumed the unity of the Epistle, Eusebius removed the contradiction. Lightfoot's view that the original Greek contained no time reference and therefore could refer to a period after the death of Ignatius was not therefore the view of Eusebius, who after all had the original Greek before him which the modern scholar has not.[1] This would therefore appear to be a further support for Harrison's theory that the references in Chs. ix and xiii are in fact irreconcilable and belong to two distinct letters written at different times. It is extraordinary that Harrison, with his acute perception, while repeatedly referring to Eusebius' quotation of Ch. xiii, made no reference to the omission of the last sentence.[2]

We may then accept the thesis that the Epistle of Polycarp is in fact two letters which came later to be fused together, Ch. xiii and the postscript Ch. xiv having been written while Ignatius was still alive.

Chapters I—XII

We now pass to a consideration of Chs. i—xii which are, on Harrison's theory, a letter written *c.* A.D. 135. The main arguments put forward in support of this dating are as follows:

(A) The reference in i. 1 to the Philippians having helped on their way 'those who were bound in chains, which become the saints, and are the diadems of those who have been truly chosen by God and our Lord' refers to an event which happened some twenty years earlier when Ignatius and his companions visited Philippi on their fateful journey. While this is not impossible it seems more probable, as with St. Paul in Phil. i (cf. Ep. Barn. i) that a more recent event is referred to.[3] Polycarp rejoices that the Philippians, not so long before, assisted Ignatius and his friends on their way to martyrdom. Memory soon fades. Polycarp wishes to remind them of their moment of glory.

(B) Ch. vii, according to Harrison, refers to an earlier stage of Marcion's teaching and this could not have arisen before *c.* A.D. 135. The advent of this heretic was in fact the *raison d'être* of the second letter which Polycarp writes to counteract the 'crisis' which had

---

[1] The only way of evading this conclusion is to assert that the Latin is a later interpolation. But I know of no competent authorities prepared to support this. On the Latin version, now contained in the Latin *Corpus Ignatianum*, see Lightfoot, op. cit., Vol. I, pp. 534-5.

[2] Lawler and Oulton, Eus.*E.H.*, Vol. II, p. 110, likewise make no comment on the omission.

[3] Harrison seems to sense this: 'True, the mere fact that the letter opens with a reference to that visit may, at first sight, seem to suggest that the visit had taken place recently' (op. cit., p. 158).

arisen due to his activities and teaching. It would appear that Harrison emphasized too much the 'crisis' atmosphere of Chs. i–xii.[1] Heretical teaching was not the foremost reason why Polycarp wrote to the Philippians. He says that he writes 'concerning righteousness, not at my own instance, but because you first invited me' (iii. 1). In Ch. iv he warns against the love of money and in Ch. v gives Christian obligations to a virtuous life; in Ch. vi come the duties of the presbyters—especially are they to be compassionate, merciful and forgiving. The fair fame of the Philippian Church had been sullied by the sin of one Valens, a presbyter, and his wife, who had apparently been guilty of some act of fraud and dishonesty (Ch. xi). This had made a deep impression on Polycarp who constantly warns his readers against the sin of avarice. Only in Ch. viii is there a warning against heretical teaching of a Docetic type similar to that found elsewhere in early Christian literature.[2] It is thus not true to say that this letter has a 'crisis' atmosphere—Docetism was after all a widespread phenomenon in the early Church. What then are we to make of Harrison's theory that Marcion is referred to in the Epistle?

vii. 1 reads:

> 'For everyone who does not confess that Jesus Christ has come in the flesh is an anti-Christ; and whosoever does not confess the testimony of the Cross is of the devil: and whosoever perverts the oracles of the Lord for his own lusts, and says that there is neither resurrection nor judgement, this man is a first-born of Satan.'

There is nothing specifically Marcionite in the doctrines attacked in this passage. Marcion's dualism, his doctrine of the two gods, his rejection of the Old Testament nowhere appear. Neither did Marcion deny the judgement—in fact he held as firmly as any Catholic that men would be rewarded or punished hereafter according to their deeds in this life, although it was the Demiurge who would be their Judge. The death of Christ was very important to him although he was a Docetist.[3] Moreover Marcion excised rather than perverted the scriptures and he certainly did not do this for his own lusts (πρὸς τὰς ἰδίας ἐπιθυμίας) which denotes the antinomian license known to have been practised by certain Docetic groups. Marcion's conduct was above suspicion and even Tertullian, his doughty opponent,

[1] Noted by E. J. Goodspeed, *A History of Early Christian Literature*, p. 25.
[2] Cf. 1 Cor. xv. 12; 2 Tim. ii. 18; 1 John iv. 2–3; 2 John vii; Rev. ii. 6, 14ff., 20ff.; Ign. *ad Smyrn.* i–vii.
[3] See the important observation of Harnack, *Marcion* (1924 edn.), p. 125: 'To conclude from this that the sufferings and death of Christ were to him a mere shadow-show is incorrect.'

bears decisive witness to his moral rectitude.[1] Harrison attempted to get round these damaging facts by arguing that Ch. vii referred to an earlier phase of Marcion's teaching before he went to Rome, where he derived his characteristic doctrines from Cerdo. But we have no other information as to this earlier phase of his activity or that he had ever been at Philippi. If there was an earlier phase his teaching must then have been indistinguishable from the Docetism condemned in the Johannine and Ignatian literature and contrary to much that Marcion later taught. This is the weakest part of Harrison's notable book and it seems inconceivable that he would have put it forward save for the reference to 'a first-born of Satan'. It is quite true that Polycarp's choice of this epithet seems appropriate to Marcion, as later on a famous occasion (Iren. *adv. haer.* iii. 3. 4). Yet there is surely no difficulty in believing that Polycarp may have used the phrase as a general term of abuse against Docetic heretics (is it significant that there is no definite article in the Greek?) and later in his life applied it specifically to Marcion. We have other evidence that Polycarp had a habit of repeating favourite expressions. Irenaeus in his Epistle to Florinus (Eus. *E.H.* v. 20) mentions the exclamation 'O good God' as one of these phrases. In any event the teaching of Ch. vii is so at variance with the characteristic teaching of Marcion that it is difficult to find in it any reference to the arch-heretic. Docetism was rampant in Asia Minor in the late first and early second centuries and it is against this that Polycarp warns the Philippians.

(c) Dr. Harrison's next argument in support of a late date c. A.D. 135 for Chs. i–xii is that quotations from the New Testament and 1 Clement frequently occur in these chapters, in contrast to Chs. xiii–xiv and the Ignatian Epistles, and this indicates that these chapters were written at a time when the New Testament Canon was at a fuller stage of development than in A.D. 110–15. The comparison with Chs. xiii–xiv is not decisive, as these comprise, on Harrison's theory, a brief covering note which we would hardly expect to contain biblical quotations. His other point needs further consideration. Polycarp was a rather unimaginative, conservative writer whose outlook and diction was steeped in the traditional Christian vocabulary. Unlike Clement of Rome and the writer of Barnabas he was born of Christian parents and had been familiar with Christian teaching from childhood; we should thus expect him to know some of the apostolic writings.[2] In Chs. i–xii he appears to know Matthew, Luke,

---

[1] Cf. *de praescr. haer.* xxx, 'continentia Marcionensis'; cf. *adv. Marc.*i. 1, 29, iv. 11.
[2] This is well brought out by *D.C.B.*, Vol. IV, p. 425, article 'Polycarpus of Smyrna'.

Acts, the Pauline Epistles, 1 Peter and 1 Clement as well as certain of the Ignatian Epistles. Recent discoveries at Nag Hammadi, and in particular the Gospel of Truth, have shown that the formation of the New Testament Canon was not a late development belonging to the mid-second century but had begun at an earlier date. Polycarp's quotations of the New Testament, if such they are, in Chs. i–xii, are quite consistent with a date *c.* A.D. 120. A further significant fact is that while Polycarp is familiar with the *Corpus Paulinum* he shows no aquaintance with the fourfold Gospel which a Christian leader in Asia Minor writing *c.* A.D. 135 would have been expected to have known.[1] (The widespread influence of the fourfold Gospel in the period A.D. 120–60 is evidenced by its use in Papias, 2 Peter, the Gospel of Peter, the *Epistola Apostolorum* and the writings of Justin Martyr).[2]

Furthermore recent studies of the background of early Christian writings [3] have shown that a large body of catechetical material, in oral and written forms, circulated in the early Church and was used by teachers, catechists and writers as 'pegs' on which to hang their own theological interpretations. It is not therefore to be supposed that a Christian writer is always quoting verbatim from an earlier document when similarity of subject matter occurs. It seems possible that a few of the 'quotations' from the New Testament in Chs. i–xii of Polycarp's Epistle may in fact come out of a wider background of catechesis. Thus iv. 2 reads: 'next teach our wives to remain in the faith given to them, and in love and purity, tenderly loving their husbands in all truth, and loving all others equally in all chastity, and to educate their children in the fear of God.' The relationship of husbands and wives is dealt with in 1 Pet. iii. 1–7, Col. iii. 18–19, Eph. v. 22–23, 1 Tim. ii. 9–15 and Titus ii. 4–5, and Dr. Selwyn shows that this was a catechetical theme which was developed in different ways by various writers.[4] Similarly the relationship between children and parents is the subject of Col. iii. 20–21, Eph. vi. 1–4, *Did.* iv. 9, 1 Clem. xxi. 8 where the background is the Christian home and family life; this teaching appears to derive from an early

---

[1] E. J. Goodspeed, op. cit., p. 25. Harrison, op. cit., p. 261 thinks that the Fourth Gospel was not written until *c.* A.D. 135 and that Polycarp had not seen it when he wrote the 'Crisis' Letter. Recent discoveries render this dating untenable.

[2] Note the conservative treatment of the evidence in C. F. D. Moule, *The Birth of the New Testament*, pp. 197–8: 'But at least it can be said with confidence that the fourfold Canon is well established before our earliest official lists of accredited books' (op. cit., p. 198).

[3] Especially P. Carrington, *The Primitive Christian Catechism*, and E. G. Selwyn, *The First Epistle of St. Peter*.

[4] Op. cit., pp. 432–5.

domestic code which formed part of the primitive catechesis. Compare also the younger members of the community mentioned in v. 3 (νεώτεροι) with 1 Pet. v. 5, Titus ii. 6, 1 Tim. v. 1, 1 Clem. i. 3. It is not therefore to be supposed, as Harrison thought, that Polycarp is quoting verbatim or picking up odd phrases from the New Testament and other early Christian literature. He is simply drawing on a stock of catechetical material well known in the early Church. We have no space to consider this question further but it seems likely that there are other examples of catechetical material in this Epistle.[1] It would be a profitable line of investigation, so far not carried out, to examine the whole corpus of the writings of the Apostolic Fathers for catechetical and liturgical material.

A further point, not noted by Harrison, is the presence of Jewish or Jewish-Christian catechetical material, not found in the New Testament, in Chs. i–xii of Polycarp's Epistle. Especially interesting is x. 2: 'When you can do good defer it not, for almsgiving sets free from death.' This appears to be based on Prov. iii. 27 and Tobit iv. 10. We know that Prov. iii was Jewish catechetical material which was known and used in the early Church, where it was woven into a fragment of catechumen virtues.[2] There is also much material in Polycarp's Epistle similar to the injunctions found in the Jewish-Christian 'Two Ways' which appears in the *Didache* and the Epistle of Barnabas.

These considerations suggest that Chs. i–xii should not be dated too late in the second century, for they presuppose a background of catechetical teaching similar to that found in the New Testament, *Didache*, Ep. Barnabas and the earlier parts of Hermas. On these grounds, in view of the failure to quote the fourfold Gospel, and the fact that the formation of the New Testament Canon had begun fairly early in the second century, I should not be inclined to date Chs. i–xii of Polycarp's Epistle later than *c.* A.D. 120.

(D) Another argument of Harrison for the late dating of these chapters is that quotations from the Ignatian Epistles abound in them while they are absent from Chs. xiii–xiv. This, he thinks, points to the first twelve chapters having been written at a time when the Philippians had themselves been long familiar with the Ignatian phraseology, i.e., many years after the time of Ignatius' martyrdom. This argument does not seem to bear decisively on the question of dating once we accept the thesis that Chs. i–xii were written after Ignatius' death. Both Ignatius and Polycarp were aware of the value of

[1] Cf. the primitive catechetical form (based on the *Abstinentes*), which laid special emphasis on the sins of uncleanness and covetousness, with v. 3, xi. 1–2.
[2] Selwyn, op. cit., pp. 19, 408–10.

collections of Christian letters. Ignatius speaks of a collection of the Pauline Epistles (*ad Eph.* xii. 2; cf. Polyc. *ad Phil.* iii. 2) and no doubt this stimulated the collection and circulation of his own Epistles. Polycarp had apparently collected certain of these before the Philippians asked him for them (xiii. 2) and if they received these before Ignatius' martyrdom (on Harrison's theory of Ch. xiii) there is nothing to suggest that by *c.* A.D. 120 they would not have become thoroughly familiar with the phraseology of the Saint. Since Harrison wrote, further study has been made [1] of the influence of the public reading of Christian literature in Christian worship. It seems likely that this ensured the survival of much of this literature and was also a powerful means by which telling phrases of individual writers became widely and swiftly known. The Ignatian Epistles, with their variety of subject matter and bearing the imprint of an outstanding personality, were particularly suitable for public reading. Polycarp, writing *c.* A.D. 120, can therefore assume that the Philippians will be familiar with the allusions which he makes to Ignatius' ideas.

(E) Harrison's final argument for the late dating of Chs. i–xii is based on Polycarp's age. He was born *c.* A.D. 69 and was 46–48 years of age when Ignatius passed through Smyrna on his way to Rome, shortly after which he wrote Ch. xiii. By the year A.D. 135 Polycarp was between 66 and 68 years of age and 'by that time he had attained that unique position and influence which is implied by the request of an important and historical Church three hundred miles away from Smyrna to intervene in a grave crisis in their internal affairs with which their own body of Elders had found themselves unable to cope'.[2] We have already noted that Harrison overemphasizes the 'crisis' atmosphere of the second letter—if anything it was Valens' avarice which was the main difficulty. The warning against Docetism in Ch. vii is no different from that found in many other early Christian writings. There is in fact nothing in Chs. i–xii to suggest that Polycarp is being consulted as an elder stateman who is nearing three score years and ten. The example of Damas in Magnesia (Ign. *ad Magn.* iii. 1) among his contemporaries, and Athanasius at a later epoch, witnesses to the practice of placing younger men in the highest offices of the Church in the earliest centuries. Polycarp, by

---

[1] See especially G. D. Kilpatrick, *The Origins of the Gospel According to St. Matthew*, p. 65: 'as long as a document continued to be read publicly its existence was guaranteed, but as soon as it disappeared from the worship of the Church it was in grave danger of being lost.' Cf. also pp. 72–100.

[2] Harrison, op. cit., p. 283; cf. p. 268: 'the Philippians' request . . . suggests that he must have been by this time a man of wide influence, ripe experience and advanced years'.

A.D. 120, was already over fifty years of age [1] and as a direct link with our Lord's Apostles [2] would have been venerated as a source of trustworthy information concerning the first age of the Church. We are expressly told that even before his hairs were grey he was treated with every honour by those about him (*Mart. Polyc.* xiii). It was natural for such a leader to be asked for advice by the Philippians, who may not have had a bishop of their own.[3]

In this chapter we have given some new reasons for questioning Dr. Harrison's late date for Chs. i–xii of Polycarp's Epistle—the second letter. This however should in no way temper our gratitude to him for solving one of the most vexed problems of Patristic scholarship. The thesis that Polycarp's Epistle to the Philippians is in fact two letters written on different occasions may be regarded as established beyond doubt and its wide acceptance by scholars is a mark of the importance of the author's work. His book deserves to rank as one of the most learned and acute patristic monographs so far produced in this century.

[1] The Pionian legend (late 4th century) which speaks of Polycarp's 'hoary head', the 'forerunner of old age' at the time when he was admitted to the priesthood, has no points of contact with authentic tradition.

[2] Iren. *adv. haer.* iii. 3. 4; Tert. *de praescr. haer.* 32.

[3] The silence of Polycarp's letter concerning episcopacy, in contrast to the Ignatian Epistles, may suggest that monarchical episcopacy had not yet come into existence at Philippi or that the office was vacant at the time Polycarp wrote.

V

JUDAISM IN EGYPT A.D. 70–135

The period from the fall of Jerusalem to the Bar-Kochba rising (A.D. 70–135) was one of crucial significance for Egyptian Judaism. During these years Hellenistic Judaism, which had produced so much noble literature and had made such a sustained effort to bridge the gulf between the Jewish and Greek worlds, virtually ceased to exist as an effective force, and the Christian Church and Gnosticism became its heirs. After A.D. 135, although Jewish communities continued to exist, Judaism never again rose to pre-eminence and Jews did not play even a minor role in Alexandrian politics until the fourth century A.D. The story of this intellectual and religious decline has never been written, owing to the paucity of evidence, from the Jewish side, for this transition period. After Philo there exists an unfortunate blank in our knowledge of the beliefs and literary activity of Alexandrian Judaism. We shall hope to show in this chapter that the situation is not so serious as has often been assumed and that from a Christian source it is possible to show the probable course that at least one section of Alexandrian Judaism took. But first we must trace the historical background of the Jewish communities.

Historical Background

Jewish settlements existed in Egypt from early times, one of the first being at Elephantine, the ancient Yeb, an island on the Nile in Upper Egypt. There a Jewish community in the sixth century B.C. developed a curious kind of religious syncretism which embraced the worship of Yahweh under the name of Yahu or Yaho [1] with that of other gods and goddesses including Anathyahu,[2] who was regarded as Yahweh's bride. However, we gain the impression, from the sporadic references which have come down, that before the time of Ptolemy I Jewish settlements were few and that no mass migrations had taken place. The position changed somewhat from the time of Alexander the Great, who, according to Josephus,[3] incorporated Jews among the citizens of the new city of Alexandria; later

---

[1] Cowley, *Aramaic Papyri*, 1923, Pap. 13.
[2] Op. cit., Pap. 44, 3. Five deities can be traced, corresponding to the five gateways to the temple. The colonists may have brought this polytheism with them from Judaea.
[3] *Bell. Jud.* II. xviii. 7; *contra Apion.* ii. 4.

they came to enjoy special privileges and had their own quarter. By the beginning of the Christian era the Alexandrian Jews had so multiplied that they were the largest Jewish community outside Judaea and, according to Philo,[1] constituted about two-fifths of the city's population, occupying two of the five city divisions. There were, however, no ghettoes, and some Jews lived scattered among the Graeco-Egyptian population, where they had their own synagogues for worship and religious instruction. Philo also reckoned that the total Jewish population in Egypt was, in his day, about a million, which may be considered to be confirmed by the many references to their existence in Lower, Middle and Upper Egypt which have been found.[2] The same author's remark that the Jews had their dwellings 'as far as the borders of Ethiopia' is not necessarily an exaggeration on present knowledge.[3]

The Diaspora, united as it was by a bond of loyalty to its Palestinian home, was a permanent problem to the Roman authorities. Everywhere the Jews aroused suspicion among the native population on account of their ritual practices, abstention from local social activities, refusal to join in the official worship of the locality, and strange diet. The Romans tried in earnest to respect the rights of minorities, and the Jews were not slow to take advantage of this toleration. They appealed immediately and without hesitation to the governing power whenever they suffered hostile acts or adverse decisions from local magistrates, and more often than not the Romans, as a matter of general policy, intervened in their favour. It was Julius Caesar who, as a reward for services rendered in his Egyptian campaign, gave the Jews a unique juridical status, i.e., freedom of assembly for worship, the right to collect offerings for the Jerusalem Temple, exemption from military service, and a recognition of their corporate existence according to the traditions of their fathers. The amicable relationship which existed between the Roman power and the Egyptian Jews, coupled with the consciousness that the Jews were strangers from afar, tended to embitter the non-Jewish population. Moreover the exemption which they enjoyed from the jurisdiction of the Greek courts no doubt caused discontent, and to this was added Jewish exclusiveness, intolerance,

---

[1] For Philo's references to the Jews see *in Flaccum* vi.

[2] L. Fuchs, *Die Juden Aegyptens*, 1924, pp. 43–4; H. I. Bell, *Cults and Creeds in Graeco-Roman Egypt*, 1953, pp. 34–5. The papyri are particularly helpful in illustrating the growth of Jewish communities outside of Alexandria. Cf. U. Wilcken, *Gr. Ostr.* I, pp. 523–4; P. Tebt. III, 817; P. Lond. III, pp. 18ff., no. 1177, 57–61.

[3] Cf. also Philo's statement that communities of Jewish Therapeutae were to be found in every nome (*de vita cont.* iii). Samaritan communities also existed in Egypt (Petrie, *Papyri*, II, pp. 92–3).

and consciousness of racial superiority. The wealth and commercial ability possessed by some members of the Alexandrian community, such as Alexander the Alabarch, Philo's brother, simply added fuel to the flames. These were the causes of that deep hatred of the Jews which became evident in the Egyptian metropolis.

Antipathy towards the Egyptian Jews took no violent form during the Ptolemaic period. However, after the fall of Anthony and Cleopatra relationships began to take on a more sombre aspect when Octavian, with significant lack of tact, confirmed the Jews in their privileges at the very time when he was refusing the Alexandrians the senate for which they had asked. From this time Greek-Jewish hostility became more marked and a nationalist anti-Jewish literature began to appear. During the reign of the Roman Emperor Caligula a collision occurred which was to have not insignificant consequences.[1] This happened in the spring of A.D. 38 when Herod Agrippa, the notorious spendthrift son of Herod the Great, set out from Rome surrounded by an escort of soldiery with the intention of calling at Alexandria *en route* for Palestine. The local Jews decided to make his visit the triumphal entrance of their ruler. This greatly embittered the Greek population, who retaliated by dressing up a local idiot to resemble Agrippa and insulting him with coarse wit and shouts of *Marin*, the Syrian word for Lord—an added 'insult' in view of Agrippa's Syrian origin.[2] The Greeks then demanded that the Jews should pay divine honours to Caligula, who had been deified, insisting that his statue should be set up in their synagogues. A riot followed in which Jewish shops and houses were plundered in the traditional eastern manner, many Jews being slaughtered in the streets. Flaccus, the weak Roman Governor, did nothing to stop the pogrom, and the unfortunate survivors were huddled together in a ghetto in the delta quarter of the city, although later, when the Emperor heard about the incident, Flaccus was condemned to death. On the Alexandrian side there were some trials in the imperial courts, and a whole patriotic literature, the *Acta Alexandrinorum*, grew up around the local heroes who are represented as treating the Emperor with great boldness and courage. The Alexandrians came to cherish the memory of their martyrs as much as the Jews and Christians that of their own. This pogrom had a great effect upon the imagination of the Jews, who swore vengeance for the outrage which had been committed. Embassies were sent to other Jewish centres, with the result that armed reinforcements flocked into the Egyptian capital. Claudius'

[1] Philo *in Flaccum* v–vi.
[2] Agrippa was well known to the Alexandrian money-lenders. J. G. Milne, *A History of Egypt* (3rd edn. 1924), p. 17.

command to the Jews [1] 'not to introduce or invite Jews who sail down from Syria or Egypt, thus compelling me to conceive the greater suspicion; otherwise I shall by all means take vengeance on them as fomenting a general plague for the whole world' may conceivably refer to these reinforcements. The Jewish communities were, however, by no means united within themselves and internal strife reared its ugly head, if we may judge by the embassies which two factions sent to Claudius concerning an unknown matter.

Further conflicts between Jew and Greek took place in Alexandria in A.D. 53,[2] and at the time of the Jewish war against Rome during the years A.D. 66–70 when the cry of 'spies' was raised against the Jews.[3] After the destruction of the Temple in A.D. 70 a number of fugitives came from Jerusalem to Alexandria and sought to stir up trouble against the Romans, which the orthodox leaders resisted. In the ensuing turmoil these revolutionaries put to death certain of the orthodox leaders. However, their success was short lived, for the Jewish Gerousia soon crushed the faction, taking some six hundred prisoners in the process. Another clash between Jews and Greeks took place in A.D. 110 when the Jews appear to have had the ear of Trajan. The position was reversed in A.D. 115 when the Egyptian Jews rose against this Emperor [4] (when he was engaged in his Parthian war), as part of a concerted movement of revolt which had its origin in Cyrene. This brought more strife to Alexandria, where a terrible conflict took place with the Greek population in which the Jews suffered heavy losses. During this period, as we shall see later, relations between Jews and Christians of Jewish descent also worsened and violent feeling was aroused. After A.D. 135 the Egyptian communities declined in influence, and eventually St. Cyril of Alexandria expelled the Jews *en masse* from the metropolis after some seven centuries' existence in the city.

This historical background has been dwelt on at some length because it is indispensable for the understanding of the path which Egyptian Judaism took in the little-known period from A.D. 70–135. Strife between Jew and Greek, between Jew and Jew, and Jew and Christian, often accompanied by violent massacres and upheavals, formed the political background of the age. It was in such a setting as this that hellenistic Judaism of the philosophic type, which had sought to present Jewish ideas in Greek dress and to provide a bridge

---

[1] Hunt and Edgar, *Select Papyri*, II, p. 86, ll. 96–100.
[2] H. I. Bell, *Juden und Griechen im römischen Alexandreia*, 1924, pp. 27–30.
[3] Bell, op. cit., p. 31.
[4] P. Oxy. IX, 1189 shows that the Oxyrhynchus Jews were especially engaged in this struggle. Eighty years later the inhabitants of the city still celebrated their victory over the Jews at an annual festival; see P. Oxy. 705.

between the Graeco-Oriental and Jewish worlds, gradually disappeared. It was, however, destined to survive as a living force within the Christian Church, where it later flowered in the writings of Clement and Origen. Gnosticism and the Hermetic writings, to judge from recent work on this subject,[1] also laid their claim to its treasures.

Developments in Judaism

The problem presented by the eclipse of Philo and Jewish philosophical speculation is of signal importance for the path that Egyptian Judaism took in this period. Why was it that Philo's works, to say the least, were not preserved by the Jews? [2] It is of course possible that this great thinker was never typical of Alexandrian Judaism as a whole, perhaps representing only a small philosophically-minded circle—although it is an interesting fact that in one place [3] Philo is concerned to combat Jews who carried his allegorical method to the extreme of denying altogether the relevance of the Torah to their faith, an indication of the existence of a Jewish group or groups who yielded even more than he did to an accommodation to current thought. However, the main reason for the eclipse of Philo was the resurgence of Pharisaic Judaism, which began at Jamnia after A.D. 70 and continued unabated, in its literary activity, until about A.D. 600. The Rabbis looked with disfavour on the attempt which had been made in Alexandria to bridge the gulf between the Jewish and Greek worlds and gradually exerted their influence against this. Thus Judaism, which earlier had been of a varied character wherein, both in Palestine and in the Diaspora, Pharisaic, hellenistic, and sectarian beliefs existed side by side, now slowly conformed to the path of Rabbinism. However, this change of emphasis was not effected immediately upon the reconstruction of Judaism at Jamnia, as the textbooks used to suggest. There was in Palestine and the Diaspora a transition period, covered approximately by the years A.D. 70–135, during which hellenistic and Rabbinic ideas continued to exist side by side in Greek documents, and the linguistic frontier between the Greek and Semitic worlds had not yet been identified with the cultural frontiers between hellenism and Judaism. It is the merit of Professor G. D. Kilpatrick's outstanding work on St. Matthew's Gospel that this fact is recognized and given full weight.[4]

[1] R. McL. Wilson, *The Gnostic Problem*, 1958, pp. 172–255.
[2] The first Jew to mention Philo by name after his time is A. de Rossi (A.D. 1573). The preservation of Philo's works was undoubtedly the achievement of the Christian Church.
[3] *de migr. abr.* 16, 89 f.
[4] *The Origins of the Gospel according to St. Matthew*, 1946, pp. 101–23.

He shows that in Matthew we have a Greek document whose thought is closely connected with, and is evidence for, the Rabbinical Judaism of the end of the first century A.D. and, more recently, Professor K. Stendahl [1] has provided evidence that this Gospel was produced within a school of exegetes who worked on the lines of the Rabbinical schools attached to the synagogues. Rabbinical Judaism in Syria, if Matthew had its origin there, was a force to be reckoned with in this transition period. However, when we turn to Egypt it has usually been said that evidence for the beliefs of the Jewish communities in this period, from both Jewish and Christian sides, is totally lacking and that therefore it is impossible to gain any clear view as to their development or otherwise. *A priori* we should expect in the years A.D. 70–135 the hellenistic element in Egyptian Judaism to decline and the Pharisaic to rise to the ascendancy as the influence of Jamnia was exerted.

We wish to suggest that one piece of evidence for the understanding of Egyptian Judaism in this period has been overlooked. This is the Christian document known as the Epistle of Barnabas, which is usually classed with the writings of the Apostolic Fathers of the Church. Barnabas, an epistolary tract of unknown Jewish-Christian authorship, was probably written in Alexandria during the early years of the reign of Hadrian (A.D. 117–38),[2] and its significance for

---

[1] *The School of St. Matthew*, 1954, p. 35.

[2] Recently P. Prigent, *L' Épitre de Barnabé I–XVI et Ses Sources* (Paris, 1961) has cast doubts on this Epistle's Alexandrian provenance, believing it to come from a Syrian milieu. Against this however is the strong literary connexion with Alexandria. Clement of Alexandria, the earliest witness to the Epistle, frequently quotes it and gives it an authority equal to the Catholic Epistles, which suggests it had already gained recognition in the Alexandrian Church—perhaps through public reading. Following Clement, Origen, A.C.O. (*c.* A.D. 300) and Codex Sinaiticus, all Egyptian witnesses, knew the Epistle. On the other hand there are no African witnesses before St. Augustine and no Syrian witnesses before the fifth century. The supposed connexions with the Odes of Solomon, Ascension of Isaiah and the Gospel of Peter are too vague to bear critical examination. It is true that early Christian allegory had more in common with Palestinian Rabbinic typological exegesis than with that of Philo—but with the significant exception of Ep. Barnabas. In this Epistle the typical features of Alexandrian allegorism appear—e.g., the argument that the *Torah* was never meant to be obeyed literally, the undervaluing of the historical meaning of Old Testament history and ordinances, the allegorizing of the smallest details of the LXX to yield a higher, spiritual meaning (e.g. Barn. vi. 1–11, viii. 1–7, ix. 8, xi. 1–11). The Epistle is so full of this method that the writer presupposes that his readers will understand his arguments. This suggests that the work comes from a *Sitz im Leben* where allegorizing, as distinct from historical typology, was not an innovation. Alexandria certainly fits this picture better than any other centre. See further L. W. Barnard in CQR 159 (1958), pp. 211–29 and JEA 44 (1958), pp. 101–7.

us lies in the fact that its arguments are so thoroughly Jewish that the specifically Christian elements are pushed into the background. J. B. Lightfoot [1] said that the writer treats the Jewish scriptures with a degree of respect which would have satisfied the most devout Rabbi. If this is the case, we may have first hand evidence for the beliefs of at least one section of Alexandrian Judaism in the early decades of the second century A.D., just before the triumph of Pharisaism.

We may give briefly the arguments for regarding the author as a converted Rabbi who brought into Christianity the exegetical and homiletic traditions of the Alexandrian synagogue. The first is the strongly Jewish character of the Epistle's argument and its familiarity with Jewish rites. We may mention also the designation of Satan as the Black One (iv. 9, xx. 1),[2] the invisibility of God (v. 10),[3] the land of milk and honey (vi. 8), the ritual of the Day of Atonement (vii. 1–11),[4] the shrub 'Rachel' (vii. 8), the sacrifice of the red heifer (viii. 1–2), the 'Kingdom of Jesus on the wood' (viii. 5), the gematria on the 318 servants of Abraham (ix. 8),[5] the interpretation of Psalm i (x. 10),[6] Moses and Amalek (xii. 1–11) [7] Jacob and Esau (xiii. 1–7), the celebration of the Sabbath (xv. 1–9) [8] and the allegorical interpretation of the six days of the creation as the 6,000 years of the world's history (xv. 4). However, it is the author's exegetical method which, for our purpose, is of the greatest interest.

(A) This is strongly Rabbinic

This is shown by the division made by the author into Haggadah (Chs. i–xvii) and Halakhah (Chs. xviii–xx) and by the fact that the Epistle as a whole is a Talmud, i.e., *didache*. Thus in ix. 9 immediately following the bold gematria on Abraham's servants, come these words: οἶδεν ὁ τὴν ἔμφυτον δωρεὰν τῆς διδαχῆς αὐτοῦ θέμενος ἐν ἡμῖν. οὐδεὶς γνησιώτερον ἔμαθεν ἀπ' ἐμοῦ λόγον· ἀλλὰ οἶδα, ὅτι ἄξιοί ἐστε ὑμεῖς. And in xvi. 9 the author says that God dwells in us by ὁ λόγος αὐτοῦ τῆς πίστεως, ἡ κλῆσις αὐτοῦ τῆς ἐπαγγελίας, ἡ σοφία τῶν δικαιωμάτων, αἱ ἐντολαὶ τῆς διδαχῆς....

[1] *St. Clement of Rome*, Vol. II, p. 503.
[2] Kidd. 30a. Rabbi Güdemann, *Zur Erklärung des Barnabasbriefes*, p. 128, holds that this expression would only be possible on the lips of a Jew.
[3] Chullin 60a. This conception was also held by a long tradition of Greek thought from the time of Plato onwards.
[4] Mishna, Menach. II; Talmud, Menach. 100a; Yoma vi. 1–6, 66b; Jos. *Ant.* iii. 10. 3.
[5] Beresh. rabba 43, 44; Nedar. 32a.
[6] Succa 21b; Abod. sar. 19b.
[7] Mishna, Rosh Hash. iii. 8. In the first two centuries A.D. Amalek, for the Jews, was the eternal enemy. Cf. Justin *Dial.* xlix.
[8] Cf. Berachoth 57b.

The division between the Haggadic and Halakhic sections of the Epistle is marked by the words, Μεταβῶμεν δὲ καὶ ἑτέραν γνῶσιν καὶ διδαχήν (xviii. 1). Moreover passages from the LXX are broken into their component parts and explained piece by piece, as in the Rabbinical method of writing midrash (a good example of this is Chapter iv); it is this method which largely accounts for the lack of unity and the presence of *membra disjecta* in the Epistle. Indeed some of the writer's interpretations have close parallels in Rabbinical exegesis. Thus the belief that the Jews fell from grace when Moses broke the tables of stone at Sinai (iv. 8, xiv. 3) is also found in a tradition in Mekilta, and the subject is further discussed in the Talmudic Aboda Zarah iv[b]–v[a]. There was a Jewish fast day on Tammuz 17 which commemorated the dark day of the golden calf incident. Another indication of the Epistle's Rabbinical style is the author's fondness for the rhetorical question, a didactic device much used by the Rabbis. These considerations suggest that the Alexandrian synagogue, in which the author was nurtured before his conversion, knew and practised in the early second century A.D. a type of exegesis and homiletic exposition closely parallel in many ways to that of the Rabbis of Jamnia. The only difference was that this exegesis was somewhat more free than that of Palestinian Rabbinism, being based on the Greek Bible as a whole and on certain of the pseudepigraphical writings. As yet the school associated with Rabbi Akiba, with its passion for minute accuracy and devotion to the letter of the Hebrew text, which reflected badly on the frequent loose phraseology of the Greek version, had been unable to prevent the use of the LXX in the Hellenistic synagogues of Alexandria. In Egypt the LXX probably ceased to be copied by Jews at a slightly later date than that of this Epistle.

(B) Allegorical Interpretation

It is a well-known fact that the Epistle adopts *in toto* the allegorical method of interpretation. Examples may be picked at random, the most striking being in ix. 8 where Abraham's 318 servants are made to refer to Jesus and the Cross (IHT = 318). The writer's usual procedure is to break up passages from the LXX into their component parts, as in the Rabbinical midrashim, and then explain them allegorically. His use of this method far exceeds anything known in Rabbinical Judaism and the New Testament, where it is used only with the greatest caution, and in none of the passages classified by Dr. C. H. Dodd as primary sources of testimonia.[1] We are therefore justified in believing that the writer knew

[1] *According to the Scriptures* (1952), pp. 107–10.

of this method from the teaching of the Hellenistic synagogue before his conversion.

Philo's type of allegorization must therefore still have been practised in Alexandria in the early second century A.D. although it may have been used only to serve the purposes of midrashic exposition.

(c) The Pesher Method

Embedded in the Epistle's Rabbinical mode of thought is a method of interpreting the Old Testament which has been found in the Qumran Scrolls. This is the quotation of an Old Testament text followed by an application to contemporary events—an interpretation which was believed to have a profound significance for those who could understand. Thus Barn. v. 3–4 reads:

'Therefore we ought to give hearty thanks to the Lord that he has given us knowledge of the past, and wisdom for the present, and that we are not without understanding for the future. And the Scripture says, "Not unjustly are the nets spread for the birds". This means that a man deserves to perish who has a knowledge of the way of righteousness, but turns aside into the way of darkness.'

Barn. xvi. 3–4:

'Furthermore he says again, "Lo, they who destroyed this temple shall themselves build it". That is happening now. For owing to the war it was destroyed by the enemy; at present even the servants of the enemy will build it up again.'

This method of interpretation is reminiscent of that found in the Qumran commentaries on the Books of Micah, Nahum, Habakkuk and Psalm xxxvii, and in the Damascus Document. For instance, with the first passage quoted above may be compared Com. Ps. xxxvii. 8–9 (fragment A, col. 1): 'Refrain from anger and abandon wrath; fret not thyself, it tendeth only to evil doing. For evildoers shall be cut off. This applies to those who return to the Torah and do not refuse to repent their evil-doing. Those, however, who are defiant about repenting their iniquity will be cut off.' With the second compare 4 Qp. Nah. ii. 11: 'Where is the abode of the lions, which was the feeding place of the young lions. (This refers to Jerusalem which has become) an abode for the wicked men of the heathen.' Barnabas' use of this method recalls the Qumran word *pesher*, used frequently in these commentaries to indicate the interpretation of texts, the true significance and application of which is only known by those who possess understanding. Professor Stendahl [1] has plausibly

[1] Op. cit., pp. 183–202. *Pesher* is also used in the Aramaic part of the Book of Daniel, cf. Dan. iv. 9. I have discussed the *pesher* method further on pp. 87–8.

connected the *pesher* type of citation with the formula quotations of St. Matthew's Gospel, and it could be argued that Barnabas took over this method from there. However, the fact that his interpretations never refer to the fulfilment in our Lord, and the close parallel with the Qumran citations, suggest that the method may have been already known in the Alexandrian Judaism in which he was cradled.

(D) The Religious Life

In this Epistle the distinctive Christian virtues of faith, hope and love play a subordinate role, the main emphasis of the writer being on spirituality (iv. 11, xvi. 10) and upon knowledge, (gnosis), which is used in three senses:

(i) Knowledge is often coupled with faith and has ethical consequences (i. 5, v. 4, xviii. 1, xix. 1).
(ii) Sometimes this knowledge refers to the interpretation of events in the past, present, and eschatological future (ii. 3-4, v. 4).
(iii) Knowledge is also mediated through the allegorical interpretation of the Old Testament (vi. 9, xiii. 7) and is also the gift of God (i. 7, ix. 8).

This idea of knowledge is not that of Gnosticism, where it refers to the comprehension of the soul's origin and nature by a mystical enlightenment, but is fundamentally Jewish. This is shown by the marked affinities which the connotation of knowledge in Barnabas has with the idea of *da'ath* in the Qumran texts, where it also has a strong ethical content [1] and an eschatological reference.[2] However as W. D. Davies [3] points out, the emphasis which the Dead Sea sect placed on *da'ath*, in comparison with other Jewish literature, may well reflect, in a subtle way, hellenistic influences which had been entering Palestine since the Maccabaean period. It is therefore possible that the emphasis upon knowledge in Barnabas, while fundamentally Jewish,[4] also owed something to the hellenistic milieu of Alexandria, where the idea of knowledge formed part of the intellectual climate of the age.

While no claim is made that the Jewish background of this Epistle necessarily represents the whole of Alexandrian Judaism in the early decades of the second century A.D., it is at least evidence which deserves to be taken into consideration. It shows that, in certain

[1] I QS ix. 17f; cf. I QS iii. 2, v. 9, 12, vi. 9, vii. 3-4.
[2] I QS iv. 18f; I Qp. Hab. ii. 14.
[3] HTR 46 (1954), p. 135.
[4] Qumran influence on Barnabas was in all probability indirect; see pp. 87-99. I have discussed more fully 'knowledge' in Barnabas and the Dead Sea Scrolls on pp. 90-92.

Jewish circles, some hellenistic influences and ideas, parallel to those found on Palestinian soil at Qumran, continued to exist side by side with Rabbinic conceptions. However, the Rabbinical caste of thought and exegetical methods are clearly central to the Epistle's arguments and overlay these other influences. It therefore appears that in the crucial period A.D. 70–135 Alexandrian Judaism, while having affinities on one side with Philonic allegorism and other hellenistic modes of thought, was not unaffected by the pattern and requirements of Rabbinism which, no doubt, had been exerting pressure on Diaspora Judaism.[1] The triumph of Pharisaism had, however, not yet fully come.

The Struggle with Christianity

We have already seen that strife between Jew and Greek reached ugly proportions during this period. In particular the terrible losses suffered by the Alexandrian Jewish community following on the revolt against Trajan in A.D. 115 must have had serious consequences. A time of political upheaval such as this would not have been conducive to consolidation, and Egyptian Judaism slowly began to decline in influence. However, in the period from A.D. 70–135 the Jews were still a force in Egypt, and we must now study their relations vis-à-vis the Christian Church.

As is well known, the origins of Egyptian Christianity are bathed in obscurity. It has been suggested [2] that in origin it was of Gnostic character and that this accounts for the silence of later orthodox writers. There is no real evidence to substantiate this view—especially in view of the fact that Basilides and Valentinus now appear to have been more Christian and less Gnostic than previously thought.[3] Again, our earliest certain evidence for Christianity in Egypt is the Epistle of Barnabas, c. A.D. 117–19, which has behind it a long tradition of worship, catechesis,[4] and liturgy, and presupposes the

[1] E. R. Goodenough, *Jewish Symbols in the Graeco-Roman Period*, 1953, ff, has argued that a form of hellenistic Judaism existed side by side with Rabbinic Judaism in Egypt down to the fourth or fifth centuries A.D. His evidence, however, is mostly drawn from funerary inscriptions, which are notoriously conservative, and cannot be taken as evidence for the continuance of an independent hellenistic Jewish philosophy. However, his work is a warning against making too rigid a dichotomy between hellenistic and Rabbinic Judaism.

[2] W. Bauer, *Rechtgläubigkeit und Ketzerei im ältesten Christentum*, 1934, pp. 49 f.

[3] See especially the *Gospel of Truth* in the Jung Codex, which is probably the composition of Valentinus. Text in Ed. M. Malinine, H-C. Puech, and G. Quispel, *Studien aus dem C. G. Jung Intitut* VI (Zürich, 1956).

[4] A comparison of the structure of the Epistle with that of the Tannaitic catechism might well yield interesting results. See my paper in ATR 41 (1959), pp. 177–90.

use of St. Matthew's Gospel and several of the New Testament epistles. Moreover the use of an earlier Two Ways catechesis in this work, almost certainly Jewish-Christian, suggests that Christians of Jewish descent existed in Egypt at an earlier period. We may also believe that Gentiles formed an element in the Church, as the earliest Christian Gnostics, who appear in the reign of Hadrian, could hardly have arisen *in vacuo*. Basilides in particular had behind him earlier Christian speculations. There is also some evidence for a connexion between the Roman and Egyptian Churches at an early period which was, no doubt, facilitated by trading contacts between the ports of Puteoli and Alexandria. Quite apart from Eusebius' reference to St. Mark, the historical value of which is disputed,[1] we have the recognition of the connexion by Julius I,[2] the similarity between the Canons adopted by the two Churches and the readings found in the Sahidic version of the New Testament which are also found in Codex D and in the old Latin versions. It appears probable that both Jewish and Gentile Christians were to be found in Egypt in the first century A.D., and perhaps the Roman Church had taken a share in bringing the new faith to the country.

Relations between Jews and Christians during the period A.D. 70–135 took on a more sombre aspect. From the Christian side we have the evidence of the Gospels of St. Matthew, St. John, and the Apocalypse,[3] i.e., evidence from Syria and Asia Minor, which shows that antagonism was most marked where Christians were of Jewish descent. This is also supported by explicit statements from Jewish sources which have been collected by Professor Kilpatrick[4] who quotes, as the most informative piece of evidence, the Birkath-ha-Minim composed by Samuel the Small at Jamnia *c.* A.D. 85. In its earliest form it reads: 'For the excommunicate let there be no hope and the arrogant government do thou swiftly uproot in our days; and may the Christians and heretics suddenly be laid low and not be inscribed with the righteous. Blessed art thou, O Lord, who humbles the arrogant.' This insertion in the liturgy henceforth made it impossible for Christians of Jewish descent to attend the synagogue,[5]

[1] *H.E.* ii. 16. Mr. C. H. Roberts' demonstration in JTS 50 (1949), pp. 155–68, that the Alexandrian Church's custom of writing biblical texts on papyrus leaves, rather than on rolls, was taken over from Roman usage also supports the view that the two Churches were connected. His further view that Eusebius' reference is a reminiscence of the arrival of St. Mark's Gospel in the Egyptian metropolis demands careful consideration.

[2] Athan. *Apol. contra Arian.* xxxv.

[3] Matt. xxvii. 25; John v. 17 f., vi. 32–35, vii. 19, 37–39 *inter alia*; Rev. ii. 9, iii. 9.

[4] Op. cit., pp. 109–13.

[5] Matt. iv. 23, ix. 35, x. 17, xii. 9, xiii. 54 (συναγωγῇ followed by αὐτῶν) and John ix. 22, xii. 42, xvi. 2 are relevant here.

as undoubtedly some of them had done up to that time, and the breach was made absolute before A.D. 100 by the sending out of letters from Palestine to all synagogues informing them of the necessity of excluding Christians from their assemblies. Further evidence of the persecution measures taken by Judaism is provided by a statement in Justin Martyr which may well belong to an earlier period.[1] Relevant also are two stories found in Jewish sources dating from the period A.D. 100–130. The first concerns a man called Ishmael who prevented Jacob, a follower of Jesus ben Pandera, from healing a man who had been bitten by a snake. The second is about a certain Eliezer ben Hyrkanos who admits to his error in applauding a specious halakhah of Jesus which had been recounted to him by the Christian Jacob of Kephar Sekhanya. These stories show that by the early second century A.D. religious contact between Jews and Jewish Christians had been condemned, which applied also to the reading of Christian literature. A ruling which dates from the period A.D. 90–120 ran: 'The book margins and the books of the Minim (i.e., the Jewish Christians) are not saved but they with the divine names in them are burned where they are.' [2] A further indication of the controversy between the two bodies is to be found in the Rabbinical polemic against the doctrine of the two powers, which had been held in earlier Judaism and is found in the Qumran Scrolls.[3] This attack began in the first quarter of the second century and would certainly have been invoked against the Christian doctrine of the Person of Christ. The above evidence will have shown that in the period A.D. 70–135, and especially from c. A.D. 90, Rabbinical Judaism took active measures against Jewish Christianity which included the expulsion of Christian Jews from the synagogues, the prohibition of religious intercourse between the two groups, and the reading of Christian literature by Jews. A Jew had to be either a Christian or a Jew; he could not be both at the same time.

The evidence from the Jewish side so far considered is Palestinian in origin, while the Christian evidence comes in the main from Syria and Asia Minor. Can we generalize from this to the position obtaining in the Egyptian Diaspora? How far, in fact, were the instructions of the Rabbis of Jamnia, which begin with the promulgation of the Birkathha-Minim, carried out in Egypt, in view of the somewhat

[1] *Dial. cum Trypho.* xvii. 1.
[2] Kilpatrick, op. cit., pp. 111–12.
[3] I QS iii. 13–iv. 26. This conception is ultimately Iranian. Cf. Yasna xxx. 3. 5. H. Michauda, 'Un mythe zervanite dans un des manuscripts Qumran', VT 5 (1955), pp. 137–47, believes that Zervanism, a special branch of Zoroastrianism, was the determining influence on the Qumran theology.

freer attitude adopted by Alexandrian Judaism in matters of homiletic and midrashic exposition? Were there any violent contacts between Church and Synagogue during this transition period which saw the slow decline of hellenistic Judaism from the pinnacle to which Philo had brought it? Again it is the Epistle of Barnabas which throws some light on this difficult question.

Commentators on Barnabas have often been puzzled by the violent reaction which it exhibits against Jewish institutions and beliefs, exceeding anything known elsewhere in early Christian literature, although in itself the Epistle is based closely on a Rabbinical method of exegesis. A good example of this is the polemic against the Temple in xvi. 1–2, where the Jews are not only castigated as 'wretched men' for putting their hope in the building but are also stated to have consecrated God in the Temple almost like the heathen. In the same chapter we have an exultation over the destruction of the Temple and the Holy City which is almost unbelievable on the lips of a Jew (xvi. 5). Similar to this is the writer's polemic against Jewish sacrifices and fasts (ii. 4–10, iii. 1–6) and against circumcision, which he regarded as the work of an evil angel (ix. 4). While the political upheavals of the age favoured fanaticism, these views appear to have been born of the consciousness that, as a Christian convert, he was finally excluded from Judaism and its worship, never to return. The very fact that he had written a Christian Epistle, only fit for burning as a book of the Minim, would have widened the breach; and the same applies to the writer's employment of a Two Ways catechesis, with its doctrine of the two angelic guides, which to the Jews would have savoured of the hated 'two powers' doctrine. This Epistle reflects a breach between the two religions which had become absolute, and this is the explanation of its references to 'we' and 'they' (iv. 6; xiv. 4) to the 'former people' and the 'new people' of God (v. 7, xiii. 1), and to the covenant which has been taken away from the Jews and given to the Christians (iv. 7, xiv. 4). The writer sees no continuity between Judaism and Christianity, such as is found in the Epistle to the Hebrews, but only antagonism. The very fact that he could advocate such violent and extreme views, although elsewhere appearing as a kindly and humane man of real pastoral gifts,[1] is an indication of the feeling which existed between Jews and Jewish Christians in Egypt in the early part of the second century A.D. We are thus justified in believing that the Palestinian Rabbis by this time had been able to exert their views in the Egyptian metropolis on the question of religious intercourse and that Jewish Christians had been expelled from the synagogues in accordance with the Birkathha-Minim. In many ways the situation in

[1] i. 1–5, 8, iv. 9, xxi. 5–9.

Alexandria was then similar to that of the milieu which produced St. Matthew's Gospel. This Gospel, like the Epistle of Barnabas, is strikingly Jewish; its structure is based on the five books of the Torah and its arguments are essentially Talmudic. Yet this same Gospel reflects also a breach between the two religions which was becoming absolute.

In this chapter we have sought to use a Christian source for the elucidation of an obscure, although nevertheless crucial, transition period for Egyptian Judaism. Caution is obviously needed in generalizing from its evidence about the beliefs and actions of Judaism *in toto*; some variety of approach may have continued to exist to a later date,[1] as was certainly the case with second-century Egyptian Christianity. However, our results seem to support the view that in Egypt, as in Palestine and elsewhere in the Diaspora, Rabbinical Judaism was slowly and successfully enforcing the pattern laid down at Jamnia. During the period A.D. 70–135 the way for the triumph in Egypt of Pharisaic Judaism over hellenistic and sectarian Judaism was being prepared, although the point of no return had not yet been reached—except in the question of social and religious relations between Jews and Christians.

[1] We should perhaps be wary of speaking of a 'normative' Judaism.

VI

ST. STEPHEN AND EARLY ALEXANDRIAN CHRISTIANITY

The message of St. Stephen and its relationship to first-century Judaism and early Christian theology has recently been the subject of several studies.[1] It is, I suppose, universally agreed that Stephen was a hellenistic Jew of the Diaspora who came into acute conflict with other Diaspora Jews of a more conservative kind domiciled in Jerusalem and that these took the initiative in effecting his arrest and trial. But that is as far as agreement goes. The attempt to understand further Stephen's message and influence has produced the widest divergence of opinion. To some[2] he is the originator of the mission to the Gentiles and Christian universalism whose conception of Christianity was adopted by later preachers and teachers with momentous consequences for Christian history. To others[3] he remained in essence a Jew, albeit of a liberal kind, even after his conversion, whose aim was to propogate a type of Judaism which was strongly anti-Temple and anti-cultus. On this view Stephen stands in the line of Nathan, Hosea, Trito-Isaiah, the Rechabites, some Essene circles and the Ebionites, as pictured in the Pseudo-Clementine writings, in asserting a non-material form of worship, independent of the Temple cultus, as being authentic Judaism. Still others[4] believe that Stephen cleverly preached Jesus in his interpretation of Joseph, Moses and Joshua; on this view he is a typologist whose aim is to show that Jesus' passion has been prefigured in the persecutions which God's righteous servants have always had to endure. It is not our purpose here to examine and criticize these conflicting opinions in detail but to seek to answer two questions, namely (i) Was Stephen's position an isolated one in first-century Judaism and in the early Church? (ii) And, if so, is it yet possible to trace his influence on Alexandrian Christianity

---

[1] L. M. Menchini, *Il discorso di S. Stefano Proto-martire nella Letteratura e Predicazione Christiana Primitiva* (Rome, 1951); W. Manson, *The Epistle to the Hebrews* (1951), pp. 25–46; W. Foerster, *Stephanus und die Urgemeinde in Dienst unter dem Wort* (1953), pp. 9–30; M. Simon, JEH 2, no. 2 (1951), pp. 127–42; M. Simon, *St. Stephen and the Hellenists in the Primitive Church* (1958), to which I am especially indebted.

[2] Manson, op. cit., pp. 25, 37.

[3] Simon, JEH 2, p. 141; Simon, *St. Stephen*, p. 111.

[4] R. B. Rackham, *The Acts of the Apostles* (1904), pp. 92–5; R. P. C. Hanson, *Theology* 50 (1947), p. 142 f.; C. S. C. Williams, *The Acts of the Apostles* (1957), pp. 100–102.

when it comes into historical perspective in the early second century of our era?

(1)

This we answer in the affirmative. In the first place Stephen's speech (Acts vii. 2–53) undoubtedly rests upon good historical tradition. The very fact that scholarly opinion as to the purpose of the address is so diverse is convincing proof of this, for a mere fabricator would have left his readers in little doubt as to his *Tendenz*.[1] E. Jirku,[2] followed by M. Simon,[3] has shown that the speech follows a literary pattern well known in the Old Testament and Pseudepigrapha, which was used for catechetical purposes; cf. Ps. cv. 12–43, cvi. 6–42; Josh. xxiv. 2–13; Neh. ix. 7–31; Judith v. 6–18. These summaries tell the story of the chosen people from the days of Abraham and the patriarchs with an emphasis on God's mercies towards the nation; He always hears their cry in times of affliction even though they may have provoked him to anger. Stephen's speech, though it follows a similar pattern to the above, has one significant difference. It lays a great emphasis on the unworthiness and rebelliousness of the Jews, especially towards their chosen deliverers (Acts vii. 35, 39, 51, 52), which culminates in their apostasy in building the Temple which is not the dwelling place of God (Acts vii. 46–50). The conclusion which Stephen draws is that God has abandoned his people because of their persecution of their deliverers:

'Ye stiffnecked and uncircumcised in heart and ears, ye do always resist the Holy Ghost: as your fathers did, so do ye. Which of the prophets did not your fathers persecute? and they killed them which shewed before of the coming of the Righteous One; of whom ye have now become betrayers and murderers' (Acts vii. 51–52).

Stephen's fierce hostility to the Temple and cultus is in line with his attitude towards the Torah. He believed that Moses on Sinai had received living oracles (λόγια ζῶντα, Acts vii. 38), that is the Torah, which the Jews since had never kept (Acts vii. 53). This extreme position is confirmed by the accusation at his trial, 'This man ceaseth not to speak words against this holy place and the Torah' (Acts vi. 13).

This attitude towards Old Testament history and institutions is

[1] H. J. Schoeps, *Theologie und Geschichte des Judenchristentums* (1949), p. 441, believes that the ideas developed in Stephen's speech are those of James, Jesus' brother, and that Stephen himself is a mythical figure. Such a radical view, which plays fast and loose with Acts, seems to me to be wide of the mark.
[2] *Die älteste Geschichte Israels im Rahmen lehrhafter Darstellungen* (1917).
[3] Simon, *St. Stephen*, pp. 40–41.

more extreme than anything found in the Hebrew prophets or in sectarian Judaism. Even the Qumran sect did not oppose the Temple and its cultus *per se*; it merely disputed the legitimacy of the priests then in control of the Temple. Indeed in all probability the sect regarded the sacrificial laws as still binding and believed that temple worship would be resumed in the eschatological future.[1] The only approximation to Stephen's views is found in the hellenistic Judaism of the Diaspora, and even there in only a few texts. Thus Trypho,[2] a representative of Ephesian Greek-speaking Judaism, distinguishes between the inferior type of Jerusalem worship, associated with sacrifices and the cultus, and the worship 'in spirit and in truth' which is practised in the synagogues of the Diaspora. The Sibylline Oracles Bk. IV, which probably are an Asia Minor composition, also express a similar idea; God does not dwell in a stone temple, because he is invisible,[3] and those who turn away from such futile buildings, soiled as they are with the blood of sacrifices, are to be commended.[4] But these passages date from after A.D. 70, when the temple lay in ruins, and I should not feel as confident as Schoeps and Simon are in asserting that such views were well known in Palestinian and Diaspora Judaism before A.D. 70. This may have been so, but decisive proof is lacking. In any case such radical views would have been held by only a small minority of 'advanced' thinkers. It is perhaps not without significance that such a thorough hellenist as Philo had no doubt that the temple and its cultus was of God although the use of allegory was needed to plumb the deeper meaning of the rites. Stephen's position is at best a minority view within first-century Diaspora Judaism approximating in many respects to Greek criticism of the pagan temples and idols. Whether some unfortunate experience of the Temple and Pharisaic Judaism had coloured his judgement we cannot tell. But the lack of specific Christian content in the speech, often noted by commentators, makes it probable that Stephen had developed the main lines of his attack on orthodox Judaism before his conversion to Christianity. The evidence of the witnesses at the trial (Acts vi. 14) shows that he had picked upon one element in Jesus' reported teaching [5] as supporting his views, while ignoring much else, and especially the practice of the Apostles in continuing their association with the Temple (Acts ii. 46–47). Stephen, when placed against a background of Pharisaic,

[1] M. Burrows, *More Light on the Dead Sea Scrolls* (1958), pp. 258, 363–5.
[2] Justin Martyr, *Dial.* cxvii. 2.
[3] IV, 8—12. Simon, JEH 2, pp. 136–7.
[4] IV, 27–30.
[5] The *verba Christi* concerning the destruction of the Temple which appear on the lips of the false witnesses in Mark xiv. 58.

sectarian and hellenistic Judaism, is something of a unique figure even within the wide limits which Judaism embraced before A.D. 70. He does not quite fit any mould.

When we consider his position vis-à-vis the early Church the same judgement must be recorded. The New Testament records many conflicts with Jews but nowhere, in the earlier documents, is it suggested that the Jews had consistently disobeyed their lawful teachers and failed to keep the Torah. St. Paul, like Stephen, treats Jewish history in outline, but his emphasis is on David as the progenitor of Jesus and the Christian κήρυγμα as the culmination and fulfilment of the whole process (Acts xiii. 16–41). We remember, too, that Paul was not beyond performing a religious purification in the Temple when expediency so demanded (Acts xxi. 26), an example of becoming a Jew unto the Jews in order to win them (1 Cor. ix. 20). The Torah, for the great Apostle, was a leader or guide (παιδαγωγός) unto Christ and was absolutely valid and binding until Jesus came (Gal. iii. 24–25). The Pauline theology is at the furthest remove from that of Stephen who regarded the history of the Jews, from the time of the golden calf incident, as one long apostasy deserving only of rebuke. And it is no different with St. Peter, who held a more developed Christology than Stephen, to judge from 1 Peter and the speeches in Acts. For him the Jews had acted through ignorance in crucifying Jesus, having misunderstood their own scriptures (Acts iii. 17–18). When we turn from Acts to other types of theology found in the New Testament an equal variance with Stephen's position appears. The late W. Manson [1] sought to show that the Epistle to the Hebrews took up and extended his message which, he believed, contained the seeds of universalism. Manson makes great play with their supposed identity of attitudes towards the cultus and Torah.[2] But Hebrews regards the tabernacle, cultus and Torah as valid for their age although but shadows of heavenly things.[3] The new and better covenant wrought in Jesus has now superseded the first which, although not faultless, was yet binding on the Jews.[4] The Platonism of Hebrews, often undervalued nowadays in the interests of 'biblical theology', is something quite different from the radical discontinuity of Stephen, who exalts the tabernacle because it belongs to the Mosaic age, and condemns the Temple because it is the fruit of that Jewish apostasy which began with the disobedience reflected in the golden calf incident.

[1] Op. cit., pp. 25–46.
[2] Op., cit. p. 36. Simon's further criticisms in *St. Stephen*, pp. 100–104, seem to me decisive.
[3] Cf. Heb. viii. 5: οἵτινες ὑποδείγματι καὶ σκιᾷ λατρεύουσι τῶν ἐπουρανίων.
[4] Heb. viii. 7, 13.

Stephen's position was an isolated one in the early Church. His attitude towards the Temple and Torah was very different from that of the first disciples who are recorded as, 'day by day, continuing steadfastly with one accord in the Temple, and breaking bread at home, they did take their food with gladness and singleness of heart, praising God, and having favour with all the people' (Acts ii. 46–47). The fact that he was quoted at the trial as buttressing his anti-Temple and anti-Torah polemic with some reported *verba Christi* along the same lines may have added fuel to the flames but in itself was not the cause of his death. He was condemned first and foremost as a Jewish left-wing critic of the *status quo*. Can it be that Luke has provided a clue to the historical situation in the summarizing verse Acts vi. 7 [1] which is significantly placed between the setting apart of the seven hellenists, Stephen among them, and the description of his arrest and trial?: 'And the word of God increased; and the number of disciples multiplied in Jerusalem exceedingly; and a great company of the priests were obedient to the faith.' Was Stephen's polemic the cause of unrest among the priesthood which resulted in many embracing the new faith? And was this the real reason for the drastic action taken by the conservative hellenistic Jews against him? In any event Stephen's position was anathema to Judaism, both Pharisaic and hellenistic, in Jerusalem, and also perhaps to Jewish Christianity which would regard him as a disruptive element intent on a breach with the ancestral faith. To the Jews he was a liberal extremist; to many Christians his views did not suit their present position vis-à-vis Judaism. He was a man born before his time.

We have already examined [2] the evidence that in the period A.D. 70–135, and especially from c. A.D. 90, Christian Jews were expelled from the synagogues and the final breach between Rabbinical Judaism and Christianity occurred. The Church in reply developed an anti-Jewish polemic, based on collections of Old Testament testimonia, which sought to show that Jesus was the Messiah of Hebrew prophecy. Stephen, whose influence in the early Church, apart from the Ebionite backwater,[3] was negligible, would

---

[1] On the summaries see H. J. Cadbury, *The Beginnings of Christianity*, V, note 30; C. J. Cadoux, JBL 56 (1937), p. 177 f.; P. Benoit, *Mélanges Goguel*, 1, note 1. The historical value of the summaries has often been called in question. No doubt there was a natural tendency to exaggerate the growth of Christianity; on the other hand the brevity of the reference to the priests here may imply that Luke's knowledge rests on more information than we now possess. See further the cautious conclusions of Cadbury, op. cit., p. 402 and Williams, op. cit., p. 35.

[2] pp. 51–5.

[3] Cf. especially Clem. *Rec.* i. 38; Simon, JEH 2, pp. 139–40.

have made an admirable theological ally during this period when extreme views as to the apostasy of the Jews would have received a ready welcome. This was a period of political upheaval when a revolutionary position vis-à-vis Pharisaic Judaism would not have seemed outrageous. Moreover the Temple issue remained a live one both in Palestine and in the Diaspora and a problem for the Church. There is nothing to which the Tannaim hold more strongly than the hope of the rebuilding of the Temple and the resumption of material sacrifices.[1] In many Mishnahs [2] and Baraithas [3] mention of the Temple is accompanied by the prayer, 'May it speedily be rebuilt in our time'. Many ordinances which had no real meaning after A.D. 70 were still accounted obligatory for one reason only: 'The Temple will be speedily rebuilt, and its ritual restored.' [4] The Church was thus still obliged to treat the Temple question seriously during the period A.D. 70–135 and it developed its earlier teaching that Jesus, in some way, had brought about the end of the Jerusalem shrine. According to John ii. 19–22 the Temple of Jesus' body replaces the Temple of stone, a fact not fully grasped by the disciples until the post-resurrection period. Barnabas has a theory that the Temple is essentially the divine indwelling of the human heart (xvi. 6–10). Stephen could have provided another, namely that the Most High dwelleth not in houses made with hands and that the building of stone temples, whether those of the past, or as proposed in the future, is an act of apostasy from the true traditions of Israel.

(2)

We must now go on to consider whether, in fact, the views of Stephen found any response in the period A.D. 70–135. Several commentators have noted connexions with the Epistle of Barnabas only to discount them. Thus Professor Simon writes: 'the affinities here are very clear and precise', only to conclude: 'Thus in spite of some real points of contact, Stephen diverges from pseudo-Barnabas, who comes closer to Hebrews than to him. Both Epistles belong to that Alexandrian line of thought represented in pre-Christian times by the Epistle of Aristeas and the works of Philo, which have undoubtedly influenced them. Stephen seems to stand in another line.' [5] Against this we shall now seek to show that the Alexandrian Barnabas, almost alone among Christian writers in this period, was *directly*

[1] J. Klausner, *The Messianic Idea in Israel* (1956), p. 513.
[2] Taanith iv. 8; Tamid vii. 3.
[3] Cf. Baba Metsia 28b, b.
[4] Sukkah 41a; Menahoth 25b; Rosh ha-Shanah 30a; Betsah 5b; Taanith 17b; Sanhedrin 22b; Bekhoroth 53b.
[5] *St. Stephen*, pp. 104 and 107.

influenced by Stephen's views, embodying them in his work; and the reason for his partiality for Stephen lies in the particular historical situation which produced the Christian Epistle.

The dating of this Epistle hinges on the interpretation of two passages, iv. 4–5 and xvi. 3–4. The latter we refer to conditions at the beginning of Hadrian's reign when the Emperor had adopted a lenient policy towards the Jews, holding out to them a promise that the temple would be rebuilt [1]—or at least rumours to this effect were then current.[2] On this theory the ὑπηρέται of xvi. 4 are the craftsmen and workers who accompanied many of the legions in Hadrian's time and who were to be engaged in actual building operations, together with some Jews, if the reading of ℵ is adopted. After the terrible conflict between Jews and Greeks in the time of Trajan, which resulted in Jewish losses on a vast scale, this promise must have appeared of great significance to Egyptian Judaism, for many of the Egyptian Jews, especially in country areas, had looked towards Jerusalem since their own replica of the Temple at Leontopolis had been closed in A.D. 73. Barnabas, with his Jewish background and knowledge, knew of Hadrian's proposal, the fulfilment of which he believed to be imminent—hence his use of γίνεται and ἀνοικοδομήσουσιν in xvi. 4. The enigmatic passage iv. 4–5 is not really at variance with this dating if, in the enumeration of the ten emperors, Julius Caesar is put aside; though he claimed the *praenomen Imperatoris* [3] he was a dictator rather than an Imperator in the later sense. Also Galba, Otho and Vitellius (whose reigns covered but nineteen months) should be omitted, as in Rev. xvii. 10, as unworthy to rank with the Augusti.

If, then, we date Barnabas c. A.D. 117–19 and set the Epistle against a background of a renewed interest, among Jews and certain Christians, in the Jewish Torah and Temple—an interest which was becoming a threat to Christianity—then we have a situation in which Stephen's anti-Torah and anti-Temple views would have been useful in Christian polemic. We must now see if, in fact, such was the case.

Specific Parallels

(A) Attitude towards the Temple

[1] Epiph. *de mens. et pond.* xiv.
[2] Cf. Sibyl. Or. V, 48, 421; X, 163. On Hadrian's pro-Jewish policy see the valuable study of K. Thieme, *Kirche und Synagogue* (1944), pp. 22–5 and J. A. Kleist, *A.C.W.* (1948), pp. 31–2. This policy is also illustrated by the Alexandrian Acts of the Martyrs—see Von Premerstein in *Philologus*, Suppl. 16, 2 (1923).
[3] Suet. *Jul.* 76. I have dealt with the dating of Barnabas in JEA 44 (1958), pp. 101–7 where fuller details are given.

Stephen
Acts vii. 48–50;

ἀλλ' οὐχ ὁ ὕψιστος ἐν χειροποιήτοις κατοικεῖ· καθὼς ὁ προφήτης λέγει, <u>Ὁ οὐρανός μοι θρόνος, ἡ δὲ γῆ ὑποπόδιον τῶν ποδῶν μου· ποῖον οἶκον οἰκοδομήσετέ μοι; λέγει Κύριος, ἢ τίς τόπος τῆς καταπαύσεώς μου;</u> οὐχὶ ἡ χείρ μου ἐποίησε ταῦτα πάντα;

Epistle of Barnabas
Barn. xvi. 1–2:

Ἔτι δὲ καὶ περὶ τοῦ ναοῦ ἐρῶ ὑμῖν, ὡς πλανώμενοι οἱ ταλαίπωροι εἰς τὴν οἰκοδομὴν ἤλπισαν, καὶ οὐκ ἐπὶ τὸν θεὸν αὐτῶν τὸν ποιήσαντα αὐτούς, ὡς ὄντα οἶκον θεοῦ. σχεδὸν γὰρ ὡς τὰ ἔθνη ἀφιέρωσαν αὐτὸν ἐν τῷ ναῷ. ἀλλὰ πῶς λέγει κύριος καταργῶν αὐτόν, μάθετε· Τίς ἐμέτρησεν τὸν οὐρανὸν σπιθαμῇ ἢ τὴν γῆν δρακί; οὐκ ἐγώ; λέγει κύριος· <u>Ὁ οὐρανός μοι θρόνος, ἡ δὲ γῆ ὑποπόδιον τῶν ποδῶν μου· ποῖον οἶκον οἰκοδομήσετέ μοι, ἢ τίς τόπος τῆς καταπαύσεώς μου;</u> ἐγνώκατε, ὅτι ματαία ἡ ἐλπὶς αὐτῶν,

The quotation from Isa. lxvi. 1 f. occurs in both writers, significantly with the same slight variation from the text of the LXX, namely ἢ τίς τόπος for καὶ ποῖος τόπος. It may be thought that both writers are drawing on a common testimony source; cf. Justin, *Dial.* xxii. 2–5, 11 where Amos v. 25 f. and Isa. lxvi 1 f. are brought together. On the other hand the Isaiah quotation is nowhere else found within or without the New Testament before Barnabas, where the context of thought is very similar to Acts. Thus χειροποίητος is used most frequently of idolatrous temples and certainly carries that derogatory meaning in Stephen's speech; cf. the similar expression of the idolatrous worship of the golden calf in vii. 41: ἀνήγαγον θυσίαν τῷ εἰδώλῳ, καὶ εὐφραίνοντο ἐν τοῖς ἔργοις τῶν χειρῶν αὐτῶν. Barn. xvi. 2 is very close to this: σχεδὸν γὰρ ὡς τὰ ἔθνη ἀφιέρωσαν αὐτὸν ἐν τῷ ναῷ. ἀφιεροῦν is found in hellenistic religious literature with the meaning 'consecrate';[1] Barnabas therefore castigates the Jews for consecrating God by or in the Temple like the pagans, that is, building a temple which is the equivalent of a pagan temple and therefore a place of idolatry (cf. xvi. 1); this is stated explicitly in xvi. 7: ὡς ἀληθῶς οἰκοδομητὸς ναός διὰ χειρός, ὅτι ἦν πλήρης μὲν εἰδωλολατρείας καὶ ἦν οἶκος δαιμονίων διὰ τὸ ποιεῖν, ὅσα ἦν ἐναντία τῷ θεῷ. Stephen implies, in Acts vii. 48–9, that, as God does not dwell in a human οἶκος made with hands, his οἶκος must be in heaven.[2] Barnabas again states this more explicitly in denouncing

[1] Diod. Sic. i. 90. 4; Philo Bybl. (c. A.D. 100) in Eus. *Praep. ev.* i; x. 16, 20, 21; 4 Macc. xiii. 13; Jos. *Ant.* xv. 364.

[2] A distinction already implied in the LXX; cf. 2 Chron. vi. 21. The LXX uses the verb κατασκηνῶσαι of the divine temporary dwelling in the temple, but reserves κατοικεῖν for God's permanent dwelling in heaven. See further Simon, JEH 2, pp. 132–3.

the Jews for putting their hope on the building, καὶ οὐκ ἐπὶ τὸν θεὸν αὐτῶν τὸν ποιήσαντα αὐτούς, ὡς ὄντα οἶκον θεοῦ (xvi. 1). The attitude towards the Temple in Stephen's speech and the later Epistle is identical and more extreme than anything found elsewhere in early Christian literature. Is it probable that both developed their views independently in view of the similarity of argument and verbal agreements?

(B) Moses, the Torah and the Jews

Stephen's speech is an impassioned attack on the conduct of the Jews in rebelling against their appointed leaders. And it is not without significance that at least twenty of the fifty-three verses of the speech are concerned with Moses. For Stephen the culmination of Jewish perverseness is found in the incident of the golden calf. Thus Acts vii. 38–42a:

'This is he (i.e., Moses) that was in the church in the wilderness with the angel which spake to him in the mount Sinai, and with our fathers: who received living oracles (λόγια ζῶντα) to give unto us: to whom our fathers would not be obedient, but thrust him from them, and turned back in their hearts unto Egypt, saying unto Aaron, Make us gods which shall go before us: for as for this Moses, which led us forth out of the land of Egypt, we wot not what is become of him. And they made a calf in those days, and brought a sacrifice unto the idol, and rejoiced in the works of their hands. But God turned, and gave them up to serve the host of heaven.'

(Cf. Acts vii. 53: 'Ye who received the Torah as it was ordained by angels, and kept it not.')

Stephen's underlying contention is that the Torah was given to Moses as the true Word of God, but that the Jews, by their rebelliousness, never kept it. Whatever was ordered after the golden calf incident was idolatrous—'God turned and gave them up to serve the host of heaven'. There will be no renewal of the Covenant, for God has abandoned the Jews once and for all. Their history, from the time of the making of the calf onwards, is a proof of this fact.

With this cf. Barnabas iv. 7–8:

'It (i.e., the covenant) is ours: but in this way did they finally lose it when Moses had just received it, for the scripture says: "And Moses was in the mount fasting forty days and forty nights, and he received the covenant from the Lord, tables of stone written with the finger of the hand of the Lord". But they turned to idols and lost it. For thus saith the Lord: "Moses, go down quickly, for thy people, whom thou broughtest forth out of the land of Egypt, have broken the Torah." And Moses understood and cast the two tables out of his hands, and their covenant was broken, in order that the covenant of Jesus the Beloved should be sealed in our hearts in hope of his faith.'

(Cf. xiv. 4–5: 'Moses received it (i.e. the covenant) but they were not worthy. But learn how we received it. Moses received it when he was a servant, but the Lord himself gave it to us, as the people of the inheritance, by suffering for our sakes. And it was made manifest both that the tale of their sins should be completed in their sins, and we through Jesus, the Lord who inherits the covenant, should receive it.')

The underlying idea here is the same as in Stephen's polemic. Moses received the true Torah and Covenant, but the Jews immediately lost it by worshipping the golden calf, so causing Moses to cast the tables of stone out of his hands in anger (Exod. xxxii. 19);[1] Barnabas interprets this as the moment when the Covenant made by God was broken and mystically transferred to the Christians. In his view there is no renewing of the Covenant in Judaism or Christianity but only one Covenant which God has taken away from the Jews because of their rebelliousness—'they were not worthy'—a view at variance with the Christian idea of the new and better Covenant wrought in Jesus. The only difference between the two writers is that Barnabas has introduced a certain amount of allegorical interpretation into his argument which is not found in Stephen's speech. This is because he is not delivering an impassioned speech to Jewish elders but writing a treatise for Christians. He is seeking to find a Christian meaning in Jewish ordinances through the use of Alexandrian principles of interpretation, rather than to recount Jewish history *per se*. And we also note a sharpening of the anti-Jewish polemic. The Jews, who have persecuted the prophets (Acts vii. 52; Barn. v. 11), have the total of their sins completed by the coming of Jesus in the flesh (Barn. v. 11, xiv. 5).

(c) Sacrificial worship

The attitude of Stephen towards sacrificial worship is found in Acts vii. 41–3 where the idolatrous worship of the golden calf results in God giving up the Jews to the service of the host of heaven.[2] This is buttressed with a quotation from the LXX of Amos v. 25f.:

[1] Found also in a Rabbinical tradition in Mekilta; cf. also Aboda Zarah 4b–5a.
[2] Cf. Jer. vii. 18, viii. 2, xix. 13; Zeph. i. 5; 2 Chron. xxxiii. 3, 5; Deut. iv. 19; xvii. 3; 2 Kings xxiii. 5.

'as it is written in the book of the prophets, Did ye offer unto me slain beasts and sacrifices forty years in the wilderness, O house of Israel? And ye took up the tabernacle of Moloch, and the star of the god Rephan, the figures which ye made to worship them: and I will carry you away beyond Babylon' (Acts vii. 42-43).

Stephen's view is that the sacrificial cult is not the will of God but fundamentally an act of idolatry—the worship of false gods. Justin Martyr [1] significantly quotes this same passage from Amos in conjunction with Jer. vii. 21-2: 'Thus saith the Lord, Gather your burnt offerings and your meat-offerings, and eat flesh. For I spoke not to your fathers, nor commanded them in the day wherein I brought them up out of the land of Egypt, concerning burnt offerings and sacrifice.' However Justin somewhat qualifies this prophetic denunciation by stating that subsequently God had to accept Jewish sacrifices in order to prevent the Jews from continuing in idolatry.[2] The levitical regulations concerning sacrifice have, in his view, a therapeutic value. Stephen is more radical than Justin. Just as the Jewish Temple is the equivalent of a pagan temple filled with idols so sacrifice is not the will of God.

Barnabas' view is given in Ch. ii of his epistle:

'For he has made plain to us through all the prophets that he needs neither sacrifices nor burnt offerings nor oblations, saying in one place, What is the multitude of your sacrifices unto me? saith the Lord. I am full of burnt offerings and desire not the fat of lambs and the blood of bulls and goats, not even when ye come to appear before me. For who has required these things at your hands?... These things then he abolished (κατήργησεν) in order that the new law of our Lord Jesus Christ, which is without the yoke of necessity, might have its oblation not made by man (ἀνθρωποποίητον). And again he says to them, Did I command your fathers when they came out of the land of Egypt to offer me burnt offerings and sacrifices? Nay, but rather did I command them this: Let none of you cherish any evil in his heart against his neighbour, and love not a false oath (ii. 4-8).

This is plain enough. καταργεῖν here means 'to put an end to', 'abolish', as at xv. 5,[3] where it is used eschatologically of the Son's putting an end to the time of the wicked one; cf. also 1 Cor. xiii. 2; 2 Thess. ii. 8. The use of ἀνθρωποποίητος is also significant and is synonymous with the χειροποίητος which Stephen applied, in a

[1] *Dial.* xxii. 2-6.
[2] *Dial.* xix. 6.
[3] ὅταν ἐλθὼν ὁ υἱὸς αὐτοῦ καταργήσει τὸν καιρὸν τοῦ ἀνόμου.

derogatory sense, to the earthly temple (Acts vii. 48). Sacrifice, being a human thing, is therefore no part of the will of God—and indeed has been abolished by him, being replaced by the Christian oblation of a humble and loving heart (ii. 8, 10). The attitude of Stephen and Barnabas towards the sacrificial cult is therefore identical, although Barnabas goes further in stating the Christian meaning of sacrifice.

(D) Christology

Stephen's Christology is primitive and Palestinian. Jesus, in his exalted state, is Son of Man and Lord (vii. 56, 59–60); in his earthly existence he is a prophet like unto Moses [1] and the Righteous One (vii. 37, 52). All of these designations are found elsewhere in the New Testament in early passages. But for our purposes the last is the most interesting. The term ὁ δίκαιος is used in Acts in a messianic sense here, at iii. 14 and at xxii. 14, all—significantly—in speeches. Unlike other New Testament passages where it is used of Jesus,[2] it has in each case the article and no name, which suggests that it is used as a title rather than as a simple descriptive adjective; apparently it belonged to the earliest Jerusalem apostolic κήρυγμα and formed part of the archaic terminology of the Palestinian Church.[3] Apart from Enoch xxxviii. 2 there is no indisputable use of the term as a messianic title in pre-Christian Judaism, and even this reading is uncertain, as we cannot be sure that ὁ δίκαιος lies behind the Ethiopic text. However, scriptural roots were soon found in Isa. iii. 10 (LXX) and Wisdom ii. 18. As it was, the title passed out of use in the primitive Church and it has been suggested [4] that the Qumran sect's veneration for its founder, the Teacher of Righteousness, was one reason for this as, according to the Damascus Document, this Teacher will arise at the end of the days—possibly as the priestly Messiah of Aaron.[5] It seems, however, more probable that the Christian disuse of the title was a natural result of the Church expanding its mission into the Graeco-Roman world when the Person of Christ had to be interpreted in different categories of thought, such as Son of God and Logos. In the event δίκαιος, according to

[1] Based on Deut. xviii. 15 and found later in the Ebionite Clem. *Rec.* i. 36, 43 where Jesus is described as 'propheta quem Moyses praedixit, qui est Christus aeturnus'. Apart from Christian sources the only evidence for this designation is found among the Samaritans in their doctrine of *ta'eb* (the Restorer). The Samaritan attitude to the Jerusalem Temple was the same as that of Stephen and Barnabas.
[2] Matt. xxvii. 19; Luke xxiii. 47; 1 Pet. iii. 18, iv. 18; 1 John ii. 1.
[3] V. Taylor, *The Names of Jesus* (1953), pp. 80–3.
[4] C. S. C. Williams, op. cit., p. 78.
[5] CDC vi. 11.

Hegesippus,[1] came to be applied to James the Lord's brother in a non-messianic sense.

Early Christian literature up to c. A.D. 150 shows no trace of the use of ὁ δίκαιος as a title apart from two writers. The earliest is in the Epistle of Barnabas [2] where it appears in a direct quotation from Isa. iii. 9–10 (LXX) in a context referring to the manifestation and suffering of Jesus in the flesh: 'For the prophet says concerning Israel, Woe unto their soul, for they have plotted an evil plot against themselves, saying, Let us bind the Righteous One, for he is unprofitable to us.' (Δήσωμεν τὸν δίκαιον, ὅτι δύσχρηστος ἡμῖν ἐστίν). The other is the similar quotation from Isaiah in Justin, Dial. cxxxvi. 2, which suggests that both writers may be drawing on the same testimony source.[3] In Justin, Dial. xvi. 4 ὁ δίκαιος occurs in a passage which speaks of the cursing of Christians in the synagogues, from which we infer that the term came to belong to the conflict with Judaism, which would certainly fit the background of Barnabas. However we still have to ask why Barnabas picked on this particular archaic testimonium when his own Christology is so much more developed? Jesus, for him, is essentially the Son of God (vii. 9, xvii 9–10) and Lord of all the world, to whom God spoke before the foundation of the world (v. 5). Although Barnabas does not employ the Logos or Wisdom Christologies of John or Paul he firmly holds to the pre-existence of Jesus. Why then did he take up the primitive title ὁ δίκαιος, even in a quotation, and apply it to Jesus in his Passion? We suggest that he used it because it had been used by Stephen, whose polemic against the golden calf and the Temple he had found so congenial. And it is perhaps not without significance that in a similar passage referring to the Incarnation and Passion of the Son of God the Jews are described as persecuting his prophets to death (v. 11)—an act which Stephen directly links with the persecution of the Righteous One (Acts vii. 52).

(E) Other contacts

A few further points may be noted. Stephen places a great emphasis on Joseph, Moses and Joshua, in whose ill-treatment by the Jews he may conceivably have seen a type of Jesus' sufferings. Barnabas likewise is greatly interested in Moses and Joshua and allots them a whole chapter emphasizing the type of Jesus' Passion and Cross (xii. 1–11, cf. iv. 7–8).

[1] Eus.E.H. ii. 23–24: Διαδέχεται δὲ τὴν ἐκκλησίαν μετὰ τῶν ἀποστόλων ὁ ἀδελφὸς τοῦ Κυρίου Ἰάκωβος, ὁ ὀνομασθεὶς ὑπὸ πάντων δίκαιος ἀπὸ τῶν τοῦ Κυρίου χρόνων μέχρι καὶ ἡμῶν· ἐπεὶ πολλοὶ Ἰάκωβοι ἐκαλοῦντο.
[2] vi. 7.
[3] The *testimonium* is found later in Melito, *Homily on the Passion* l. 72; cf. also Cyprian *Test.* iii. 14; Lact. *Div. inst.* iv. 16; Hippolytus *adv. Jud.* ix.

We have already referred to the catechetical use to which summaries of Old Testament history, which followed a similar literary pattern, were put. Barnabas also incorporates much Jewish catechetical material into his epistle—and not only in the 'Two Ways' section (xviii–xx). A careful comparison of the structure of the epistle with the scheme of the Tannaitic catechism would, I believe, show a close correspondence.[1]

The word σοφία, which is used four times in the account of Stephen (vi. 3, 10, vii. 10, 22) and nowhere else in Acts, is also a favourite word of Barnabas (cf. ii. 3, vi. 10, xvi. 6, xxi. 5). However perhaps not too much should be made of this, as Stephen's and Barnabas' use may simply be the natural usage of hellenistic Jews of the Diaspora. We remember that it was the Alexandrian Apollos who introduced the conception of Wisdom into the Church at Corinth. Moreover the Qumran Scrolls have shown that the similar idea of knowledge (*da'ath*) was already known on Palestinian soil before the beginning of the Christian era. It was not confined to the Diaspora.

The above parallels will be variously estimated. Some may feel that Barnabas, *c*. A.D. 117–19, is simply drawing on a stock of teaching, both Jewish and Christian, known in the Alexandrian Church of his day, which included a strand of theology represented, at an earlier date, by Stephen. However we have to remember that Stephen's was an isolated and extremist position in the early Church which, on the whole, rejected his anti-Jewish polemic in favour of a more reasonable approach. Thus the fulfilment of Judaism in the new religion came to be emphasized rather than its total abrogation; the Old Testament was the preparation for the Gospel and the Torah was a leader unto Christ. Barnabas, as we have shown, also represents an extremist anti-Jewish position which is in marked contrast to his employment of so much traditional Jewish exegesis.[2] Indeed although his epistle came to be highly valued in Alexandria and nearly found its way into the New Testament canon it cannot be

---

[1] The Tannaites divided their instruction into five parts (i) The Test; (ii) the Commandments; (iii) Charity; (iv) the Penalties; (v) The Reward and World to Come. Cf. with:
  (i) Barn. i–iv, esp. iv. 9.
  (ii) Barn. v—xvi with its emphasis on suffering, commandments, baptism, circumcision, sacrifice and covenant.
  (iii) Barn. xviii—xx.
  (iv) Barn. x.
  (v) Barn. xxi.

[2] The Rabbinical character of the epistle is shown by the division into Haggadah and Halakhah, by its literary style and knowledge of Jewish rites, and by its frequent use of the rhetorical question as a didactic device. See pp. 47–48.

said that his extreme position vis-à-vis Judaism and Jewish institutions found much favour in the patristic age.[1] If, then, both Stephen and Barnabas held the same views as to the apostasy of the Jews—which had reached a climax in the golden calf incident and the building of the Temple—on the Torah and on the abrogation of the sacrificial cult, and both used a primitive Messianic title for Jesus, can both have come to these views independently? Can both interpretations have arisen *in vacuo*?

It seems then probable that Barnabas, in the second decade of the second century, drew directly on the theology of Stephen and wove it into the texture of his allegorizing. We have suggested that the immediate cause of his adopting Stephen's position was Hadrian's proposal to rebuild the Jerusalem Temple *c*. A.D. 118 which had proved an attraction for Christians of Jewish descent in a particular Christian community somewhere in Egypt. It was this proposal which was the final stumbling block (τὸ τέλειον σκάνδαλον—iv. 3) against which, in Barnabas' view, Christians ought to stand firm. Stephen's anti-Temple polemic was ready to hand to aid Barnabas in his cause. After A.D. 135 the question of the Temple was a dead issue so far as Judaism and Christianity were concerned and the breach between the two religions became absolute. Hellenistic Judaism virtually disappeared and the ascendancy of Rabbinism, begun earlier at Jamnia, became undisputed. A mixed type of Judaism, such as is found in Stephen and Barnabas, now became an impossibility and Pharisaism reigned supreme both in Palestine and the Diaspora.

It is possible, but cannot be proved, that Stephen had connexions with Alexandria, which is almost certainly the provenance of the Epistle of Barnabas. He emphasizes that Moses had been instructed in all the wisdom of the Egyptians (Acts vii. 22), agreeing on this point with Philo (*Vita Mosis* i. 5).[2] The doings of Joseph and Moses in Egypt are the subject of a lengthy peroration—the words Egypt, Egyptian, occurring no less than sixteen times in the speech. Possibly Stephen originally belonged to the more liberal wing of the hellenistic synagogue in the Egyptian metropolis. But of this we cannot be sure. It is certainly strange that the Alexandrian Church, when it came into historical purview early in the second century, did not claim Stephen as one of its martyrs. Instead a tradition that Mark,[3] rather than Stephen, had been associated with this Church was

---

[1] The *Epistle to Diognetus*, the *Apology* of Aristides and the Ebionite literature are the only possible exceptions to this statement.
[2] This subsequently plays a considerable part in Jewish legends about Moses. A full list is given in E. Schürer, *G.J.V.* II, pp. 34f.
[3] Eus.*E.H.* ii. 16.

handed down. We simply do not know if Stephen's followers came to Alexandria after his death and there prepared the soil for the later use of his theology by Barnabas.

We must therefore err on the side of caution and believe that the Alexandrian writer of Barnabas took over and adapted Stephen's theology directly from the Book of Acts. Basilides and Valentinus, who are only slightly later than this Epistle, knew this book and Barnabas himself knew St. Matthew's Gospel and several of the New Testament epistles. In any event the resurrection of Stephen's position in the later Christian Epistle had no widespread influence on patristic theology.

VII

IS THE EPISTLE OF BARNABAS A PASCHAL HOMILY?

In recent years, as is well known, new evidence for the Easter celebration in the pre-Nicene Church has come to light and this has been conveniently summarized by Professor F. L. Cross in his study of 1 Peter :[1]

(i) Melito of Sardis' *Homily on the Passion*, edited by Dr. Bonner of Michigan in 1940,[2] is a carefully composed text for an actual Easter celebration as held in the third quarter of the second century which may well reflect primitive practice.

(ii) The *Apostolic Tradition* of Hippolytus, with its detailed account of the Paschal baptism, confirmation, eucharist and paschal fast, is evidence for the Easter celebration as held in Rome in the late second century, and to this may be added: (a) the Paschal homily attributed to the same writer which appears to possess an Hippolytean basis; (b) the last two chapters of the *Epistle to Diognetus*, which may be fragments of a liturgical sermon for Easter Day delivered by Hippolytus; [3] (c) the fragments of Hippolytus' discourse περὶ τοῦ πάσχα which belong to a Paschal vigil sermon.

(iii) Other references in Irenaeus, Origen and Athanasius.[4]

While this new evidence is of the greatest value in filling out the information provided by the Quartodeciman controversy it must be recognized that first hand documentation of the Easter Feast for the first century and the early part of the second century is still lacking unless we accept Professor Cross' view that 1 Peter is a Paschal Liturgy compiled for the celebrant's part of the Paschal Vigil—the most solemn occasion of the Church's year. Yet, as Cross [5] points out, it is certain that Easter was celebrated from the earliest days, as

---

[1] *1 Peter: A Paschal Liturgy* (1954) pp. 8–11. I am much indebted to his illuminating work.

[2] In *Studies and Documents*, ed. K. and S. Lake, XII (1940); B. Lohse, *Die Passa-Homilie des Bischofs Meliton von Sardes* (1958); for a Latin version see H. Chadwick, JTS 11 (April 1960), p. 76–82.

[3] Cf. ad Diogn. xii. 9, καὶ τὸ κυρίου πάσχα προέρχεται. On the other hand 11. 5, οὗτος ὁ ἀεί, ὁ σήμερον υἱὸς λογισθείς has seemed to some exegetes more appropriate to a Feast of the Nativity. I do not subscribe to the theory of Hippolytean authorship of these chapters.

[4] Iren. *Demonstr. Apost. Preaching* xxv; Orig. Toura Fragment *On the Pasch*; Ath. *Festal Eps.*

[5] Op. cit., p. 7. A number of scholars have maintained that the Markan Passion narrative contains indications of a Sunday Paschal Feast; see M. H. Shepherd, *The Paschal Liturgy and the Apocalypse*, pp. 34–37.

is proved by the universality of its observance when it appears and still more by the Semitic name Pasch (or Passover) which it bears.[1] The purpose of this chapter is to point to certain indications of the celebration of the Feast in Egypt in the early part of the second century A.D. which are, I believe, contained in the Epistle of Barnabas.

This Epistle is taken as an Alexandrian production by the majority of commentators and probably dates from the early years of the reign of Hadrian (A.D. 117–38).[2] The writer was, I believe, a converted Jew who continued to employ the catechetical, homiletical and exegetical methods of the synagogue in his role as a Christian teacher. The personal references and character of the introductory and closing chapters seem to preclude the theory that the Epistle is a pseudepigraphical work. Rather it is, as the writer states, a letter addressed to a definite Christian community somewhere or other in Egypt, which was in danger of falling back into Judaism as the result of the activity of militant Judaizers. Was then the Epistle composed solely for the leaders of the community—or was it designed to be read at corporate gatherings for public worship? We wish to suggest that the Epistle was designed to be read at the paschal Feast which culminated in the Easter baptism and eucharist—a solemn occasion when large numbers of Christians were gathered together; and that the writer has adapted older catechesis and homiletic material (based on Jewish models) with this Feast in mind. We must now put this hypothesis to the test.

THE EMPHASIS ON SUFFERING

The number of references to suffering in the Epistle is remarkable. The verb πάσχω is used thirteen times [3] (twelve times with reference to Jesus' sufferings) as against seven times in the whole *Corpus Paulinum*, four times in the Epistle to the Hebrews and twelve times in 1 Peter. Coupled with πάσχω is the use of ὑπομένω which occurs five times.[4] A favourite theme of the writer—indeed it becomes almost a refrain—is that Jesus endured to suffer. Professor Cross has observed that the primitive kerygma did not normally include an explicit reference to Jesus' sufferings and this also appears to have been the case with the credal formulae

[1] ὥστε ἑορτάζωμεν in 1 Cor. v. 8 is not certainly a reference to the Christian Pasch; rather it is a figure of the Christian life as a whole. It is interesting that painted Easter Eggs were originally called Pasch Eggs.
[2] Perhaps I may be permitted to refer to my papers in CQR 159 (April 1958), pp. 211–30; 160 (July 1959), pp. 320–34 and in JEA 44 (1958), pp. 101–7 where the statements in this paragraph are discussed in detail.
[3] Four times in Ch. v; twice in Ch. vi; five times in Ch. vii and twice in Ch. xii. τὸ πάθος is found at vi. 7 and ἡ πληγὴ at vii. 2.
[4] All in Ch. v.

underlying the writings of the Apostolic Fathers.[1] However, in the Paschal Orations of Melito and Hippolytus, where the Old Testament types of the Paschal redemption are worked out, the theme of suffering is constantly found; cf. Melito 46: 'What is the Passover? It is so called from what befell—that is from "suffer" and "be suffering" (ἐκ γὰρ τοῦ παθεῖν καὶ πάσχειν). Learn then who is the sufferer and who suffers with him. Behold the Lord comes to the world, to the sufferer to heal. . . . But the Lord had by a previous dispensation ordained his sufferings in the patriarchs and prophets and all the people, sealing them through the law and the prophets. . . . So also the Passion of the Lord, manifested of old from afar and seen through a type is thus today fulfilled.' Cf. also Hippolytus *Paschal Homily* 49: 'This was the Passover (πάσχα) which Jesus desired to suffer (παθεῖν) on our behalf. By suffering he freed us from suffering and by death He conquered death . . .'[2] We can hardly doubt that 'Pasch' was believed to derive from the verb πάσχω and that this was a leading theme of the Easter celebration. The frequent use of this verb in connexion with Jesus' sufferings in the Epistle of Barnabas, in contrast to the rest of the Apostolic Fathers, would therefore be appropriate if the writer had this Feast in mind. For him Jesus' sufferings were central to the fact of redemption and had been foretold in the prophetic tradition: 'Since therefore he was destined to be manifest and to suffer (πάσχειν) in the flesh the passion (τὸ πάθος) was foretold. For the prophet says concerning Israel, 'Woe unto their soul, for they have plotted an evil plot against themselves, saying "Let us bind the Just one, for he is unprofitable to us".' (Barn. vi. 7, quoting Isa. iii. 9.) The writer also held that Christians suffer in mystical union with Christ although he does not develop this theme to the extent found in 1 Peter; cf. vii. 11: 'But why is it that they put the wool in the midst of the thorns? It is a type of Jesus placed in the Church because whoever wishes to take away the scarlet wool must suffer much (πολλὰ παθεῖν) because the thorns are terrible and he can gain it only through pain. Thus, he means, those who will see me, and attain to my kingdom must lay hold of me through pain and suffering (θλιβέντες καὶ παθόντες λαβεῖν με)'— a theme appropriate to the solemn Paschal gathering and especially to a community which was suffering from the assaults of a militant Judaism.

---

[1] Ign. *ad Trall.* ix. 1-2; *ad Smyrn.* 1. 1-2 where ἀφ' οὗ καρποῦ ἡμεῖς ἀπὸ τοῦ θεομακαρίστου αὐτοῦ πάθους appears to be an insertion made by the writer into the kerygmatic formula; *ad Eph.* xviii. 2 where τῷ πάθει seems to refer to the baptism; Polyc. *ad Phil.* ii. 1.

[2] I owe these references to Professor Cross, op. cit., pp. 14-15, whose translations are given above.

The Nature of the Feast

F. E. Brightman, in an article on the Quartodeciman dispute,[1] was the first to show that the Paschal celebration commemorated the whole redemptive work of Christ in his death, resurrection, ascension and second advent. For the early Church the observance of Good Friday was not separated in time from that of Easter Day and Ascension Day but all were fused together in a single Paschal commemoration which was both a solemn and joyous occasion and one which was attended by every Christian worthy of the name. We have already mentioned the strong emphasis placed by the epistle on suffering; but the other aspects of redemption are not forgotten as the following examples will show:

(a) v. 6–7: 'Learn: the Prophets who received grace from him prophesied of him, and he, in order that he might destroy death and show forth the resurrection from the dead, because he must needs be manifested in the flesh, endured, in order to fulfil the promise made to the fathers, and himself prepare for himself the new people and show while he was on earth that he himself will raise the dead and judge the risen.' While this is not wholly clear it would seem that the writer regards Jesus' endurance, suffering, resurrection and the bringing into existence of the Church as parts of a single redemptive process.

(b) vi. 2–4: Here the testimonia concerning Christ as the Stone, which were well known in the early Church,[2] occur as part of a larger series of proof texts which are referred, *inter alia*, to the plotting of the Jews against Jesus, the entry into Christ through baptism, the second creation and Christian worship. Barnabas' version is interesting in that it contains differences from the version in 1 Peter ii. 6–8 and Rom. ix. 33. The introduction in vi. 2, 'And again the prophet says that he was placed as a strong stone for crushing (εἰς συντριβήν) appears to be a free rendering of Isa. viii. 14 (LXX) or Dan ii. 34, 45 in view of the fact that συντριβή means 'rubbing away', 'crushing', 'destruction'.[3] The thought is of Christ, as a λίθος ἰσχυρός, destroying those who dash against him. This is following an exact quotation of Isa. xxviii. 16 (LXX) as far as ἔντιμον, in contrast to 1 Peter and Romans who quote a version nearer to the Hebrew text. vi. 3, 'And whosoever shall hope on it shall live forever', appears to be another reference to Isa. xxviii. 16–17 (LXX) although

---
[1] JTS 25 (1923-4), pp. 254–70.
[2] Mk. xii. 10–11, Lk. xx. 18, Acts iv. 11, Rom. ix. 33, 1 Pet. ii. 6–8, Cyprian *Test.* i. 16, etc.
[3] As in Vett. Val. lxiv. 4; Heliodorus x. 28; not elsewhere in early Christian literature.

the connexion is loose. ℵ, C and L certainly understood it so for they read ὁ πιστεύων εἰς αὐτόν under the influence of the LXX. To the question 'Is our hope then upon a stone?' the explanation is given that the Lord set (τέθεικεν)[1] his flesh in strength, which is an introduction to a loose quotation from Isa. l. 7 (LXX) which now appears.[2] vi. 4 then quotes Ps. cxviii. 22 (LXX) exactly, although verse 23 is omitted,[3] following it with a loose quotation of Ps. cxviii. 24 which has ἡ μεγάλη καὶ θαυμαστή for the LXX ἀγαλλιασώμεθα καὶ εὐφρανθῶμεν ἐν αὐτῇ, θαυμαστή perhaps being a glance at verse 23.

The Epistle's treatment of this series of testimonia is instructive; in accordance with his practice elsewhere the writer's quotations from the LXX are often loose paraphrases—although he can quote exactly. The fact that he quotes the LXX of Isa. viii. 14 and xviii. 16, as against the Hebrew of the source behind 1 Pet. ii. 6-8 and Rom. ix. 33, and also introduces allusions to Isa. xxviii. 17, l. 7 and Ps. cxviii. 24 which are not found in the earlier testimonia, does not suggest that he is using a written Greek testimony source or that he is directly quoting the New Testament Epistles. Rather, around the original testimonium of Christ as the Stone rejected by the Builders yet made the Cornerstone, Barnabas has woven his mosaic of texts from the LXX which he has adapted to his purpose, which is clearly to emphasize the centrality of the death and resurrection of Christ. In this connexion I would especially point to the change which the writer makes in vi. 4 from the LXX of Ps. cxviii. 24 in order to emphasize that the day which the Lord made is 'great and wonderful'. There is no reason why this change should have been made if the Epistle had only been intended for the leaders of a Christian community to be read at their leisure or if it was to be read at ordinary gatherings for public worship. I suggest that the writer had in mind not simply the day of crucifixion, or any day for ordinary worship, but the day of the Paschal celebration which was the great and wonderful occasion when Christ's death and resurrection were solemnly and joyfully remembered. We know, too, that the Easter baptism formed a significant part of the Pasch and it is perhaps not mere coincidence that allusions to baptism are very prominent in this chapter.[4]

[1] J. Rendel Harris, *Testimonies*, I, p. 31 thinks that the appearance of ἐτέθη, τέθεικεν and ἔθηκεν in Barn. vi. 2-3 is proof that Barnabas knew, but did not use, Isa. xxviii. 16 in the version used by 1 Peter and Romans. However, his use of τίθημι might well have come from Isa. l. 7 (LXX).

[2] This has been previously quoted in more exact form, at v. 14.

[3] Quoted in the *verba Christi* Mk. xii. 10-11.

[4] vi. 8, 10, 11, 13, 14, 17. The Stone testimonium also appears in a baptismal context in 1 Pet. ii. 1-10.

(c) xv. 9: 'Wherefore we also celebrate with gladness the eighth day in which Jesus also rose from the dead, and was made manifest, and ascended into heaven.'

The celebration which the writer has in mind is, according to xv. 8, an anticipation of the spiritual 'eighth day', the day of eternity, which is to dawn at the end of the millennium or sabbath rest. But what are we to make of the mention of the resurrection, manifestation and ascension of Christ in close juxtaposition? This is a well known *crux interpretum*. Many exegetes hold [1] that the verse implies that the resurrection and ascension took place on the same day, i.e., on a particular Sunday, a theory in direct conflict with Luke-Acts, although not an isolated opinion in the early Church.[2] Another view is that Barnabas believed that the resurrection and the ascension took place on a Sunday but with an interval of time separating them, καὶ φανερωθείς then referring to the post-resurrection appearances recorded in the Gospels.[3] There is nothing in the Greek to compel us to accept the first view; the second is not excluded by the construction; however against both views is the conflict with the forty days tradition of Acts [4] which eventually triumphed. We wish to suggest another solution, viz., that the writer had in mind the whole drama of the redemption—death, resurrection, and ascension, without considering the chronological interval between these events. The various historical 'moments' stood for him together as part of the good news revealed in Christ. Such a combination would have been especially appropriate for the Paschal Feast which in Egypt would then have been held on a Sunday.[5] In support of this is the close connexion drawn in this chapter between the Parousia and Christian worship, for there is evidence, up to the third century, that

[1] Hilgenfeld, Volkmar, Weizsäcker, Gebhardt, Kirsopp Lake, *inter alia*.
[2] Cf. Aristides ii, μετὰ δὲ τρεῖς ἡμέρας ἀνεβίω καὶ εἰς οὐρανοὺς ἀνῆλθεν; Gospel of Peter 35–42; Codex Bobbiensis on Mk. xvi. 3; *Ep. Apostolorum* 51; see further F. J. Dölger, *Sol Salutis*, pp. 212 ff.
[3] Various traditions as to the duration of the post-resurrection appearances are found in the early centuries. Chryst. *Hom.* iii. 1 held that the ascension occurred on a Saturday, apparently deducing this from Acts i. 12 'a Sabbath day's journey'. Another tradition associated the ascension with the Day of Pentecost—*Etheria peregrinatio ad loca sancta* 43.
[4] A number of scholars have challenged the authenticity of this tradition. Among the most recent is P. H. Menoud 'Remarques sur les textes de l'ascension dans Luc-Actes' in *Neut. Stud. für R. Bultmann* (1954), pp. 148 f.
[5] The celebration of the Paschal Feast on a Sunday, in opposition to the Quartodeciman position, may have been associated with the acceptance of St. Matthew's Gospel; see further M. H. Shepherd, op. cit., pp. 43–4. Later evidence from Egypt (see *Letter of Dionysius of Alexandria to Bishop Basilides of Cyrenaica*) suggests that the character of the Egyptian celebration was similar to that of Rome.

the Parousia was expected at Eastertide.[1] Our multiplication of Christian Festivals makes it difficult for us to grasp the fact of a single celebration which embraced the whole drama of the redemption.[2] We find it hard to realize that there was no separate Festival of the Ascension until the latter part of the fourth century and no Whitsun celebration until the time of Tertullian.

(d) The Exodus setting: The deliverance of Israel through the Exodus and entry into the promised land was, from the earliest times, a leading type of the Easter deliverance. It is found in the New Testament underlying 1 Pet. i. 13-21 and ii. 9-11 and regularly in the Paschal homilies of Melito of Sardis and Hippolytus. It is significant that the events of the Exodus and the entry into the promised land are prominent in the Epistle of Barnabas although they are used not so much as historical types but to yield allegorical meanings; cf. especially iv. 7-8, vi. 8-17, xii. 2-9, xiv. 1-4.

The writer has his own theory concerning the Jews—viz., that Moses received the covenant on their behalf but they lost it through their disobedience and worship of the golden calf [3] whereby God has given the covenant to Christians as the people of the inheritance. This theory, born of the writer's violent antipathy to his ancestral faith, and reflecting the conflict between Christianity and Judaism in Egypt in the early decades of the second century, prevented his using the Passover as a historical type—for that showed the Jews in too good a light. However, the strong emphasis placed on the work of Moses and on the entry into the promised land was appropriate to the Easter celebration. Cf. especially xiv. 1-9 where, after a section dealing with Moses and the covenant, the writer goes on to speak of the redemption from darkness wrought by Christ; the verb λυτρόω is used four times in xiv. 5-8; cf. xix. 2.

Another theme of the early Easter celebration is the co-existence of suffering with joy and gladness which belongs to the time when Good Friday and Easter Day had not been separated in theology or liturgy. The Epistle's strong emphasis on suffering has already been noted; yet the note of gladness, joy, hope and thanksgiving is not absent and does much to counteract the writer's somewhat arid exegesis of the Old Testament found in long stretches of the work; cf. i. 6, v. 3, x. 11, xi. 11, xix. 2, xxi. 9.

The Paschal theology of the Epistle is embodied in words which,

[1] *Ep. apostolorum* 6; Tert. *de bapt.* 19; Hippolytus Comm. on Dan. 4, 55, 1ff.

[2] The Eastern Orthodox Churches have preserved this emphasis. Their hymns and prayers commemorating Christ's nativity, baptism, transfiguration, death and resurrection usually begin with the words: *Today* Christ is born, *today* He has risen from the dead, etc.

[3] There appear to be affinities between the theology of St. Stephen and that of the writer. See pp. 62-72.

if not so profound as those found in 1 Pet. iii–v, yet express the meaning of the celebration: 'And it was manifest . . . that we, through Jesus the Lord who inherits the covenant, should receive it, for he was prepared for this purpose, that when he appeared he might redeem from darkness our hearts which were already paid over to death, and given over to the iniquity of error, and by his word might make a covenant with us. For it is written that the Father enjoins on him that he should redeem us from darkness and prepare a holy people for himself. The Prophet therefore says, "I the Lord thy God did call thee in righteousness, and I will hold thy hands, and I will give thee strength, and I have given thee for a covenant of the people, for a light to the Gentiles, to open the eyes of the blind, and to bring forth from their fetters those that are bound and those that sit in darkness out of the prison house". We know then whence we have been redeemed.' (xiv. 5–7.)

The Baptismal Setting of the Epistle

In the early Church the regular season for baptism was Easter and the celebration of the baptismal-eucharist was central to the Paschal liturgy. If therefore the arguments of this chapter are sound we should expect to find baptism mentioned and baptismal language used in an epistle intended to be read at the Paschal gathering.

(a) Explicit references to baptism: These occur in vi. 11, 14, xi. 1–11, xvi. 8. Indeed the allocation of a whole chapter of the Epistle (Ch. xi) to the prefiguring of the sacrament in the Old Testament illustrates the importance which it held in the eyes of the writer. Baptism is, for him, being 'made new' (ἀνακαινίσας in vi. 11; ἐγενόμεθα καινοί in xvi. 8); being 'created afresh' (ἀναπλάσσοντος in vi. 11; ἐξ ἀρχῆς κτιζόμενοι in xvi. 8) and 'receiving the remission of sins' (vi. 11, xi. 11, xvi. 8). This language denotes the change wrought in the spiritual condition of the believer by baptism and is parallel to the use of ἀναγεννάω in 1 Pet. i. 3, 23 and ἀρτιγέννητος in 1 Pet. ii. 2.

(b) References to baptismal practice: After quoting in xi. 1–7 a series of texts from Jer. ii. 12–13; Isa. xvi. 1–2, xlv. 2, 3, xxxiii. 16–18 and Ps. i. 3–6 which are believed to prefigure baptism, the writer continues: 'Mark how he described the water and the cross together. For he means this: blessed are those who hoped on the cross, and descended into the water (κατέβησαν εἰς τὸ ὕδωρ) . . . He means to say that we go down into the water full of sins and foulness and we come up (ἀναβαίνομεν) [1] bearing the fruit of fear in our hearts, and

[1] For immersion in baptism see Acts viii. 38; Hermas *Mand.* iv. 3. 1; *Sim.* ix. 16. 4–6. The moment of 'coming up' carried a profound meaning

having hope in Jesus in the Spirit (τὴν ἐλπίδα εἰς τὸν Ἰησοῦν ἐν τῷ πνεύματι ἔχοντες, xi. 8 and 11)'. Clearly baptism is by immersion, rather than affusion, and the descent into and ascent from the waters effect the change from a life of sin and foulness to the new life in Christ with its fruits of faith, hope and love (xi. 8b). The mention of hoping on the Cross and hoping in Jesus, with which may be associated the hoping on the Name of xvi. 8, suggests a stereotyped formula. Certainly there is other evidence that baptism in the Name of Jesus or Jesus Christ was not unknown in the early Church [2] and, even in the third and fourth centuries, there were those who held the one name to be sufficient.[3] The archaic features of this account appear to reflect primitive practice. The close connexion drawn between baptism and the Cross is also to be noted.[4]

(c) Catechetical background: A regular preparation of candidates prior to the Easter Baptism must have been established early in the history of the Church if we are to judge from the almost universal existence of the catechumenate in the third century.[5] In the last decades the researches of Drs. Carrington, Selwyn and Moule [6] have shown that much catechetical material is to be found underlying the New Testament Epistles and undoubtedly some of this was used prior to the Easter Baptism. These scholars have shown that Christianity, to some extent, was indebted to Jewish models in the working out of its catechetical forms and I have sought to show elsewhere [7] that the Epistle of Barnabas reflects very closely the order and substance of the instruction given by the Tannaim to proselytes to Judaism. In this respect the Epistle stands closer to Judaism than the New Testament Epistles, where instruction in the specific Christian virtues is more prominent.

---

in Jewish proselyte baptism which many regard as the precursor of Christian baptism; cf. Bab. Yeb. 47b, 'when he has undergone baptism and come up (*tabhal we 'ala*) he is like an Israelite in all respects'. According to D. Daube, *The New Testament and Rabbinic Judaism*, p. 112, the 'coming up' of Jesus after His baptism (Mk. i. 10, Mt. iii. 16) is proof that Christian baptism originated in the Jewish rite.

[2] Acts ii. 38, viii. 16, x. 48; cf. also the early confession attributed to the Ethiopian Eunuch in Acts viii. 37 (D).

[3] Cyprian *Ep.* lxxiii. 4, lxxv. 5; Ambrose *de spiritu sal.* i. 3.

[4] Cf. Jn. vii. 38, xix. 34; Rom. vi. 3; Ign. *ad Eph.* xviii. 2. We do not know if the custom of signing with the cross was yet in use. Certainly by the time of Tertullian it was widely practised—cf. *de coron. militis* iv.

[5] Cross, op. cit., pp. 30–31.

[6] *The Primitive Christian Catechism*; *The First Epistle of St. Peter*; JTS 1 (New Series) 1950, pp. 29–41.

[7] ATR 41 (July 1959) pp. 177–90.

A good example of this Jewish catechetical material is the section on the Two Ways of Light and Darkness (Barn. xviii–xx) which is also found in *Didache* i–v. The question of the relationship between these versions has been frequently discussed in the last forty years without a final decision; however the discovery of a section headed 'On the Two Spirits in Man', containing similar material, in the Qumran Manual of Discipline [1] seems to have proved that a pre-Christian Two Ways instruction lies behind the later Christian versions.

Barnabas' version is certainly appropriate to the preparation of catechumens for baptism. We especially note the social groupings he had in mind. Thus: 'Thou shalt not withhold thy hand from thy son or from thy daughter, but shall teach them the fear of God from their youth up. . . . Thou shalt obey thy masters as a type of God in modesty and fear; thou shalt not command in bitterness thy slave or handmaid who hope in the same God, lest they cease to fear the God who is over you both; for he came not to call men with respect of persons, but those whom the Spirit prepared.' (xix. 5 and 7.)

Codes of social relationships are also found underlying the catechetical teaching of the New Testament Epistles [2] and the version here is of interest in showing that the Christian community, in Barnabas' time, was of mixed social grouping containing not only slaves but wealthy people who were slave-owners. Daily gatherings for instruction, perhaps at a Christian 'school', or at daily public worship, are also enjoined upon catechumens (xix. 10). The Way of Life which the Christian was expected to follow was laid down in detail.

(d) Credal references: The use of a creed at baptism is very ancient as is shown by Acts viii. 37 (D) and possibly by 1 Pet. iii 18–22.[3] Barnabas is not a systematic writer and his thought is overlaid with the allegorical interpretation of the smallest Old Testament incident —yet nevertheless traces of credal formulae are perhaps to be found in the Epistle; cf. v. 6–7, vii. 2 and xv. 9.

(e) The baptismal-eucharist: At the baptismal-eucharist, which formed the climax of the Paschal liturgy, the newly-baptized, according to the rite of Hippolytus, received three cups in succession —of water, milk and honey mingled, and wine (*Ap. Trad.* xxiii. 2). Apart from the reference to milk in 1 Pet. ii. 2, which is not certainly a reference to the rite,[4] possibly the only mention of it in Christian

---

[1] I QS iii. 13–iv. 26.
[2] Selwyn, op. cit., pp. 426–39.
[3] Cross, op. cit., pp. 31–2.
[4] Cross, op. cit., pp. 32–3 thinks that it is. The absence of any mention of honey, however, suggests caution.

sources prior to the time of Hippolytus [1] is in this Epistle. Thus vi. 8: 'What does the other Prophet, Moses, say to them? "Lo, thus saith the Lord God, enter into the good land which the Lord sware that he would give to Abraham, Isaac, and Jacob, and inherit it, a land flowing with milk and honey".' This is a quotation based on Ex. xxxiii. 1, 3 (LXX) and Lev. xx. 24 (LXX) and that the entry into the good land signified, for the writer, entry into the Christian Church through baptism is conclusively shown by vi. 10, 11, 14. The phrase ἄνθρωπος γὰρ γῆ ἐστιν πάσχουσα in vi. 9 has created difficulties for commentators and it seems best to take πάσχουσα in the sense of 'capable of suffering change', 'capable of being moulded into a human being',[2] in which case the reference is to Adam, moulded from the dust of the earth, and, by a play on the words, to Jesus who suffers. And as γῆ in vi. 10, 11 refers to the land flowing with milk and honey, i.e., entry into Christ through baptism, the writer regards baptism as having its origin in the Passion of Christ—an association we have already found in xi. 2, 8. The writer returns to the milk and honey theme in vi. 17: 'What then is the milk and honey? Because a child [3] is first nourished with honey, and afterwards with milk. Thus therefore we also, being nourished on the faith of the promise and by the word, shall live and possess the earth'.

In the light of the writer's elusive method of referring to Christian doctrines and practices and the strong baptismal associations in this chapter we are probably justified in finding here an allusion to the practice of administering the cup of milk and honey to the newly baptized—one of the earliest references to the custom in Christian literature. And in support of this is the fact that the direction for the benediction over the milk and honey in the Hippolytean rite contains a reference to the Israelites of the exodus period and their entry into the promised land—a mystical connexion found here. Traces of the baptismal-eucharist are perhaps also to be found in ii. 6, 9, 10 where προσφορά, προσαγεῖν and θυσία are used against a background

[1] Clem. Alex. *Paed.* i. 6, 34ff. and Tert. *de Cor.* iii, *adv. Marc.* i. 14 are further witnesses to the cup of honey and milk. Less certain is the testimony of Justin 1 *Apol.* lxv, 3. That the custom is an early one is however suggested by Gnostic sources; thus Tert. *adv. Marc.* i. 14 says that Marcion did not reprove 'the water of the Creator whereby He washes them, nor the oil wherewith He anoints them, nor the mingling of the honey and milk with which He nourishes them as children, nor the bread by which He represents His own Body'. Cf. also Logion 23 of the Gospel of Thomas (c. A.D. 140): 'Jesus saw little ones receiving milk. He said to His disciples, these little ones receiving milk are like those who enter into the Kingdom.'

[2] J. A. Kleist, *A.C.W.*, VI, p. 173, note 70.

[3] This association is also found in Hippolytus where the faithful are likened to little children.

of worship and spiritual offerings. We may also note the reference to worship in vi. 16 in a baptismal context.

(f) The theme of Darkness and Light: A prominent feature of baptismal imagery has always been that of a passage from darkness to light and this received concrete expression in the Paschal Vigil which began in darkness and ended in broad daylight. In later times the light of baptism came to be symbolized by the liturgical use of a Paschal candle. It is significant that the Two Ways instruction in this Epistle is preceded by a short section which describes them as 'Two Ways of teaching and authority, one of Light and one of Darkness' (xviii. 1) in contrast to the *Didache*'s Way of Life and Death (*Did.* i. 1). Other references to the redemption from darkness occur in xiv. 6 and in xvii. 7, 8 where Christians are to be a light to the Gentiles (quoting Isa. xlii. 6, 7, xlix. 6, 7).

The evidence assembled above will be variously estimated and any one item, by itself, may be thought insufficient to establish the Epistle's Paschal setting. However, cumulatively they seem to be of considerable weight. The themes of the Epistle of Barnabas, which shine through much allegorism, are suffering, resurrection and redemption, catechetical instruction and moral duties, baptism and perhaps the eucharist—the whole set against the background of the Exodus and entry into the Promised Land. This combination is very remarkable and contains just those elements which appear in the celebration of the Paschal Feast when it comes into historical perspective. The Epistle, I submit, would have been appropriate to that great occasion when every member of the Christian community addressed, including many whom the writer knew (i. 4), would have been present for the celebration of their redemption and the baptism and first eucharist of new converts. This Epistle is *not* the liturgy of the celebrant but is a homily to be read at the Paschal Vigil [1] reminding older Christians, at this solemn yet joyous time, of their own catechumenate and baptism and of their duty to stand firm

[1] G. D. Kilpatrick, *The Origins of the Gospel according to St. Matthew*, p. 65, emphasizes the importance of the public reading of Christian literature as a guarantee of its survival. He believes that, with the exception of Papias, Hegesippus and the Apologists, the whole of Christian literature before Irenaeus was used for reading in the services of the Church. Considerable liberty existed in the choice of books to be read in the earliest period. Cf. Justin I *Apol.* lxvii. 3 ff.; Eus.*E.H.* iv.23; Rufinus in *Symb. apost.* xxxviii; Jerome *de vir. illustr.* xvii. In later times homilies were normally read at the pro-anaphora which consisted of lections from the LXX, homilies, prayers and psalmody—a sequence taken over from the synagogue service. There is however no evidence from the pre-Nicene period that the pro-anaphora formed part of the Paschal rite as such; lections, homilies and instructions were usually given at the Paschal Vigil.

against the assaults of a militant Judaism. This was a time when this community was at the 'crossroads' and Barnabas, with great respect and charity, seeks to keep them on the right path. The Epistle's exegesis, which to our eyes is so strange, should not blind us to its strong practical motive. Moreover, the frequency with which Clement of Alexandria cites it and the high authority he ascribes to it, suggest that it had long been read in public worship and we may surmise that it was the importance ascribed to it by its original recipients, and the occasion on which it was first read, which led to its survival in the Church.

The evidence for the celebration of the Paschal Feast in Egypt in the early decades of the second century fills out the later unequivocal evidence of Melito of Sardis and Hippolytus and the references in Irenaeus and Origen. We can hardly doubt that Easter was celebrated from the earliest times, whatever view we may take of the New Testament evidence.

VIII

THE DEAD SEA SCROLLS, BARNABAS, THE *DIDACHE* AND THE LATER HISTORY OF THE 'TWO WAYS'

(1)

The discovery of the Qumran texts, as is well known, has produced a whole spate of books and articles many of which deal *inter alia* with affinities between the doctrinal formularies of the sect and the New Testament and between its organization and practice and that of the Apostolic Church in Jerusalem. However, in all this literature, which has now reached unmanageable proportions, it would seem that insufficient attention has been paid to affinities between the texts and Christian post-Apostolic literature.[1] We consider firstly parallels between the Scrolls and the Epistle of Barnabas.

(A) Method of Biblical Exegesis

The Epistle of Barnabas adopts *in toto* the allegorical method of interpretation which had reached its zenith in the voluminous writings of Philo. Indeed it is not improbable that the Epistle played a role in the preservation of Philo's writings for posterity, for these were certainly preserved by Christians rather than Jews. However, embedded in the writer's fanciful allegorization is another method of interpretation which has been found at Qumran. This is the quotation of the Old Testament texts, followed by an application to contemporary events, which were believed to have a profound significance for those who could understand and interpret them. Some illustrations of this method may be given, chosen almost at random:

Barn. v. 3–4:

'Therefore we ought to give hearty thanks to the Lord that he has given us knowledge of the past, and wisdom for the present, and that we are not without understanding for the future. And the Scripture says, "Not unjustly are the nets spread out for the birds".[2] This means that a man deserves to perish who had a knowledge of the way of righteousness, but turns aside into the way of darkness.'

[1] The only writer known to me who has discussed this question at length is J.-P. Audet, O.P., 'Affinités littéraires et doctrinales du Manuel de Discipline', RB (1952), pp. 219–38; (1953) pp. 41–82. He has expanded his views in his important study *La Didaché: Instructions des Apôtres* (Paris 1958).
[2] Prov. i. 17.

Barn. xv. 8–9:

'Furthermore he says to them, "Your new moons and the sabbaths I cannot away with." [1] Do you see what he means? The present sabbaths are not acceptable to me, but that which I have made, in which I will give rest to all things and make the beginning of an eighth day, that is the beginning of another world. Wherefore we also celebrate with gladness the eighth day in which Jesus also rose from the dead, and was manifest, and ascended into Heaven.'

Barn. xvi. 3–4:

'Furthermore he says again, "Lo, they who destroyed this temple shall themselves build it." [2] That is happening now. For owing to the war it was destroyed by the enemy; at present even the servants of the enemy will build it up again.'

This method of interpretation is strikingly reminiscent of that found in the Qumran Commentaries on the Books of Micah, Nahum, Habakkuk and Psalm xxxvii and in the Damascus Document where Old Testament texts are frequently quoted followed by a contemporary interpretation. For instance, with the first passage quoted above may be compared the Qumran Commentary on Psalm xxxvii. 8–9 (Fragment A, Col. i): 'Refrain from anger and abandon wrath; fret not thyself, it tendeth only to evil-doing. For evildoers shall be cut off.' This applies to those who return to the Torah and do not refuse to repent their evil-doing. Those, however, who are defiant about repenting their iniquity will be cut off.' [3] With the third passage compare the Commentary on Nahum, 4 Qp Nah. ii. 11, 'Where is the abode of the lions, which was the feeding place of the young lions. (This refers to Jerusalem which has become) an abode for the wicked men of the heathen.'

Barnabas' use of this method recalls the Qumran word *pesher*, used frequently in these Commentaries, which means the interpretation of Old Testament texts the true significance and application of which is only known by those who possess knowledge and understanding.[4] The author of the Epistle is essentially an interpreter of the Old Testament, as were the scribes who wrote the Qumran texts.

[1] Isa. i. 13.
[2] Isa. xlix. 17.
[3] I have used Gaster's translations.
[4] *Pesher* is also used in the Aramaic part of the Book of Daniel, e.g. Dan. iv. 9. K. Stendahl, *The School of St. Matthew* (1954), pp. 183–202, connects the *pesher* type of citation with the 'formula quotations' of St. Matthew's Gospel.

(B) The idea of the Community

One of the major differences between the Dead Sea sect and the Apostolic Church is that the former was an exclusive esoteric group which carefully guarded its special doctrines and shunned contact with outsiders, and especially with those who did not reach its standard of purity, while the early Christians, following the example of Jesus, took the Gospel to all and sundry and in particular consorted with sinners. However, in the Epistle of Barnabas we find advocated ideas of exclusiveness which are in striking contrast to the practice of the Apostolic Church. Thus Barn. iv. 1-2:

'We ought, then, to inquire earnestly into the things which now are, and to seek out those which are able to save us. Let us then utterly flee from all the works of lawlessness, lest the works of lawlessness overcome us, and let us hate the error of this present time, that we may be loved in that which is to come. Let us give no freedom to our souls to have power to walk with sinners and wicked men, lest we be made like unto them.'

Barn. x. 5:

' "Thou shalt not eat", he says, "the lamprey nor the polypus nor the cuttle-fish." [1] Thou shalt not, he means, consort with or become like such men who are utterly ungodly and who are already condemned to death, just as these fish alone are accursed, and float in the deep water, not swimming like the others but living on the ground at the bottom of the sea.'

Barn. xix. 2, cf. xix. 6:

'Thou shalt not join thyself to those who walk in the way of death.'

With these may be compared two passages from the Manual of Discipline I QS v.:

'This is the rule for all the members of the community—that is, for such as have declared their readiness to turn away from all evil and to adhere to all that God in His good pleasure has commanded. They are to keep apart from the company of the froward.'

'He that so commits himself is to keep apart from all froward men that walk in the path of wickedness; for such men are not to be reckoned in the covenant inasmuch as they have never sought nor studied God's ordinances in order to find out on what more arcane points they may guiltily have gone astray, while in regard to the things which stand patently revealed they have acted high-handedly.'

[1] Lev. xi. 11.

The idea of the Christian community as a closed group involved, for the Epistle of Barnabas, a mutual sharing. So xix. 8: 'Thou shalt share all things with thy neighbour and shalt not say that they are thy own property; for if you are sharers in that which is incorruptible, how much more in that which is corruptible?' This recalls the Qumran insistence that those entering the covenant should share their possessions. Indeed to lie in this matter was a serious matter and involved a severe penalty—the holding back of a quarter of the offender's food ration for a year (I QS vi.). The Epistle envisages Christians as a 'new people' in contrast to the 'former people', the Jews, who had lost their privileges and the blessings of the covenant (v. 7, xiii. 1), much as the Qumran sect believed that its members were the true Israel of the Covenant in contrast to the Judaism of the urban centres of Palestine. The introduction of such exclusive ideas into Christianity, which find only a limited support in the New Testament, has usually been explained as due to a legalistic spirit which came to the fore in the sub-apostolic Church. The Qumran texts show that these ideas may have been present in the Judaism in which the writer of Barnabas was nurtured and which he may have carried over into his interpretation of Christianity.

(c) The Religious Life

In the Epistle the distinctive Christian virtues of faith, hope and love play a subordinate role. The main emphasis of the writer is on spirituality as the aim of the Christian life—see the use of πνευματικὸς in iv. 11 and xvi. 10. The Qumran texts in a similar way emphasize spirituality as the hallmark of the members of the covenant. Thus I QS ix: 'Everyone is to be judged by the standard of his spirituality. Intercourse with him is to be determined by the purity of his deeds, and consort with him by the degree of his intelligence. This alone is to determine the degree to which a man is to be loved or hated.'

A prominent feature of the Epistle is the emphasis upon knowledge, which is used in three senses:

(i) 'Knowledge' is often coupled with 'faith' and has ethical consequences (i. 5, v. 4, xviii. 1). The practical nature of this knowledge is illustrated by xix. 1: 'Therefore the knowledge given to us of this kind that we may walk in it is as follows. . . .'

(ii) Sometimes this knowledge refers to the interpretation of events in the past, present and eschatological future. Cf. v. 3: 'Therefore we ought to give hearty thanks to the Lord that He has given us knowledge of the past, and wisdom for the present, and that we are not without understanding for the future.' (Cf. ii. 3–4.)

(iii) This knowledge is mediated through the allegorical interpretation of the Old Testament (e.g. vi. 9, xiii. 7) and is also the gift of God (i. 7, ix. 8).

The idea of knowledge (*da'ath*) in the Qumran texts [1] shows marked affinities with that found in the Epistle of Barnabas. With (i) we may compare I QS ix. 17, ff.:

> 'With those however that have chosen the right path everyone is indeed to discuss matters pertaining to the knowledge (*da'ath*) of God's truth and His righteous judgements. The purpose of such discussion is to guide the minds of the members of the community, to give them insight (*b^eda'ath*) into God's inscrutable wonders and truth, and to bring them to walk blamelessly each with his neighbour in harmony with all that has been revealed to them.'

Cf. I QS iii. 2, v. 9, 12, vi. 9, vii. 3-4.

Knowledge has an inexorable connexion with the way of life to be followed by the members of the sect. The idea of knowledge as the interpretation of past, present and future (ii above) is found in a number of passages in the scrolls. Thus I QS iv. 18 ff.: 'Howbeit God, in His inscrutable wisdom, has appointed a term for the existence of perversity.... Then truth will emerge triumphant for the world.... Like waters of purification He will sprinkle upon him the spirit of truth, to cleanse him from all the abominations of falsehood and of all pollution from the spirit of filth; to the end that, being made upright, men may have understanding of transcendental knowledge and of the lore of the sons of heaven and that, being made blameless in their ways, they may be endowed with inner vision.' A similar eschatological reference for *da'ath* is found in the Habakkuk Commentary I Qp Hab. ii. 14: 'For the earth shall be filled with the knowledge of the glory of the Lord as waters cover the sea.' This statement refers to the fact that when God eventually restores them to their former glory '(. . . . . .) falsehood (will) (. . . . . .), and thereafter knowledge will be revealed to them, abundant as the waters of the sea.' With (iii) above may be compared the close association of *da'ath* in the scrolls with the Torah (cf. I QS iii. 1).

The Qumran conception of knowledge gives an insight into ideas which existed on Palestinian soil coeval with the rise of the Church. The sect was not concerned with the anthropological and cosmological doctrines beloved of the later Gnostics but with that knowledge of the Torah which issued in obedience to God's commands in the present and in the future—a thoroughly Jewish idea. However, as W. D. Davies points out,[2] the strong emphasis which the sect

---

[1] The most detailed study of this is by W. D. Davies in HTR 46 (1953), pp. 113-39.
[2] Op. cit., p. 135.

placed on *da'ath*, in comparison to other Jewish literature, may well reflect, in a subtle way, hellenistic influences which had been entering Palestine since the Maccabaean period, much as St. Paul and St. John use terms prominent in the Mystery Religions and Gnosticism without essentially modifying the Hebraic connotations of their thought. It is now increasingly recognized that a sharp dichotomy based on language and culture between the hellenistic Judaism of the Diaspora and Palestinian Judaism did not exist prior to A.D. 135. This fact throws some light on the background of the Epistle of Barnabas. It is remarkable that its author hardly draws on New Testament ideas of knowledge; we find no subordination of knowledge to love and no focusing of knowledge upon the person of Christ. Indeed most of what is said about knowledge in the Epistle might have been written by a Palestinian Jew rather than a Christian. It is a reasonable inference that the author brought over his conception of knowledge into Christianity from Alexandrian Judaism. It follows then that the Judaism of the Egyptian metropolis in the early decades of the second century was of a mixed character—not solely Greek and hellenistic but also containing ideas which can be paralleled in pre-Christian Palestinian sectarian Judaism. The new discoveries reinforce the opinion of Professor G. D. Kilpatrick given before the advent of the scrolls: 'It is natural to make a division in the Judaism of this time, one side being Greek in speech and Alexandrian in culture, the other Aramaic in speech and Rabbinic in culture. . . . The two Gospels (i.e., St. Matthew and St. John) warn us against identifying the linguistic frontier between the Greek and Semitic worlds with the cultural frontier between Hellenism and Judaism.'[1] The Epistle of Barnabas is of significance in being a document, later than the Gospels, which reflects this mixed background before the triumph of Pharisaism produced a more rigid demarcation between the cultural and linguistic boundaries.

(D) Other Parallels

A few other affinities between the Epistle and the Qumran texts may be briefly noted. Both exhibit an antipathy towards the Jerusalem Temple and its cultus—indeed the Epistle goes as far as to say that the Jews before A.D. 70 consecrated God in the Temple almost as the heathen (xvi. 2). The Epistle here presents a closer parallel to the scrolls than that provided by the Apostolic Church, for the latter did not entirely separate itself from the Temple although the group associated with St. Stephen appears to have adopted a more independent policy. In eschatological teaching the Epistle and the

[1] *The Origins of the Gospel according to St. Matthew* (1946), pp. 105-6.

Qumran texts exhibit a similar outlook. Both believed that the last times had dawned when the works of evil were everywhere in the ascendant, Satan and his hosts having been let loose. The prime need in the present was therefore to guard against the entry of Satan (described in the Epistle as the Black One and in the scrolls as Belial) into the human heart. It is, however, noticeable that the Epistle exhibits a greater reserve in its eschatological teaching than the scrolls; this is especially true of the picture drawn in the War Scroll.

The Two Ways Section: As is well known, Chs. xviii–xx of the Epistle contain a section on the Two Ways of life which bears a marked similarity to a section in the *Didache* (Chs. i–v). The question of the exact relationship between these versions has been much discussed during the past forty years, particularly in the pages of the Journal of Theological Studies. A group of English scholars, among them Dom Connolly, Dr. Armitage Robinson, Professor F. E. Vokes and Dr. W. Telfer, has maintained with great conviction that no Jewish pre-Christian manual containing Two Ways teaching ever existed; that the author of the Epistle of Barnabas was the first to compose such a manual which he added as Halakhah to the Haggadic section of his work (Chs. i—xvii); and that the author of the *Didache* had the Epistle before him when composing his treatise. The main argument of these scholars was the silence of Jewish sources as to the existence of a Two Ways manual and the alleged chaotic order of Barnabas' Two Ways section which, in the *Didache*, is brought into a more formal order by careful rearrangement. However, many scholars were dissatisfied with this somewhat tidy theory and have continued to maintain that both versions of the Two Ways in the Christian documents were based on a Jewish-Christian manual suitable for the instruction of catechumens, which itself went back to an earlier Jewish manual or manuals used by the Rabbis for the teaching of proselytes and perhaps in the synagogue exposition. In 1945 Dr. E. J. Goodspeed [1] made the brilliant suggestion that the source used by Barnabas and the *Didache* was none other than the Greek original of the Latin text entitled *de doctrina apostolorum* which, he believes, shows primitive traces incompatible with its being a later Latin translation of *Did.* i–vi. It is beyond our purpose here to enter into the details of this debate [2] except to observe that one of the main planks of the English scholars' argument, viz., that a Jewish Two Ways never existed, cannot now be maintained in the light of a section headed 'Of the Two Spirits in Man' found in the Qumran Manual of Discipline, [3] which was, in all probability, an expository

---

[1] ATR 27 (1945), pp. 239–47.
[2] See the present writer's article in CQR 49 (1958), pp. 211–30.
[3] I QS iii. 13–iv. 26.

sermon used by the priests of the community.[1] We now proceed to compare Barnabas' Two Ways section with this version:

(a) The introduction: Barn. xviii. 1–2 reads:

'There are Two Ways of teaching and power, one of Light and one of Darkness. And there is a great difference between the Two Ways. For over the one are set the light-bringing angels of God, but over the other angels of Satan. And the one is Lord from eternity to eternity, and the other is the ruler of the present time of iniquity.'

With this may be compared this passage in the Manual:

'Now, this God created man to rule the world, and appointed for him Two Spirits after whose direction he was to walk until the final inquisition. They are the Spirits of truth and perversity. The origin of truth lies in the fountain of Light, and that of perversity in the wellspring of Darkness. All who practise righteousness are under the domination of the Prince of Lights, and walk in ways of Light; whereas all who practise perversity are under the domination of the Angel of Darkness and walk in ways of darkness.'

The resemblance here is superficially impressive—especially the occurrence in both versions of the realms of Light and Darkness presided over by the angels of God and Satan. However, the metaphor of Light and Darkness, representing good and evil, was well known in Judaism where it had probably come in under Iranian influence.[2] It is also prominent in the New Testament and, at an early date, came to be associated with baptismal instruction.[3] Later it passed into patristic thought where it became especially congenial to Alexandrian thinkers.[4] Moreover the Qumran conception of the Two Spirits, created by God, struggling for the possession of men's hearts, which is ultimately based on Iranian teaching,[5] is not found in the Epistle of Barnabas.

(b) The Way of Light: Barn. xix. 2–7a reads:

'Thou shalt love thy maker, thou shalt fear thy Creator, thou shalt glorify Him who redeemed thee from death, thou shalt be simple in heart, and rich in spirit; thou shalt not join thyself to those who walk in the way of death, thou shalt hate all that is not pleasing

---

[1] On the meaning of the title 'for the Maskil' see T. H. Gaster, *The Scriptures of the Dead Sea Sect*, p. 47.

[2] Test. Levi. xix. 1; Slav. Enoch xxx. 15.

[3] Eph. v. 8; Heb. vi. 4; 1 Pet. ii. 9; cf. Luke xvi. 8 and John xii. 36.

[4] Clem. Alex. *Exh. to the Greeks*, xi. The metaphor is also prominent in the *Enneads* of Plotinus.

[5] Cf. Yasna xxx. 3, 5.

to God, thou shalt hate all hypocrisy; thou shalt not desert the commandments of the Lord. Thou shalt not exalt thyself, but shall be humble minded in all things; thou shalt not take glory to thyself. Thou shalt form no evil plan against thy neighbour, thou shalt not let thy soul be froward. Thou shalt not commit fornication, thou shalt not commit adultery, thou shalt not commit sodomy. Thou shalt not let the word of God depart from thee among the impurity of any men. Thou shalt not respect persons in the reproving of transgression. Thou shalt be meek, thou shalt be quiet, thou shalt fear the words which thou hast heard. Thou shalt not bear malice against thy brother. Thou shalt not be in two minds whether it shall be or not. Thou shalt not take the name of the Lord in vain. Thou shalt love thy neighbour more than thy own life. Thou shalt not procure abortion, thou shalt not commit infanticide. Thou shalt not withhold thy hand from thy son or from thy daughter, but shalt teach them the fear of God from their youth up. Thou shalt not covet thy neighbour's goods, thou shalt not be avaricious. Thou shalt not be joined in soul with the haughty but shalt converse with humble and righteous men. Thou shalt receive the trials that befall thee as good, knowing that nothing happens without God. Thou shalt not be double-minded or talkative.'

There follows a social code governing the relationship between masters and slaves (xix. 7b) which is also found in the New Testament Epistles; this was based on the *imitatio Christi*. Then comes further teaching about the sharing of private property and the duty of almsgiving with the command to love 'as the apple of thine eye all who speak to thee the word of the Lord' (xix. 9). The Way of Light ends with a request to hold fast the traditions and to abstain from schism.

The Qumran list is as follows:

'This is the way those spirits operate in the world for the enlightenment of man's heart, the making straight before him all the ways of righteousness and truth, the implanting in his heart of fear for judgements of God. A spirit of humility, patience, abundant compassion, perpetual goodness, insight, discrimination, a sense of Divine power that is based at once on an apprehension of God's works and a reliance of His plenteous mercy, a Spirit of Knowledge informing every plan of action, a zeal for righteous government, a hallowed mind in a controlled nature, abounding love for all who follow the truth, a self-respecting purity which abhors all the taint of filth, a modesty of behaviour coupled with a general prudence and an ability to hide within oneself the secrets of what one knows—these are the things that come to men in this world through communion with the spirit of truth. And the guerdon of all that walk in its ways is health and abundant well-being, with long life and fruition of seed along with eternal blessings and everlasting joy in life everlasting, and a crown of glory and a robe of honour, amid light perpetual.'

The resemblance here is not so close. The Qumran list, which is much shorter than that of the Epistle, deals with the inner attitude required of members of the sect which is in line with the devotional spirit of their Thanksgiving Psalms. Here was a community of pious individuals who believed in religious inwardness. Barnabas' list, on the other hand, is more externalized with the emphasis on correct behaviour. The use of so many negative prohibitions reflects a tendency towards the codification of ethical precepts which came to the fore in sub-apostolic Christianity.

(c) The Way of Darkness: Barn. xx. 1 reads:

'But the Way of the Black One is crooked and full of cursing for it is the way of death eternal with punishment, and in it are the things that destroy their soul: idolatry, frowardness, arrogance of power, hypocrisy, the double heart, adultery, murder, robbery, pride, transgression, fraud, malice, self-sufficiency, enchantments, magic, covetousness, the lack of the fear of God.'

The Qumran list reads:

'But to the spirit of perversity belongs greed, remissness in right doing, wickedness and falsehood, pride and presumption, deception and guile, cruelty and abundant insolence, shortness of temper and profusion of folly, arrogant passion, abominable acts in a spirit of lewdness, filthy ways in the thraldom of unchastity, a blasphemous tongue, blindness of eyes, dullness of ears, stiffness of neck and hardness of heart, to the end that a man walks entirely in ways of darkness and of evil cunning.'

The resemblance here is closer than in the corresponding sections of the Way of Light. We know that the Jews drew up catalogues of sins one of which, known as the Vidui, was recited on the Day of Atonement. It is an interesting fact that the Vidui list contained twenty-two sins, the same number as appears in the Qumran way of darkness,[1] in the lists in Rom. i. 29 and *Did.* v. 1; five of the six sins

[1] There appears to have been some connexion between the beliefs of the sect and those of the Jerusalem Temple, where the Vidui originated. See further K. G. Kuhn in in *The Scrolls and the New Testament*, ed. K. Stendahl (1958), p. 69.

which Rendel Harris [1] thought might belong to the original Vidui are found at Qumran. Whatever be the explanation of the connexions between these lists it is clear that the list in the Epistle of Barnabas, which only contains seventeen sins, cannot be directly derived from the Vidui, although an indirect connexion is not excluded.

(d) The social code: Both the Epistle and the Manual of Discipline contain a code dealing with social relationships. In Barnabas the slave-master theme, familiar from the social codes underlying the New Testament Epistles, appears within the Two Ways section. The command to slaves to obey their masters is probably pre-Christian although in Christianity it was given special emphasis as an opportunity for the practice of the *imitatio Christi*. Such social relationships did not apply in the case of the Qumran community, whose members had surrendered their wealth and status on entering the covenant. Accordingly the Qumran Social Code, contained in a section [2] separate from that on the Two Spirits, deals with the relationships appropriate to the members of an exclusive sectarian group. In particular the covenanters are exhorted to obey the decisions of their priests, the sons of Zadok, who have the deciding word in all doctrinal, economic and judicial matters.

The evidence given above does not appear to prove that the author of the Epistle of Barnabas, in his Two Ways section, was directly acquainted with the corresponding Qumran version. The differences are too great to be explained in this way. However the Manual of Discipline version is of great value in demonstrating, for the first time, that a *written* Two Ways manual or expository sermon, containing lists of virtues and vices, was known in Judaism in the pre-Christian era. What had long been suspected is now removed from the realm of conjecture. The resemblances, in general, between the later Christian and the earlier Jewish versions are to be explained as due to the vicissitudes of oral and written transmission. We know that in late Judaism instruction was given by the Rabbis and naturally varied in accordance with the audience addressed. Sometimes it took the form of expository discourses, based on passages of the Torah, delivered in the synagogue service; at other times it formed, with circumcision and baptism, the conditions for the acceptance of a proselyte to Judaism. It is likely that this teaching sometimes took the form of a Two Ways discourse described metaphorically as the ways of Light and Darkness. This teaching circulated among the Rabbis in the pre-Christian era in both oral and

[1] *The Teaching of the Apostles* (1887), pp. 82–86.
[2] I QS v. 1–7.

written forms and one example of the latter is found in I QS iii. 13–iv. 26, an expository sermon which the sect may have taken over from the usage of the synagogue, although the Qumran scribes subsequently worked this over and incorporated into it certain theological ideas of their own. The exact form of this Two Ways teaching probably varied from place to place and teacher to teacher —sometimes it may have contained a code dealing with social relationships. Christianity, which was otherwise heavily indebted to Judaism, as it developed its mission in the Graeco-Roman world took over from the Diaspora Jewish forms of ethical instruction. Among these was a Two Ways teaching which may have been known to the early Church in both oral and written forms. One such Jewish written version was the source of the original Greek text of the *de doctrina apostolorum* which is now only known in a Latin version. The writer of the Epistle of Barnabas used this Two Ways, which formed the substance of the Greek *Doctrina*, when compiling the Halakhic section of this work. Thus between the Qumran version and that of Barnabas lies a number of oral and written stages which accounts for the similarities and differences which exist between the two versions.

The evidence given so far in this chapter will be variously estimated according to the predisposition of the reader. The parallels do not seem to me to prove a *direct* influence of the Qumran theology on the Epistle of Barnabas. Others may judge differently and believe that some survivors of the Qumran community came to Alexandria [1] after the destruction of their headquarters in A.D. 68 and there propagated distinctive sectarian doctrines which later became known to the writer of the Epistle. However great caution is needed in estimating the influence of the doctrines of one set of documents on another and it seems best to withhold judgement on this difficult question. In any case the discovery of the scrolls has thrown a flood of new light on the Jewish background of early Christianity and in the study of this fascinating subject we venture to think that the Epistle of Barnabas will repay careful examination. As suggested earlier, it appears to reflect closely a mixed type of Judaism which flourished in Alexandria in the early second century A.D. This Judaism had affinities on the one side with the hellenism of Philo yet also embraced doctrines which have now been found on Palestinian soil in the teachings of the Qumran sect. The Epistle of Barnabas reflects this interesting Jewish background with greater clarity than the New Testament documents. This is because its

---

[1] Y. Yadin, *The Message of the Scrolls*, p. 131, asserts that members of the sect lived in the Diaspora on the basis of the reference in the War Scroll to the 'wilderness of the peoples'. This, however, is quite uncertain.

writer was less markedly under the influence of the life, teaching and example of Christ than the early Christian writers. In spite of the violence of his anti-Jewish polemic he remained in outlook a Jew and brought with him into the Christian fold the exegetical methods and traditions of the synagogue.

(2)

We have already suggested that the writer of Barnabas used the Greek original of the *Doctrina apostolorum* when composing his work c. A.D. 117–19. However he re-wrote his sources as a midrash halakhah suitable for homiletic use in the community he was addressing. We know that the Alexandrian Church in the time of Hadrian was seeking to baptize pagan thought and culture into Christ and that a freedom of approach, in matters of doctrine and practice, existed. It is therefore no surprise that Barnabas allowed himself some freedom in using a catechism of his own Church.[1]

The constant contacts between the different centres of the early Church, which were facilitated by the well known trade routes along which missionaries and teachers travelled, render it likely that by c. A.D. 100 a number of written versions of the original Greek 'Two Ways' existed outside of Egypt. One of these versions was used by the Syrian writer of the *Didache* in the early decades of the second century [2] when compiling his manual, although he interpolated into it other material. The two titles of his work are significant—'Teaching of the Twelve Apostles' and 'Teaching of the Lord through the Twelve Apostles to the Gentiles'. *A.C.* vii. 27 seems to have had the longer title in its copy: ἄλλην διδαχὴν κηρύσσῃ παρ' ἣν ὑμῖν παρέδωκεν ὁ Χριστὸς δι' ἡμῶν. This may also have been known to the author of 2 Clement [3] and to Pseudo-Ignatius,[4] for both make

[1] J. V. Bartlet, *H.D.B.* (Extra Vol.), p. 444 thinks that Barnabas would not have treated a catechetical formula engraven on his memory in this way. This is to overlook the influence of Synagogue exposition on the writer and the fluidity of second century Christianity.

[2] I have not thought it necessary to discuss the vexed question of the date of the *Didache*. As to its venue a region of Syria has the least objections. W. Telfer boldly suggested Antioch but a N. Syrian milieu seems to me more probable (JTS 40, pp. 133–46 and 258–71). On the other hand the arguments of J.-P. Audet, *La Didaché: Instructions des Apôtres*, p. 199 for a date between A.D. 50 and 70 is clearly determined by his view that the *Didache* did not use any of the Canonical Gospels. In any event the *Didache* is not a late hole-in-the-corner production which can safely be ignored in reconstructing the history and teaching of the primitive Church. I believe that the document dates from the period A.D. 100–130 and depends on the Matthaean stream of the Gospel tradition.

[3] Ch. xiii.
[4] Ch. xi.

remarks about the Gentiles in connexion with sentiments found in the early part of the *Didache*. The longer title certainly appears to be more original for the work as a whole, for it is difficult to imagine the fuller and more personal title having been added between the more common one and the text proper.[1] The shorter title may have been the designation of the 'Two Ways' in Syria which the *Didache* took over. The phrase 'Teaching of the Twelve Apostles' is no less primitive than 'Teaching of the Apostles'. Thus in part of the Ascension of Isaiah, which dates from before A.D. 100, it is said that 'the Twelve Apostles of the Beloved' plant the Church (iv. 3); and it is 'the preaching (προφητεία) of His Twelve Apostles' that is forsaken by the mass of disciples on the eve of His approach (iii. 21). Hence the designation 'Teaching of the Twelve Apostles' may be quite early. Indeed there is nothing less primitive in the longer title which was given to his work by the Didachist. He believed that his treatise, prefaced by the 'Two Ways', expressed the mind of 'the Lord', i.e. the glorified Christ (cf. *Did.* viii. 2, ix. 5, xi. 2, 4, 8, xv. 4, xvi. 1, 7 ff.). Thus at an early date we have the original Alexandrian version of the 'Two Ways' known simply as 'Teaching of the Apostles' (*de doctrina apostolorum*, Eus.*E.H.* iii. 25, Rufinus, Athanasius' *Festal Epistles* xxxix, Nicephorus)—and also a Syrian version which went under the name 'Teaching of the Twelve Apostles' which the Didachist used in compiling his treatise on Church ordinances which he called 'Teaching of the Lord through the Twelve Apostles to the Gentiles'. The broad distinction between the Egyptian and Syrian lines of transmission of the 'Two Ways' persists throughout its later history although the textual question was complicated by the arrival in Alexandria of the fuller *Didache*.

An examination of the evidence from the early Christian centuries shows that knowledge of the 'Two Ways' is more general than knowledge of the fuller *Didache*,[2] a fact that is very strange if a Greek version of the 'Two Ways' never existed apart from its presence in the Epistle of Barnabas where it was the composition of the author. We know that in both Syria and Egypt the 'Two Ways' had a life of its own. In Syria it stood on much the same level as the fuller *Didache* down to the time of Eusebius, although after then both tended to fall out of use and were superseded by the *Didascalia* and *Apostolic Constitutions*. In Egypt and elsewhere the fuller *Didache*, which was never translated into Latin, apparently had only

---

[1] J.-P. Audet, op. cit., p. 102, holds that the original title of the *Didache* was simply: Διδαχαὶ τῶν ἀποστόλων, and a second title: Διδαχὴ κυρίου τοῖς ἔθνεσιν was, in particular, the title of the 'Two Ways'. This solution seems to raise more problems than it solves.

[2] The evidence is given in detail in *H.D.B.* (Extra Vol.), pp. 441–3.

a limited circulation, perhaps being used by scholars for historical purposes. The Teaching of the Apostles probably meant for Clement of Alexandria the Greek original of the *doctrina* (*Strom.* i. 20, 100), although he may also have known the fuller *Didache* (*Protr.* x. 108). Similarly with Athanasius, who wrote in his *Festal Letter* xxxix (A.D. 367):

ἐστὶ καὶ ἕτερα βιβλία τούτων ἔξωθεν, οὐ κανονιζόμενα μὲν τετυπωμένα δὲ παρὰ τῶν πατέρων ἀναγινώσκεσθαι τοῖς ἄρτι προσερχομένοις καὶ βουλομένοις κατηχεῖσθαι τὸν τῆς εὐσεβείας λόγον· Σοφία Σολομῶντος καὶ Σοφία Σιρὰχ καὶ Ἐσθὴρ καὶ Ἰουδὶθ καὶ Τωβίας καὶ Διδαχὴ καλωμένη τῶν ἀποστόλων καὶ ὁ Ποιμήν.[1]

This must refer to the 'Two Ways', as only this could be said to be of any use for converts who wished to be instructed in 'the word of godliness'—a fact that is confirmed by the words Διδαχὴ . . . τῶν ἀποστόλων, the same title as in the Latin *Doctrina*. In Italy, to judge from Rufinus' words, the 'Two Ways' had been given a local or Petrine setting. Thus: In Novo vero Testamento libellus qui dicitur Pastoris sive Hermae, [et is] qui appellatur Duae Viae vel Iudicium secundum Petrum. Quae omnia legi quidem in ecclesiis voluerunt, non tamen proferri ad auctoritatem ex his fidei confirmandam. (*Comm. in symb. apost.* xxxviii).[2] The above evidence supports the view that the 'Two Ways' circulated separately as a piece of instruction that was used for catechetical and homiletic purposes. Its use was so firmly rooted in Egypt that the arrival there of the fuller *Didache* and its presence, in another form, in the Epistle of Barnabas did not cause its supersession.

The later evidence of the use of the 'Two Ways' is best given as follows:

(A) Syrian Tradition

This began with a written version of the Two Ways known as the Teaching of the Twelve Apostles which was incorporated into the *Didache* c. A.D. 100–130. The *Didascalia Apostolorum*,[3] a Church Order composed in N. Syria in the first half of the third century A.D., originally written in Greek but now only surviving

---

[1] Matthaeus Blastares (A.D. 1335) quotes this, adding ταύτην δὲ καὶ ἡ ἕκτη σύνοδος ἠθέτησεν, ὡς δεδήλωται, so apparently confusing it with *Apostolic Constitutions.* Johannes Zonaras (A.D. 1120) in his commentary on Athanasius' *Festal Letters* makes the same error.

[2] We do not use as evidence the *Stichometry* of Nicephorus (c. A.D. 850), the catalogue of the 60 Canonical books of the 6th cent. (ed. Cotelerius, *Patr. Apost.* (1724), I, 197) or the list of apocryphal writings found at the end of the *Quaestiones* of Anastasius of Sinai, as their references are disputed.

[3] R. H. Connolly, *Didascalia Apostolorum* (1929). Fragments in JTS 18 (1916–17), pp. 301–9.

in Syriac and Latin fragments, shows contacts with the *Didache* in the following passages:

Did. i. 3	—	*Didascalia* i. 2-3
i. 5	—	iv. 3
ii. 4	—	ii. 6, 1
iii. 7-8	—	ii. 1, 5
viii	—	v. 14, 18-21
xiii. 3	—	ii. 26, 1 and 2
xvi. 6	—	vi. 15, 3

The presence of items from the section *Did.* i. 3-ii. 1 shows that the *Didascalia* used the fuller *Didache* and not simply the Syrian version of the 'Two Ways', although the title of the *Didascalia* may imply knowledge of this: 'The Didascalia, or the Catholic Teaching of the Twelve Apostles and holy disciples of Our Saviour'. Its first book traverses the same ground as the 'Two Ways' although expressing a fuller Christian ideal of conduct. *Apostolic Constitutions* Book vii. 1-32,[1] a collection of ecclesiastical law emanating from Syria, perhaps from the region of Antioch, in the latter half of the fourth century, embodies the whole of the *Didache*, the 'Two Ways' largely verbatim (1-21), the rest with more reserve, although many additions have been made to comply with conditions of the time. *A.C.* vii opens with Moses' reference to the choice between the Ways of Life and Death (Deut. xxx. 19), and having cited the *verba Christi*, 'No man can serve two masters', continues: 'As in duty bound, we also, following the Teacher (διδασκάλῳ), Christ, ... say that "there are Two Ways"', etc. The opening of *A.C.* i. reads: πᾶσι τοῖς ἐξ ἐθνῶν πιστεύσασιν. These suggest that the writer of *A.C.* knew the longer title of the fuller *Didache* as we have it in our MS. He also used the *Didascalia Apostolorum* as a basis for Books i-vi.

The Syrian evidence bears witness to the influence of the *Didache* on the *Didascalia* and *Apostolic Constitutions* such as to supersede, from the third century onwards, the use of the earlier written version of the 'Two Ways' which had as its title 'Teaching of the Twelve Apostles'. It is significant that a considerable use of the *Didache's* material is confined to these two documents both of which emanate from Syrian soil. This would support the view that the *Didache* itself is a Syrian and not an Egyptian composition.

(B) The Egyptian Tradition

Three versions of the 'Two Ways' were known in Egypt at an early date. The first was the original Greek 'Two Ways' of which

[1] F. X. Funk (Paderborn 1909): Migne P.G.L. I, 555-1156. English translation by J. Donaldson, Ante-Nicene Christian Library xvii (1870), part 2.

the Latin *Doctrina* is a translation; this circulated separately and was known to Clement of Alexandria and Athanasius. The second was the version of the writer of the Epistle of Barnabas, and the last was that of the Didachist whose work must have arrived in Egypt by the third century and probably earlier. All of these versions were known to the writer of the *Apostolic Church Order*[1] (*A.C.O.*) which dates from *c.* A.D. 300.[2] Originally written in Greek the work survives also in Latin and Oriental versions. This compilation achieved for the Egyptian Church what *A.C.* vii. did for the Syrian. It worked up the Egyptian recension of the *Didache*, using also Barnabas and the original Greek 'Two Ways', into a form more in accordance with local needs. The book opens with a salutation from the twelve Apostles, among whom St. Peter appears twice, once as Peter and once as Cephas; the second James and Matthias are wanting but Nathanael is added to make up the number. The Apostles speak in turn and their successive speeches are fragments of the 'Two Ways'. Much of *A.C.O.* runs parallel to the 'Two Ways' in the *Doctrina* and in *Did.* i–iv, with reminiscences of Barnabas; it is significant that *A.C.O.* has no section parallel to *Did.* i. 3b–ii. 1—which suggests that it knew a 'Two Ways' tradition lacking this section.

A.C.O. uses Barnabas' preface: χαίρετε, υἱοὶ καὶ θυγατέρες, ἐν ὀνόματι κυρίου Ἰησοῦ Χριστοῦ and also follows one of the latter's most adventurous emendations, substituting ὡς κόρην ὀφθαλμοῦ σου for ὡς κύριον. *A.C.O.* also seems to have been aware of Barn. xix. 10: μνησθήσῃ ἡμέραν κρίσεως ἡμέρας καὶ νυκτὸς since he provides the key to Barnabas' change of the *Doctrina* in the words: λόγον ὑφέξουσιν ἐν τῇ μεγάλῃ ἡμέρᾳ τῆς κρίσεως περὶ ὧν ἀκούσαντες οὐκ ἐφύλαξαν. A good example of *A.C.O.*'s method of using Barnabas is provided at the beginning of his 'Two Ways' section. Immediately after πρῶτον ἀγαπήσεις τὸν θεὸν τὸν ποιήσαντά σε *A.C.O.* adds ἐξ ὅλης τῆς καρδίας σου καὶ δοξάσεις τὸν λυτρωσάμενον σε ἐκ θανάτου from Barn. xix. 2. *A.C.O.* simply inserts here and there reminiscences of Barnabas although, in the main, it follows the version of the 'Two Ways' in the *Doctrina* and the *Didache*, which was known in Egypt *c.* A.D. 300, at least in certain scholarly circles. Traces of the *Didache* outside of *Did.* i–iv are found in *A.C.O.*'s εἰ γὰρ ὁ κύριος δι' αὐτοῦ ἠξίωσέ σοι δοθῆναι πνευματικὴν τροφὴν καὶ ποτὸν καὶ ζωὴν αἰώνιον, σὺ ὀφείλεις πολὺ μᾶλλον τὴν φθαρτὴν καὶ πρόσκαιρον προσφέρειν τροφήν which probably reveals a knowledge of *Did.* x. 3; cf. iv. 8.

---

[1] Text in Schermann, *Die allgemeine Kirchenordnung* (1914), p. 12f.
[2] The view of J. V. Bartlet, (*Church-Life and Church-Order*, p. 102) that *A.C.O.* is based on an earlier source emanating from Cilicia or Cappadocia *c.* A.D. 225–250 seems to me entirely speculative.

A trace of *Did.* xi. 11 is probably to be found in *A.C.O.* i.: πρὸς θεμελίουσιν ἐκκλησίας ἵνα τύπον τῶν ἐπουρανίων εἰδότες φυλάσσωνται κτλ.

The 'Two Ways' section of *A.C.O.* is closely based on the original of the *Doctrina* and on *Did.* i–iv with insertions from Barnabas. There is however no trace of a section parallel to *Did.* i. 3b–ii. 1 or of *Did.* v or vi. It is very unlikely that *A.C.O.* omitted the first because Barnabas omitted it; rather *A.C.O.* omitted it because it was missing from the original Egyptian 'Two Ways' catechism underlying the Latin *Doctrina*. And in any case the insertion of *verba Christi* from the *Didache* would have been unsuitable in utterances put into the mouths of Apostles. The omission of the *Via Mortis* by *A.C.O.* was probably due to a desire to avoid a repetition of what was already present, as negative prohibitions, in the *Via Vitae*. *A.C.O.* realized that a catalogue of vices was not the best way of inculcating Christian morality. *A.C.O.*, however, closely follows the *Didache*'s version of the *Via Vitae*, interpolating into it other material. Much the longest of these interpolations occurs parallel to *Did.* iii. 3 between ὁδηγεῖ γὰρ ἡ ἐπιθυμία πρὸς τὴν πορνείαν and μηδὲ αἰσχρολόγος μηδὲ ὑψηλόφθαλμος. *A.C.O.* adds here a section which expands the warning against lust which it describes as a θηλυκὸν δαιμόνιον. The reason why the writer felt free to deal in this way with his source probably lies in the *Doctrina*'s omission of *Did.* iii. 3. Previous to this point, with the exception of *Did.* i. 3b–ii. 1, the *Didache* and its *Doctrina* source have marched hand in hand. But *A.C.O.* took note of *Doctrina*'s omission and therefore felt free to expand and justify the *Didache*'s μὴ γίνου ἐπιθυμητὴς as it formed no part of the original Egyptian 'Two Ways'. *A.C.O.*, which used at least three documents in its compilation, is a most interesting witness to the Egyptian transmission of the 'Two Ways'. It confirms, as has been already suggested, that there existed an original short 'Two Ways' which was not fully superseded in Egypt by the native Barnabas or by the fuller *Didache* when it arrived.

Further evidence of the Egyptian tradition is provided by the *Panegyric* of Schnudi (Sinuthius), abbot of a monastery in Egypt, who died just before the Council of Chalcedon. This work, which was written in Coptic by Besa, Schnudi's successor, contains a homily that begins: 'The way consists of Two Ways, one to Life, and the other to Death, and there is an important difference between these two ways. And this is the way of life.' There follows a version of the Two Ways which significantly has no parallel to *Did.* i. 3b–ii. 1; the *Via Mortis* is shortened to a list of five vices concluding with the words 'every pernicious act', perhaps under the influence of *A.C.O.* The omission of *Did.* i. 3b–ii. 1 indicates that Schnudi knew a shorter version of the 'Two Ways', most probably written in Greek, to judge from the indebtedness of Coptic literature to that language. This is supported by the fact that the *Panegyric* betrays no knowledge of Barnabas who also omits the passage. The 'Two Ways' known to Schnudi was probably the Greek original of the *Doctrina*, as seventy-seven of its items can be traced in the homily,[1] largely in the same order as in the *Doctrina*. At a few places, however, the influence of the Gospels, *A.C.O.* and perhaps the longer *Didache* is discernible, e.g., in *Schnudi* i. 2 where *Doctrina*'s: 'Primo diliges deum aeternum qui te fecit' is expanded by the addition of 'from your whole heart, from your whole soul, with all your thoughts'.

The *Syntagma Doctrinae*, an Athanasian (or Pseudo-Athanasian) summary of doctrine, and the *Fides Nicaena* [2] which is dependent on it, use a version of the 'Two Ways' which again significantly has no section parallel to *Did.* i. 3b–ii. 1. However, the Syntagma has twenty-five items of the *Doctrina* which re-appear in the *Fides*. Thus the *Doctrina* is the major source behind the Syntagma's 'Two Ways' although traces of *A.C.O.* appear as in the filling-out of the command to love God, and possibly of the *Didache* in the reference to Wednesday and Friday as the Christian fast days. On occasions the *Fides* betrays an original touch, as in the addition of καὶ δίκαιος ἔσῃ from *Did.* i. 5.

The Egyptian tradition shows that a Greek 'Two Ways' was in circulation from the first century onwards. About A.D. 118 it was used by Barnabas in writing his epistle; it was known to Clement of Alexandria and Athanasius, who found it suitable for catechetical instruction, and formed one of the sources of the *Apostolic Church Order c.* A.D. 300. Schnudi based his teaching on a Coptic translation of this Greek 'Two Ways' and it also influenced the *Syntagma Doctrinae* and the *Fides Nicaena*. On the other hand extensive use of the Greek *Didache* in Egypt seems limited to the *A.C.O.* although in Syria the *Didache* was the source of the *Didascalia* and *Apostolic Constitutions* Book vii which soon superseded the shorter Syrian version of the 'Two Ways' known as 'Teaching of the Twelve Apostels'. The Egyptian preference for an independent Greek 'Two Ways' may have been due to its having been composed from *within* the Alexandrian Church as a catechesis suitable for use with converts. It met a definite local need in the first century in providing a codification of ethical principles, and being firmly rooted in the milieu of Egyptian Christianity it maintained an independent

[1] Goodspeed, op. cit., p. 237.
[2] A. Harnack, *Geschichte der Altchristlichen Litteratur*, I, p. 87, dates the *Syntagma* A.D. 350–70 and the *Fides* A.D. 375–81. Both documents are found in Migne P.G. xxviii. 835 ff. and 1637 ff.

existence for a long period, circulating among catechists and church leaders, in spite of its presence in Barnabas and the Egyptian recension of the *Didache*. In Syria however the original 'Two Ways' did not arise out of the needs of the indigenous Church but was an importation from outside. And the fact that the Didachist had reproduced it almost verbally, placing it *at the beginning* of his treatise, interpolating into it more congenial *verba Christi* and other material, meant that its value was to a great extent superseded. Hence in Syria it did not maintain for long an independent existence apart from its presence in the *Didache* and the latter's incorporation into the *Didascalia* and *Apostolic Constitutions*.

We have no exact information as to the authorship of the Latin *Doctrina* but perhaps the Greek 'Two Ways' was translated by a puritan circle such as that of Novatian and his successors,[1] who would have found these ethical precepts congenial to their outlook. Be that as it may, there is considerable evidence for the existence of the 'Two Ways' in the West. It was known to St. Augustine,[2] Rufinus and St. Jerome; in Italy it was given a Petrine setting. This knowledge of the 'Two Ways' in the West is in striking contrast to the paucity of references to the fuller *Didache*, of which no Latin translation is known. The reason for the neglect of the *Didache* lies in the latter's primitive polity and milieu which was simply out of date in regions where the authority of the Roman Church was established. The 'Two Ways', however, continued to circulate in the West and was known, in considerable detail, to medieval Rhineland preachers such as Boniface of Mainz and Severianus of Cologne.

[1] Goodspeed, op. cit., p. 232.
[2] St. Augustine was the first writer on catechetics to point out that the *norm* of Christian morality is the Decalogue, as interpreted in the two great commandments of love to God and one's neighbour (*Serm.* ix. 7, 13; *de cat. rud.* iv; most fully in *contra Faustum*). Lactantius in his *Epitome divinarum institutionum* had, however, written on the Decalogue before St. Augustine; cf. also Philo *de decalogo*. With St. Augustine's interpretation compare the hymn for Pentecost in the *Breviarum Parisiense:*
    Per quem (*Spiritum Sanctum*) *legis amor, cordibus insitus,*
        Dat quod lex iubet exsequi.

THE TEXTUAL TRANSMISSION OF THE 'TWO WAYS'

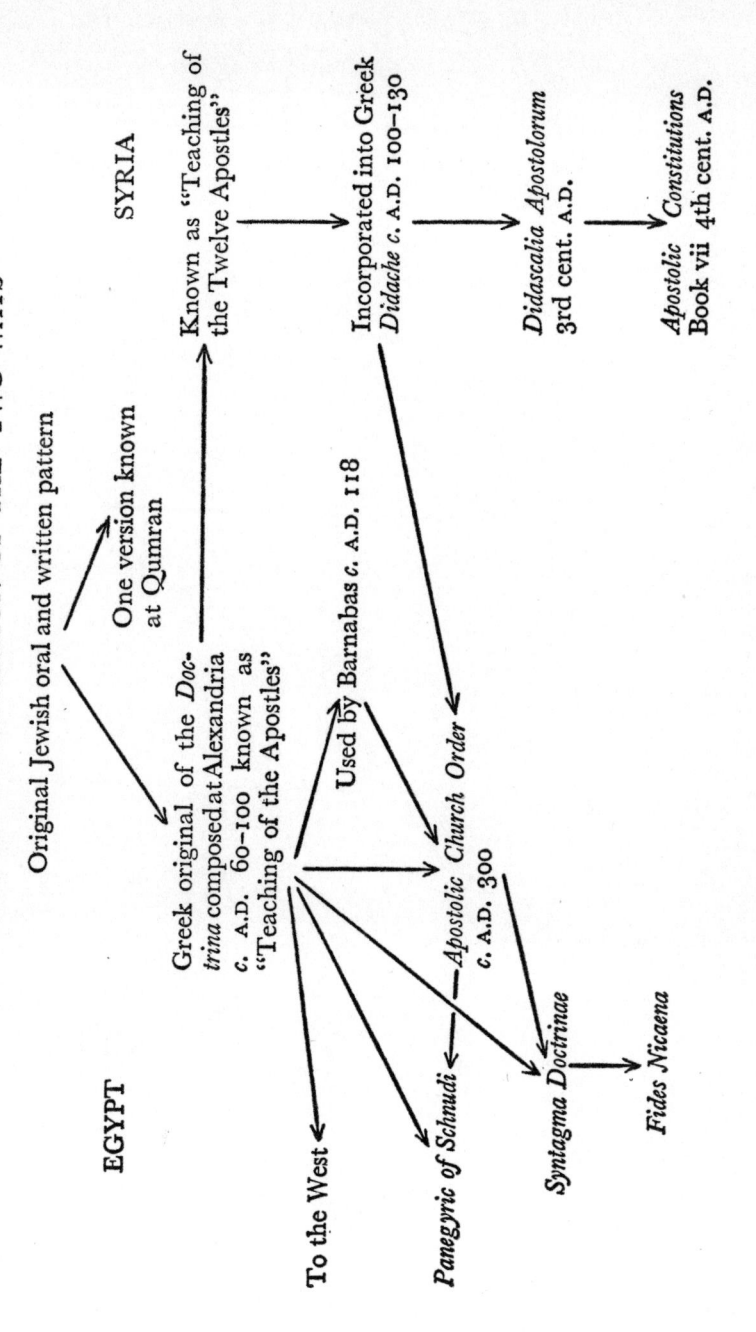

Original Jewish oral and written pattern

SYRIA

One version known at Qumran

Known as "Teaching of the Twelve Apostles"

Incorporated into Greek *Didache* c. A.D. 100–130

Didascalia Apostolorum 3rd cent. A.D.

Apostolic Constitutions Book vii 4th cent. A.D.

EGYPT

Greek original of the *Doctrina* composed at Alexandria c. A.D. 60–100 known as "Teaching of the Apostles"

Used by Barnabas c. A.D. 118

Apostolic Church Order c. A.D. 300

Panegyric of Schnudi

Syntagma Doctrinae

To the West

Fides Nicaena

IX

THE USE OF TESTIMONIES IN THE EARLY CHURCH AND IN THE EPISTLE OF BARNABAS

(1)

It has long been suggested that the phenomena of Old Testament quotations in the New Testament and the early Patristic writings were best to be accounted for by the hypothesis that a collection or collections of proof-texts from the Old Testament were compiled at an early date for the purpose of establishing the truth of the Christian Revelation and also for use against the Jews in polemical and apologetic debate. Hatch (*Essays in Biblical Greek*, p. 203), Harnack (*History of Dogma*, E.T. Vol. I, p. 175), Drummond (*Character and Authorship of the Fourth Gospel*, p. 365) were among the first to suspect the existence of such collections and the hypothesis was worked out in detail by Rendel Harris in a series of articles and later, in collaboration with Vacher Burch, in *Testimonies* (2 vols., 1916 and 1920). Harris started from the existence of three works:

(a) Cyprian's *Testimonia*, the first two books of which contain a collection of anti-Jewish testimonies classified under different headings for the use of Christian catechists and apologists [1]; (b) the collection of Gregory of Nyssa published in the *Collectanea* of Zacagni (Migne P.G. xlvi); (c) the Syriac treatise of Bar Ṣalibi against the Jews which, although late in date, contains relics of earlier controversies and sections of classified testimonia. From this base Harris worked backwards through Tertullian *adversus Judaeos*, Irenaeus *On the Apostolic Preaching*, Justin Martyr *Dial. cum Trypho*, the *Dialogue of Jason and Papiscus* (c. A.D. 135) and the Epistle of Barnabas, all of which, he believed, preserved many of the testimonia found in the later collections. Then, turning his attention to the New Testament, Harris noted that the use of Old Testament proof texts was very common and that the same passage was often quoted by more than one writer in a version different from the LXX; sometimes passages appeared in combination in different New Testament writers, suggesting the use of a source in which the quotations were already combined; and a key word would turn up in a number of passages, e.g., Christ as the Stone, which, originating in a *verbum Christi*, occurs

---

[1] Collections of proof texts formed only one part of the *adversus Judaeos* literature. Melito's *Homily on the Passion* is an example of a different type of argument which is passionate and denunciatory rather than argumentative.

in various forms in the New Testament and early Patristic writings (see below pp. 115–122) and in Cyprian *Test.* ii. 16 becomes the heading of a section: Quod idem et lapis dictus sit, which is followed by ii. 17: Quod deinde idem lapis mons fieret et impleret totam terram. Harris came to the conclusion that there existed an original *written* book of Old Testament testimonies which was the oldest literary product of the Church, ante-dating the earliest of the New Testament writings. And he further surmised that the compiler of this book which, he believed, had five sections, was the Apostle Matthew; and that the book is referred to in the enigmatic reference of Papias to the λογία composed by Matthew. Harris held that this book was drawn upon, not only by the New Testament writers, but by every patristic writer who used Old Testament proof texts, although each translated, adapted, re-edited, abbreviated or enlarged the book as seemed necessary to his purpose. The final stage of the Testimony Book is to be found in a sixteenth century MS. in the Greek monastery on Mount Athos (the same book as the Selden MS. at Oxford) which contains an anti-Jewish treatise in Five books, mainly composed of Old Testament testimonia, which is attributed to one 'Matthew the Monk'; certain of these testimonies were also known to Eusebius and St. Basil.

Harris' work was at once seen to be of fundamental importance and, with reservations on details, commanded the assent of many front-rank scholars. His unparalleled patristic learning and astonishing erudition in works of many different languages clearly showed how fundamental the use of testimonia was to the early Church—not only in controversy with the Jews but also in the development of its theology. However it must be said that Harris was under the influence of the 'documentary' theory of sources, then prevalent in New Testament and patristic studies, and that he underestimated the importance of a common method and tradition, which may have taken both oral and written forms, and may have been known to different writers. (Harris himself appears to have realized this, for in places he talks of the fluidity of the testimony tradition: cf. Vol. I, p. 100; 'We have given in the previous pages the proofs of the antiquity and the wide diffusion of the collection of prophecies employed by the early Christians in their controversies with the Jews. We have seen reason to believe that it was to some extent fluid, and that it was accommodated at various points to the needs of the time, and subject to some change, under hostile criticism or closer study'. In Vol. II, pp. 101–2, he makes a distinction in the form of the Testimony Book before and after A.D. 70 when it underwent a re-statement). Recent study of the New Testament Epistles by Drs. Carrington and Selwyn has demonstrated the existence of a pattern of Christian catechetical teaching which was common to various authors and this method, I believe, may well prove to be the key to the understanding of the use of the Old Testament in the early Church. Harris' theory of a single written testimony source underlying the New Testament and early patristic writings is also open to the damaging criticism that a work of such fundamental significance, if it existed, would surely have come to the light of day and have found a place in the New Testament Canon.

(2)

The subject of the testimonia, insofar as these were used as Messianic proof texts to establish the truth of the central facts of Christianity, has recently been the subject of an illuminating and exhaustive study by Dr. C. H. Dodd (*According to the Scriptures*, 1952). The difference in Dodd's approach from that of Harris may be stated in the former's own words: 'In much criticism of an earlier day the general presumption was entertained that the writings of the New Testament formed a series which, when arranged in correct chronological order, would reveal a more or less orderly development. . . . But much of the new work done in the last half-century has gone to show that the picture was somewhat out of focus. The early Church was not such a bookish community. The main current of its life and thought seems to have been carried by oral tradition, at least to the end of the first century, and the surviving documents are, in large measure, the deposit of a common tradition in its various stages, developed in one way or another according to the idiosyncrasy of the several authors. In certain specific cases indeed there is definite evidence that writings had some kind of literary connexion, over and above the common tradition underlying them all, but except where some such evidence can be adduced, the presumption of literary dependence is precarious, since resemblances might be so probably accounted for without it.' (op. cit., p. 29.)

After a detailed examination of the use of the Old Testament in the New Testament Dodd reaches the following conclusions which I propose to accept:

(a) The quotation of passages from the Old Testament is not to be accounted for by the postulate of a primitive Testimony Book, which was the result, not the presupposition, of the work of early Christian biblical scholars. Rather the evidence points to *a certain method* of quoting the Old Testament which, at a very early date, became part of the equipment of Christian teachers and evangelists —and this method was largely employed orally, finding only a sporadic literary expression.

(b) This method included the selection of certain large sections of the Old Testament which were understood as wholes, although only particular verses from them might be quoted by any one New Testament writer. At the same time detached Old Testament texts could be adduced to elucidate the meaning of the main section under consideration. Dodd believes that the following passages qualify for inclusion in these sections:

Primary testimonia	Supplementary sources
(i) Joel ii–iii, Zech. ix–xiv, Dan. vii.	Mal. iii. 1–6; Dan. xii.
(ii) Hosea, Isa. vi. 1–ix. 7, xi. 1–10, xxviii. 16, xl. 1–11; Jer. xxxi. 10–34.	Isa. xxix. 9–14; Jer. vii. 1–15; Hab. i–ii.
(iii) Isa. xlii. 1–xliv. 5, xlix. 1–13, l. 4–11, lii. 13–liii. 12, lxi; Ps. lxix, xxii, xxxi, xxxviii, lxxxviii, xxxiv, cxviii, xli, xlii–xliii, lxx.	Isa. lviii. 6–10.
(iv) Ps. viii, cx, ii; Gen. xii. 3, xxii. 18; Deut. xviii. 15, 19.	Ps. cxxxii, xvi; 2 Sam. vii. 13–14; Isa. lv. 3; Amos ix. 11–12.

(c) The relevant Old Testament Scriptures were interpreted on consistent principles as setting forth the determinate counsel of God which was fulfilled in the facts of the Gospel.

(d) This whole body of Testimony material is common to the main portions of the New Testament and provided the starting point for the theological constructions of St. Paul, the writer to the Hebrews and the Fourth Evangelist. It is the substructure of all Christian theology and contains already its chief regulative ideas.

This conclusion is endorsed by Archbishop Carrington who visualizes a school of oral study and a variety of partial transcripts of Old Testament testimonies which are the 'title deeds' of the Church; Books of Testimonies, if such ever existed, were the end product of this process (*The Early Christian Church*, Vol. I, p. 52).[1]

---

[1] It is only fair to add that A. L. Williams, *Adversus Judaeos* (1935), also doubted the existence of a single Testimony Book. 'The book of Testimonies, considered as one book, is a myth. But the proper meaning of 'Myth' . . . is the pictorial representation of a spiritual truth. In this case the truth denotes the permanence of a certain method which produced catena after catena of texts from the Old Testament which were regarded as Testimonies to Christ and Christianity. Words were everything; grammatical meaning and historical reference were of little account'. (p. 12).

At this point we may adduce evidence from the mission field today as being relevant to the conditions prevailing in the early Church. In U.M.C.A. areas in Central Africa catechists give simple teaching to those following the 'Hearers' course—the first part of the Catechumenate—based on an outline 'Hearers' Catechism' which contains simple proofs of the Faith. Sometimes the catechist delivers his teaching from notes; at other times orally; moreover the proofs are adapted for village catechists to suit their attainments and that of the Hearers. But always the outline of the Hearers' Catechism is the basis of the instruction given.[1] This corresponds closely to the situation of the early Church. Each New Testament writer quoted Old Testament testimonia which suited his particular approach and purpose without losing sight of the total context and meaning of the sections of the Old Testament which were regarded as fundamental proofs of the Gospel facts.

(3)

The discovery of the Dead Sea Scrolls has shown that this method of using the Old Testament had been anticipated, to some extent, in pre-Christian Judaism. The Qumran sources include commentaries (*pesarim*), which expound extended passages or entire biblical books verse by verse; collections of prophetical testimonia,[2] sometimes with expository comments appended to each, sometimes without; and historical expositions which utilized a patchwork of biblical quotations to interpret the meaning and sequence of historical events in the past and the future. This tradition of Qumran exegesis, in the opinion of many authorities, was initiated by the founder of the sect, the Teacher of Righteousness (*moreh-ha-sedeq*). The Habakkuk commentary (I Qp Hab. ii. 5–10) states that he spoke of 'all the events which were to come upon the last generation', for 'God placed (him) in the (midst of the Congregation) to expound all the words of his prophets by whose agency God has related all which is to come upon his people and (his congregation)'. Cf. I Qp Hab. vii. 4–5: 'God has informed (the Teacher of Righteousness) of the secrets of the words of his servants the prophets.' No doubt the Teacher in the beginning was indebted to earlier traditions in laying down a pattern of Biblical exegesis. And it appears that this was transmitted orally within the Qumran community and was supplemented in the regular study of the Qumran priests and

[1] I owe this information to Miss D. V. Perrott, formerly of the Zanzibar Diocese, who was responsible, in collaboration with Bishop T. H. Birley, for the development of teaching manuals in the African vernacular. The U.M.C.A. is now part of the U.S.P.G.

[2] Examples are the *Florilegium* and the *Testimonia*. See further F. M. Cross, *The Ancient Library of Qumran and Modern Biblical Studies*, pp. 82–5.

especially in the communal gatherings when the scriptures were read and systematically expounded. Only at a later period was the body of traditional exegesis committed to writing in the commentaries, testimonia and related documents which have been discovered. Thus the collections of prophetical testimonia are the result of the work of the Qumran scribes, based on communal and traditional exegesis, and not its presupposition. This would indicate that the early Church followed the same method as that used at Qumran, although it cannot be too strongly emphasized that in the New Testament the application of the testimonia is, on the whole, governed by the facts of the Christian Gospel.

(4)

We may now address ourselves to a problem which was outside the scope of Dodd's work. Did the testimonia, and in particular those *adversus Judaeos*, remain static between New Testament times and that of Cyprian when they are found grouped under specific headings? [1] Or did the testimonia grow in bulk after A.D. 70, as Christianity and Judaism became more hostile to each other, especially in regions of the Diaspora? And how far did these take written forms before Cyprian? These questions are difficult to answer but clearly they are fundamental to the study of the testimonia in the Epistle of Barnabas which we would assign to Alexandria and to a date early in the second century. Indeed, in this connexion, the significance of Barnabas and Justin Martyr lies in their being a midway stage between the testimony forms behind the New Testament and the later developed written compilations of Cyprian and Gregory of Nyssa. That the testimony material grew in bulk is, I submit, shown by an examination of Barnabas, Justin's *Dial. cum Trypho*. Irenaeus' *Apostolic Preaching* and Tertullian's *adversus Judaeos*, which contain a vast mass of Old Testament material additional to that found in the New Testament.[2] A parallel development was also taking place in Judaism where such passages as the golden calf incident and the saga of Moses

[1] It is possible that part of Cyprian's *adversus Judaeos* is a pre-Cyprianic compilation. However the exact dating of this does not affect the argument of this chapter and I have referred it to Cyprian without prejudice as to authorship. On this question see R. P. C. Hanson, *Tradition in the Early Church*, pp. 261–4.

[2] Lactantius (*c.* A.D. 300) seems to have held that Jesus was the author of these proof texts: 'He abode forty days with them and interpreted the scriptures, which up to that time had been obscure and involved' (*de mort. persec.* ii). The apocryphal Preaching of Peter, which was known to the Athenian philosopher Aristides before A.D. 148, uses testimony material which shows that, in certain circles, testimonia were thought to have the authority of St. Peter and the twelve.

and Joshua received further interpretation and expansion in Mekilta, Aboda Zarah and Taanit; St. Jerome said that he knew of many Jewish interpretations of disputed Old Testament passages. The question as to how far the Christian testimonia took a written form after A.D. 70 will be considered when we examine Barnabas' testimonia in detail.

(5)

The use of Old Testament testimonia in the Epistle of Barnabas is somewhat submerged by the author's allegorical exegesis which is carried to extreme lengths and would justify Porphyry's criticism (addressed to the Apologists) viz.: 'they made riddles of what was perfectly plain in Moses, their expositions would not hang together, and they cheated their own critical faculty', (τὸ κριτικὸν τῆς ψυχῆς καταγοητεύσαντες) (cited in Eus.*E.H.* vi. 19). Yet in spite of much fanciful allegorism the use of certain testimonia *adversus Judaeos* can be discerned in the Epistle and these must now receive detailed treatment:

(A) The Stone—Barn. vi. 2–4

We may begin with a testimonium concerning the Stone which was well known in the early Church and was applied to our Lord as the crucified and rejected Messiah who is yet raised triumphant from the dead. This testimonium takes its origin from the *verba Christi* Mk. xii. 10–11; cf. Mt. xxi. 42; Lk. xx. 17: 'have ye not read even this scripture; the stone which the builders rejected, the same was made the cornerstone: This was from the Lord, and it is marvellous in our eyes?' This is an exact quotation of Ps. cxviii. 22–3 and became one of the 'sheet anchors of the early Church' (Selwyn, op. cit., p. 269) coming, as it did, from the last of the Hallel Psalms which were among the most familiar hymns used in Jewish worship; indeed according to Oesterley (*Psalms* I, p. 101) the synagogue congregations, at the beginning of the Christian era, may well have known this psalm by heart. Its use by our Lord at the conclusion of a pointed parable which spoke of his impending passion and death ensured for it a special place in the mind of the early Church; thus St. Peter, according to Acts iv. 11, used it to clinch his argument before the Jewish High Priests and from the context we can see that these verses of the Psalm had become attached, as proof texts, to the primitive kerygma of the Jerusalem Church.

From the basis of our Lord's use of Ps. cxviii. 22–3 other Old Testament texts containing the word 'stone' soon became associated with the original testimonium. In particular Isa. viii. 14 and xxviii. 16 were drawn together, as may be seen from their use in 1 Peter and

Isaiah	Psalms	Verba Christi	I Peter
xxviii. 16			ii. 6-8
Ἰδοὺ ἐγὼ ἐμβάλλω εἰς τὰ θεμέλια Σιὼν λίθον πολυτελῆ, ἐκλεκτὸν, ἀκρογωνιαῖον, ἔντιμον, εἰς τὰ θεμέλια αὐτῆς, καὶ ὁ πιστεύων οὗ μὴ καταισχυνθῇ, καὶ θήσω κρίσιν εἰς ἐλπίδα..			διότι περιέχει ἐν γραφῇ, Ἰδού, τίθημι ἐν Σιὼν λίθον ἀκρογωναῖον, ἐκλεκτόν, ἔντιμον· καὶ ὁ πιστεύων ἐπ' αὐτῷ οὐ μὴ καταισχυνθῇ.
l. 7 δια τοῦτο οὐκ ἐνετράπην, ἀλλὰ ἔθηκα τὸ πρόσωπόν μου ὡς στερεὰν πέτραν.	cxviii. 22-24 Λίθον ὃν ἀπεδοκίμασαν οἱ οἰκοδομοῦντες, οὗτος ἐγενήθη εἰς κεφαλὴν γωνίας. Παρὰ Κυρίου ἐγένετο αὕτη, καὶ ἔστι θαυμαστὴ ἐν ὀφθαλμοῖς ἡμῶν. Αὕτη ἡ ἡμέρα ἣν ἐποίησεν ὁ Κύριος, ἀγαλλιασώμεθα καὶ εὐφρανθῶμεν ἐν αὐτῇ.	Mk. xii. 10-11 (Cf. Mt. xxi. 42, Lk. xx. 17) οὐδὲ τνὴ γραφὴν ταύτην ἀνέγνωτε· λίθον ὃν ἀπεδοκίμασαν οἱ οἰκοδομοῦντες, οὗτος ἐγενήθη εἰς κεφαλὴν γωνίας; παρὰ Κυρίου ἐγένετο αὕτη, καὶ ἔστιν θαυμαστὴ ἐν ὀφθαλμοῖς ἡμῶν;	ὑμῖν οὖν ἡ τιμὴ τοῖς πιστεύουσιν· ἀπιστοῦσι δὲ Λίθος ὃν ἀπεδοκίμασαν οἱ οἰκοδομοῦντες, οὗτος ἐγενήθη εἰς κεφαλὴν γωνίας,
viii. 14 καὶ οὐχ ὡς λίθου προσκόμματι συναντήσεσθε, οὐδὲ ὡς πέτρας πτώματι· Cf. Dan. ii. 34, 44.		Cf. Acts. iv. 11, Eph. ii. 20 and Lk. xx. 18: πᾶς ὁ πεσὼν ἐπ' ἐκεῖνον τὸν λίθον συνθλασθήσεται· ἐφ' ὃν δ'ἂν πέσῃ λικμήσει αὐτόν.	καὶ λίθος προσκόμματος καὶ πέτρα σκανδάλου, οἳ προσκόπτουσι τῷ λόγῳ ἀπειθοῦντες, εἰς ὃ καὶ ἐτέθησαν.

Romans	Epistle of Barnabas	Cyprian	Other patristic references to the Stone testimonium
	vi. 2-4 καὶ πάλιν λέγει ὁ προφήτης, ἐπεὶ ὡς λίθος ἰσχυρὸς ἐτέθη εἰς συντριβήν, 'Ἰδώ, ἐμβαλῶ εἰς τὰ θεμέλια Σιών λίθον πολυτελῆ, ἐκλεκτὸν, ἀκρογωνιαιον, ἔντιμον.... καὶ ὅς ἐλπίσει ἐπ' αὐτὸν ζήσεται εἰς τὸν αἰῶνα, ἐπὶ λίθον οὖν ἡμῶν ἡ ἐλπίς;.... καὶ ἔθηκέ με ὡς στερεὰν πέτραν.. λίθον ὅν ἀπεδοκίμασαν οἱ οἰκοδομοῦντες, οὗτος ἐγενήθη εἰς κεφαλὴν γωνίας....Αὕτη ἐστὶν ἡ ἡμέρα ἡ μεγάλη καὶ θαυμαστή, ἣν ἐποίησεν ὁ κύριος.	Testimonia i. 16 Apud Isaiam prophetam sic dicit Dominus: Ecce ego immitto in fundamenta Sion lapidem pretiosum, electum, summum angularem honoratum: et qui crediderit in eum non confundetur. Item in Psalmo cxxviii	Dial. Ath. and Zach. 112 ff.; Iren. adv. haer. iii. 21. 7; Justin Dial. cum Trypho. 34, 76, 100, 126; Gnostic Gospel of Thomas; Hippolytus de Antichristo 26; Origen in Ioann. i. 23, 41; Tert. adv Iud. 14, adv. Marc. iii. 7, v. 5. Celsus ad Vigilium cf. de Iudaica incredulitate 5; Eus. D.E. i. 7; E.P. iii. 42; Augustine Hom. in Ioann. vii. 23; Exp. pss. 188. 22-23; Sermo 51. 15, 88. 10, 95. 4, 156. 15; Gregory Nyssa viii; Methodius Orat. de Sim. vi; Cyril of Jerusalem x. 3, xii. 18, xv. 28; Firmicus Maternus de errore prof. rel. 20; Gislebert, Migne P.L. 159, 1017; Aphraates de fide 6 ff. (ed. Parisot, pp. 15ff.).
ix. 33 προσέκοψαν τῷ λίθῳ τοῦ προσκόμματος, καθὼς γέγραπται, 'Ἰδώ, τίθημι ἐν Σιὼν λίθον προσκόμματος καὶ πέτραν σκανδάλου· καὶ ὁ πιστεύων ἐπ' αὐτῷ οὐ καταισχυνθήσεται.		Testimonia i. 17 [The same stone was to become a mountain and to fill the whole earth; Cf. Dan. ii. 31–35.]	

Romans. A glance at the attached synopsis will show that 1 Pet. ii. 6–8 quotes Isa. xxviii. 16, Ps. cxviii. 22, Isa. viii. 14 in that order, while Rom. ix. 33 conflates the two Isaianic passages. The view that St. Paul is directly quoting 1 Peter or vice-versa has now been generally abandoned by scholars; quite apart from the question of 'Paulinisms' or 'Petrinisms' a weighty consideration against this is the fact that both 1 Peter and Romans introduce their quotations by 'midrashic notes'—but both of a different character; 1 Peter is concerned with Christ and the building of the Church while, for Romans, the stumbling of the unbelieving Jews is the main question. It therefore seems more probable that both writers are using a common source (so Dodd, Selwyn and most recent commentators) which they have incorporated into their books.

A significant fact is the occurrence of deviations from the LXX text which are common to both writers although both normally quote the LXX rather than the Hebrew in their Old Testament quotations. The following are the most important of these deviations:

(i) both use τίθημι instead of ἐμβάλλω in quoting Isa. xxviii. 16.
(ii) both write ἐν Σιών instead of εἰς τὰ θεμέλια Σειών in the same passage.
(iii) both write λίθος προσκόμματος and πέτρα σκανδάλου for the incorrect LXX rendering in Isa. viii. 14.

It could be argued that 1 Peter and Romans are using independently a recension of the LXX which was current in their areas,[1] but against this is the fact that the deviations have no MS. support in any known text of the LXX. In each case the two writers correctly render the Hebrew and this agreement cannot be fortuitous (note especially in (iii) that where the LXX denies the πρόσκομμα and the πτῶμα St. Peter and St. Paul presuppose a tradition which affirmed the actuality of both; cf. Dodd, op. cit., p. 42, note 1). We therefore adhere to the view that both writers made use of a series of testimonies which were current in a pre-canonical tradition in a version which was, at least in the Isaiah quotations, close to the Hebrew text. St. Peter used all three while St. Paul omitted Ps. cxviii as not germane to his argument in the context of Rom. ix. 33 (he alludes to it in Eph. ii. 20). That this testimony tradition may have reached a transcript stage is suggested by St. Peter's phrase διότι περιέχει ἐν γραφῇ (ii. 6): ἐν γραφῇ is the usual LXX word for 'in writing', cf. 2 Chron. ii. 11, xxi. 12; Eccles. xxxix. 32, xlii. 7, xliv. 5 and Selwyn's note on 1 Pet. ii. 6. (If the meaning had been 'in the passage from scripture' ἐν τῇ γραφῇ would have been used). Selwyn [2]

[1] Swete, *Introduction to the Old Testament in Greek*, p. 23.
[2] *The First Epistle of St. Peter*, p. 276.

believes that this written source was a hymn, based on a mosaic of
Old Testament texts, which the readers of 1 Peter already knew,
and that the claims of rhythm may account for some of the deviations
from the LXX text. While this is a suggestive line of approach, the
deviations from the LXX text may well be due to a desire, on the
part of the original Jerusalem Church and among Jewish-Christians,
to use testimonies to the kerygma which were close to the Hebrew
text. The earliest use of the Stone testimonia was in all probability
oral, and teachers and catechists quoted Isa. xxviii. 16, viii. 14 and
perhaps other texts in Aramaic or Hebrew; only later, with the translation of Christianity to the Greek-speaking world, did the testimonia
regularly follow the LXX. The source behind 1 Pet. ii. 6–8 and
Rom. ix. 33 may therefore have been a Greek literary transcript
which preserved the character of the earliest Stone testimonia.

As the Church's mission expanded, the use of testimonia to Christ
as the Stone remained to the forefront. This is illustrated by a statement of Justin Martyr: 'I am going to show you from all the Scriptures that Christ is King and Lord, Priest and God, Angel and man
and general and Stone, and the child that is born, and that he comes
first to suffer and then returns. . . .' (*Dial. cum Trypho.* xxxiv); and
Justin expands this by saying that Christ is the Stone which Jacob
anointed at Bethel, a testimonium found later in Cyprian. Another
development, prior to the time of Justin, was the equation of the
Stone which the builders rejected of Ps. cxviii. 22 and the stone of
stumbling of Isa. viii. 14 with the stone cut out without hands from
the mountain mentioned in Dan. ii. 34, 44–5; it is this stone which
smites and breaks in pieces the feet of the great image—which signifies,
in the vision, that God, through his chosen people, will break in
pieces the Kingdoms of evil: καὶ ἡ βασιλεία αὐτοῦ λαῷ ἑτέρῳ οὐχ
ὑπολειφθήσεται, λεπτυνεῖ καὶ λικμήσει πάσας τὰς βασιλείας, καὶ
αὕτη ἀναστήσεται εἰς τοὺς αἰῶνας· (Dan. ii. 44). The occurrence of
the same verb λικμᾶν in Lk. xx. 18, πᾶς ὁ πεσὼν ἐπ' ἐκεῖνον τὸν
λίθον συνθλασθήσεται. ἐφ' ὃν δ'ἂν πέσῃ λικμήσει αὐτόν, immediately
following a quotation of Ps. cxviii. 22, appears to indicate that Luke
has equated the Stone of Daniel with the earlier Stone testimonia;
perhaps he was the first to do this. Thus within the New Testament
there exist indications that the testimonia concerning the Stone were
growing in bulk and later, as we shall see, other testimonia, such as
Justin's [1] and Cyprian's reference to Jacob's stone, were added to

[1] J. Daniélou, *Sacramentum Futuri*, p. 187, suggests that Justin's linking of
Stone texts relies upon a Rabbinic haggadah which originally connected
these passages. With Justin *Dial.* xxxvi. 1 cf. Philo *Leg. all.* ii. 86 where the
word ἀκρότομος is applied to σοφία, perhaps recalling a similar haggadah
in Isa. xxviii. 16. See further R. P. C. Hanson, *Allegory and Event*, pp. 22–3.

the original cento of Old Testament quotations which had their origin in our Lord's use of Ps. cxviii. 22–3. How far, in the early period, these testimonia remained in an oral stage of development and how far they occurred in written transcripts cannot be ascertained with any certitude. Certainly the cento Isa. xxviii. 16, Ps. cxviii. 22 and Isa. viii. 14 existed in writing in some areas in a version different from the LXX although there is no indication of their inclusion in a written testimony book.

We now turn our attention to Barn. vi. 2–4. Here the Stone testimonia occur as part of a series of Old Testament proof texts which are referred, *inter alia*, to the plotting of the Jews against Jesus the Just One, the entry into Christ through baptism, the second creation and Christian worship. Barnabas' version is interesting in that it contains differences from the version in 1 Peter and Romans. The introduction in verse 2, 'And again the prophet says that he was placed as a strong stone for crushing' (εἰς συντριβήν) appears to be a free rendering of Isa. viii. 14 (LXX) or Dan. ii. 34, 45 in view of the fact that συντριβή means 'rubbing away', 'crushing', 'destruction' as in Vett. Val. 74, 4; Heliodorus x. 28 (and not elsewhere in early Christian literature). The thought is of Christ as a λίθος ἰσχυρὸς destroying those who dash against him. This is followed by an exact quotation of Isa. xxviii. 16 (LXX) as far as ἔντιμον, in contrast to 1 Peter and Romans who quote a version nearer to the Hebrew text. Verse 3, 'And whosoever shall hope on it shall live forever', appears to be another reference to Isa. xxviii. 16–17 (LXX), καὶ ὁ πιστεύων οὐ μὴ καταισχυνθῇ. Καὶ θήσω κρίσιν εἰς ἐλπίδα ... although the connexion is loose. ℵCL certainly understood it so for they read ὁ πιστεύων εἰς αὐτὸν under the influence of the LXX. The harder reading of G, the archetype of the eight Greek MSS. of the Epistle, may be accepted, ἐλπίσει being covered by ἐλπίς. To the question 'Is our hope then upon a Stone?' the explanation is given that the Lord set (τέθεικεν)[1] his flesh in strength, which is an introduction to a loose quotation from Isa. l. 7 (LXX) which now appears (this has been previously quoted, in a more exact form, in v. 14). Verse 4 then quotes Ps. cxviii. 22 (LXX) exactly (but omits verse 23 quoted in the *verba Christi* Mk. xii. 10–11) following it with a loose quotation of Ps. cxviii. 24 which has ἡ μεγάλη καὶ θαυμαστὴ for the LXX ἀγαλλιασώμεθα καὶ εὐφρανθῶμεν ἐν αὐτῇ. θαυμαστὴ is perhaps a glance at v. 23.

[1] I cannot agree, with Harris (op. cit., Vol. I, p. 31) who believes that the appearance of ἐτέθη, τέθεικεν and ἔθηκεν in Barn. vi. 2–3 is proof that Barnabas knew, but did not use, Isa xxviii. 16 in the version used by 1 Peter and Romans, viz: 'Ἰδοὺ τίθημι ἐν Σιὼν λίθον κτλ. His use of τίθημι might well have come from Isa. l. 7 (LXX).

Barnabas' treatment of this series of testimonia is instructive. In accordance with his practice elsewhere in the Epistle his quotations from the LXX are often loose paraphrases, although he can quote exactly. Thus in vi. 2–4 we have this sequence:

(i) Isa. viii. 14 or Dan. ii. 34, 45   loose rendering
(ii) Isa. xxviii. 16   exact
(iii) Isa. xxviii. 17   loose
(iv) Isa. l. 7   loose
(v) Ps. cxviii. 22   exact
(vi) Ps. cxviii. 24   loose

The fact that the writer quotes the LXX of Isa. viii. 14 and xxviii. 16, as against the Hebrew of the written transcript behind 1 Peter and Romans, and also introduces allusions to Isa. xxviii. 17, l. 7 and Ps. cxviii. 24, which are not found in the earlier testimonia, does not suggest that he is using a written Greek testimony source or book or that he is directly quoting the New Testament Epistles. Rather, around the original testimonium of our Lord as the Stone rejected by the builders yet made the cornerstone, Barnabas has woven his mosaic of texts from the LXX which he has adapted to his purpose. For instance, the change which he makes from the LXX of Ps. cxviii. 24 in order to emphasize that the day which the Lord made is 'great and wonderful' may conceivably indicate, in addition to the day of the Crucifixion, the day of the Christian Paschal celebration when perhaps this Epistle was read to a large number of people who were gathered together. Baptism was a significant part of the Pascha and it is perhaps not mere coincidence that allusions to baptism are very prominent in this chapter; the complex of cultus and doctrine in the Epistle certainly contains the elements which we later find fused together in the Christian Paschal celebration.[1]

Another feature of the Epistle's treatment of the Stone testimonia is that they form part of a dialogue between the writer and his readers in which he poses questions and gives the answers—much as St. Paul does in Rom. ix. The dialogue form appears to have evolved out of the earliest use of the testimonia as the foundation of the apostolic kerygma as a result of the conflict with Judaism which, in the time of Barnabas, had reached an acute stage. Indeed the best parallel to Barn. vi. 2–4 is found in the *Dialogue of Athanasius and Zacchaeus* 112 ff. where the doctrine that Christ is the Wisdom of God is worked out through various questions and protests on the part of Zacchaeus. Athanasius goes on to establish the doctrine that Christ is the Stone spoken of by the prophets. Zacchaeus listens to

---

[1] See my paper in VC 15 (Mar. 1961) pp. 8–22 and Chapter 7 of this book.

the statements that Christ was foretold to be λίθος προσκόμματος καὶ πέτρα σκανδάλου and objects that God ought not to have made Christ into a Stumbling Stone, but should have presented him so that he could be the object of faith; it is he that believes that will not be put to shame. But Christ was foretold as the Stone whom the builders (i.e., the Jews) rejected. Upon which Zacchaeus, remembering the proofs that Christ was the Wisdom of God, interjects the question: 'Do you mean that the Wisdom of God became a stone?' This type of dialogue is but a more developed example of the type found in Barnabas which reflects the deepening hostility between Christianity and Judaism after the year A.D. 70.

These considerations suggest that Barn. vi. 2–4 represents a later stage in the Stone tradition than that found in the New Testament. Other testimonia are beginning to cluster round those quoted by our Lord and in the New Testament Epistles. Yet the fact that the writer could use, amidst much extravagant exegesis, Isa. viii. 14, xxviii. 16 and Ps. cxviii. 22 remains significant and shows that he was acquainted with the fact that these passages had been used traditionally as applicable to the facts of the Gospel. But he felt free to select, adapt and supplement them to illustrate the theme of the Stone in accordance with local needs and his argument *adversus Judaeos*. This procedure does not suggest that he was drawing on any fixed, stereotyped, written testimony book. We may illustrate the development of the testimonia concerning the Stone in the following way:

Ps. cxviii. 22–23.	*Verba Christi.*
+Isa. xxviii. 16.	1 Peter.
Isa. viii. 14.	Romans.
+Dan. ii. 34, 44–45.	St. Luke.
+Isa. xxviii. 17.	Epistle of Barnabas.
Isa. l. 7.	
Ps. cxviii. 24.	

Later the Stone testimonia received further additions but these are beyond the scope of this chapter; other Patristic references are given in the last columns of the synopsis. Cyprian, in his systematic collation of the testimonies, devoted three sections to establishing (i) that Christ is called the Stone; (ii) that the same Stone would become a mountain and fill the whole earth; (iii) that in the last times this mountain would become manifest and all the Gentiles should stream into it together with the just.

(B) *The Two Peoples—Barn. xiii. 1–6*

The doctrine of the two peoples—the Jews, and the Christians who have inherited their privileges—had an important place in the arguments of early Christian writers and was developed as the Church drew apart from its Jewish cradle and became more conscious of itself as the people of God. The origin of the conception of the two peoples goes back to the earlier Gospel tradition; cf. Mk. xi. 12–14 where the fig tree symbolises the Jewish nation now superseded by Christ and the Church. It is found, too, in the New Testament Epistles where the idea of the Body of Christ, the new Israel in which national divisions are abolished, is prominent; cf. Eph. i. 22–3, iv. 4–16; Gal. vi. 16. Various Old Testament testimonies came to be used to buttress this doctrine of the two peoples. The most prominent of these are: (i) the episode of Lo-ammi and Lo-ruhamah in Hos. i and ii, understood as the way in which God adopts as His people those who were formerly no people of His, viz., the Gentiles now admitted into the Church; (ii) the story of Rebecca and the twin-children in her womb, leading up to the oracle 'the elder shall serve the younger' (Gen. xxv. 22–3); (iii) Jacob's blessing of his sons Ephraim and Manasseh (Gen. xlviii. 13–19).

LXX Hosea	Romans	1 Peter
i.6: κάλεσον τὸ ὄνομα αὐτῆς, οὐκ ἠλεημένη· διότι οὐ μὴ προσθήσω ἔτι ἐλεῆσαι τὸν οἶκον Ἰσραήλ.	ix.25: Καλέσω τὸν οὐ λαόν μου λαόν μου, καὶ τὴν οὐκ ἠγαπημένην ἠγαπημένην.	ii.10: οἱ ποτὲ οὐ λαός, νῦν δὲ λαὸς θεοῦ, οἱ οὐκ ἠλεημένοι, νῦν δὲ ἐλεηθέντες.
i.9: κάλεσον τὸ ὄνομα αὐτοῦ, οὐ λαός μου· διότι ὑμεῖς οὐ λαός μου, καὶ ἐγὼ οὐκ εἰμὶ ὑμῶν.		
ii.23: καὶ σπερῶ αὐτὴν ἐμαυτῷ ἐπὶ τῆς γῆς, καὶ ἀγαπήσω τὴν οὐκ ἠγαπημένην, καὶ ἐρῶ τῷ οὐ λαῷ μου, λαός μου εἶ σύ· καὶ αὐτὸς ἐρεῖ, Κύριος ὁ θεὸς μου εἶ σύ.		
i.10: καὶ ἔσται, ἐν τῷ τόπῳ, οὗ ἐρρέθη αὐτοῖς, οὐ λαός μου ὑμεῖς, κληθήσονται καὶ αὐτοὶ υἱοὶ θεοῦ ζῶντος.	ix.26: καὶ ἔσται, ἐν τῷ τόπῳ οὗ ἐρρήθη αὐτοῖς, Οὐ λαός μου ὑμεῖς, ἐκεῖ κληθήσονται υἱοὶ θεοῦ ζῶντος.	

(a) We may begin with Rom. ix. 25–6, which occurs in the same chapter as the Stone testimonium (ix. 32–3), which was based on a series of testimonia which were current in a pre-canonical tradition in a version close to the Hebrew text. Rom. ix. 25, introduced by ὡς καὶ ἐν τῷ Ὡσηε, is a conflation of Hos. i. 6, 9, ii. 23 while ix. 29 is an exact quotation of Hos. i. 10. 1 Pet. ii. 10 is a reminiscence of the same prophesy in Hos. i and ii but without direct quotation.

Hort believed that St. Peter's allusion was suggested by St. Paul's quotation but this appears unlikely in view of the fact that in Romans the key words are λαός and ἀγαπᾶσθαι (after Hos. i. 9, ii. 23) while in 1 Peter the key words are λαός and ἐλεεῖσθαι (after Hos. i. 6,9, ii. 1). St. Peter's approach is more general than that of St. Paul and the independence of the two writers seems certain. Selwyn (op. cit., p. 281) thinks that the data are to be explained by the hypothesis that St. Paul is quoting Hosea directly while St. Peter is quoting from a hymn in which the Hosean motif had already been incorporated. However, in view of the fact that the citations of the two writers refer to several different verses of Hos. i and ii, it seems more probable that both had in mind the whole episode of Lo-ammi and Lo-ruhamah, but that each developed it in his own way (so Dodd, op. cit., p. 75). This suggests that these chapters had been selected very early on as providing testimonia in support of the entry of the Gentiles into the Church. By the middle of the second century the testimony tradition concerning the superiority of the Gentiles, as the new people, to the Jews, in numerical strength, truth and faith had grown in bulk, as is illustrated by this quotation from Justin Martyr which is expressly stated to have been taken from the testimonies:

'I have many other prophecies to relate to you but at present I forbear, thinking the passages already quoted sufficient, . . . For how should we ever have come to believe in a crucified man, that he is the First-Born of God, and is to carry out the judgement of the whole human race, if we had not found, before his coming in human form, such testimonies declared concerning him and such as we see to have actually occurred, viz.: the desolation of the Jews' land, and men of every race persuaded, through the teaching of his Apostles, to abandon the ancient customs of their life in error, seeing, as they did, that we had become, as Gentile Christians, more numerous and more true than those who belonged to the Jews and the Samaritans? . . . for it had been foretold that the believers among the Gentiles would be more numerous than those from the Jews and Samaritans, and we will repeat the prophecies to that effect. . . . And to show you that the Gentiles were known beforehand as being more true and faithful, we will relate to you some words of the prophet Isaiah,' etc. (1 *Apol.* liii, translated by Harris op. cit., Vol. I., p. 24). Cf. 2 Clem. ii. 3 (for a similar view) and Tert. *adv. Jud.* i.)

Before considering further the use of the Hosea testimonia in the patristic writings we shall examine the testimonium concerning Rebecca and her twin-children.

(b) This is found in Rom. ix. 10–13 in close proximity to the quotation from Hos. i and ii and the Stone testimonium. In Rom. ix St. Paul replies to the view that God was bound, by his promise to Abraham, to save Israel *in toto* whatever the attitude of individual Jews might be. He insists that full weight must be given to the doctrine of Divine Sovereignty which he shared with his Pharisaic opponents. If God chooses to reject the Jews and elect the Gentiles then the true Israel is composed of those whom he elects. In the course of his argument St. Paul refers to Rebecca having conceived by Isaac twin-sons in her womb; both were born under the same conditions yet one was rejected and the other chosen—and this choice took place before their births. Thus the status of Jew and Gentile rests solely on the Divine Will and the fact that 'the elder shall serve the younger' was God's determining. It might be argued that St. Paul was the first to use the Rebecca testimonium as part of his argument for Divine Election which he developed in Rom. ix–xi. However we have already seen that the Hosea testimonies and that to Christ as the Stone circulated in an earlier, pre-canonical, tradition and it is not impossible that the Rebecca testimonium had already been selected as a suitable proof. Certainly Cyprian used it as a heading for a section of his Testimonies in close proximity to the Hosea quotations. Thus:

'Quod duo populi praedicti sint, maior et minor; id est vetus Iudaeorum et novus qui esset ex nobis futurus. In Genesi: Et dicit Dominus Rebeccae: duae gentes in utero sunt et duo populi de ventre tuo dividentur, et populus populum superabit, et maior serviet minori. Item apud Osee prophetam: Vocabo non-populum meum populum-meum, et non-dilectum dilectum: erit enim, quo loco dicetur non-populus meus, illo loco vocabuntur filii Dei vivi.' (i. 19).

(c) The fullest development of, and the best commentary on, the early Rebecca testimonium is to be found in the Epistle of Barnabas. Barn. xiii. 1 is a kind of testimony heading similar to that found in Cyprian: 'Now let us see if this people or the former people is the heir, and if the covenant is for us or for them.' This is followed (xiii. 2) by a quotation from Gen. xxv. 21–3 (LXX) with the omission of the incident of the babes' leaping in Rebecca's womb. Barnabas has δύο λαοὶ ἐν τῇ κοιλίᾳ σου for the LXX ἐκ τῆς κοιλίας. In the Hebrew 'from' is used in a temporal sense, as in Ps. xxii. 10, i.e., the two will pursue divergent, and mutually hostile, courses from their births. However, the writer is not concerned with historical accuracy but only with the phrase 'the elder shall serve the younger' which appears to be a Hebraism. This is followed (xiii. 4) with a quotation of Gen. xlviii. 11, 9 (LXX) where the writer has ἐστέρησέν for the LXX ἐστερήθην, and in xiii. 5 by a loose quotation of Gen. xlviii. 13–19 (LXX) which leads up to a repetition of the phrase 'the elder shall serve the younger' which is not found here in the LXX. Barnabas' object in this chapter is to show that Israel, the 'former people', as represented in type by Esau in Rebecca's womb and by Manasseh, Jacob's older son, is subordinate to the Church, 'this people', represented by Jacob and Ephraim. For him the covenant given to the Jews on Sinai, through their disobedience, had been mystically transferred to the Christian Church (iv. 7–8, xiii. 6, xiv. 1–4); the Jewish nation was therefore inferior to the Christian Church, as the types indicate.

This chapter represents a development in the tradition concerning the 'two peoples' and, from the fact that the testimonium concerning Rebecca and her twin-sons is not associated with Divine Election (as in Rom. ix. 10–13), we infer that Barnabas was not drawing directly on St. Paul. Probably he knew that this passage had been selected as suitable for anti-Jewish polemic and to this kernel he has added the account of the blessing of Ephraim and Manasseh as a further illustration of the 'two peoples' doctrine; Cyprian was later to take this up (*Test.* i. 21). It is however significant that Barnabas makes no use of the Hosea testimonia found in Romans, 1 Peter and later patristic writers, which he may have known. I suggest that the reason for this omission lies in the fact that the Hosea testimonia had been used in support of the entry of the Gentiles into the Church. Barnabas however was a converted Jew and he was writing to a community of mixed racial origin (note Barn. iii. 6). His primary concern was not that of St. Paul, viz., the acceptance and status of the Gentiles in the Church, but with the retention in the Church of Christians who were in danger of reverting to Judaism. The 'former people' were the Jews who had lost the privileges of the covenant; 'this people' were the Christians (both Jews and Gentiles).

(d) In later patristic writers the testimonium concerning Rebecca and her twin sons, those from Hosea i and ii and that concerning the blessing of Jacob's sons, received further elaborations and in Cyprian's tradition they are found as headings in his Testimony Book.

The patristic use may be shown as follows:

Rebecca's twin sons Gen. xxv. 21-3	Hosea i & ii	Jacob's sons Gen. xlviii. 13-19
Rom. ix. 10-13	Rom. ix. 25-6 1 Pet. ii. 10	
Barn. xiii. 2-3		Barn. xiii. 4-5
Cyprian *Test.* i. 19	Cyprian *Test.* i. 19	Cyprian *Test.* i. 21
Tert. *adv. Jud.* i	Dial. Timothy and Aquila, p. 74	
Evagrius *Altercatio Simonis et Theophili* v. 29	Bar. Ṣalibi vii. 21	

We conclude that the use of testimonies concerning the 'two peoples' occupied a not insignificant place in patristic apologetic, vis-à-vis the Jews. Barn. xiii is accordingly no *tour de force* of the writer but a development of an earlier testimonium known in the Church and is used in support of the argument that the one covenant had been taken away from the Jews and given to the Christians. Other writers use this and the other testimonia to buttress their own emphases. So Evagrius, *Alt. Sim. et Theoph.* v. 29. proves the doctrine of the 'two peoples' from Gen. xxv. 21-3. But he does not make the Jews an unbelieving, and the Christians a believing people; rather the one people are the circumcised Jews and the other the uncircumcised Christians who are both to come to the faith of Christ.[1]

(c) Other Testimonia

A few further testimonia may be briefly considered:
(a) The question of Jewish Sacrifice, and its supersession, receives treatment in Barn. ii. 4-10. The writer denounces Jewish sacrifices by a quotation from Isa. i. 1-13 which is followed by the comment: 'these things then be abolished (κατήργησεν), in order that the new law (καινὸς νόμος) of our Lord Jesus Christ, which is without the yoke of necessity, might have its oblation (προσφοράν) not made by

[1] I owe this reference to Harris, op. cit., Vol. II, pp. 18-19.

man'. In support of this Jer. vii. 22–3 is then quoted, followed by a free paraphrase of Zech. viii. 17.

That Barnabas is quoting testimony material is shown by Cyprian *Test.* i. 16 who has the Isaiah quotation with the following headings:
Quod sacrificium vetus evacuaretur et novum celebraretur.
Quod jugum vetus evacuaretur et jugum novum daretur.
Cf. also Gregory of Nyssa (*Collectanea* of Zacagni) who quotes as follows: 'Esaias' (followed by Jer. vii. 21–2) 'and again': (followed by the Isa. quotation). The displacement of the title and the ascription of the Jeremiah quotation to Isaiah will be noted and recalls Mk. i. 2 where a quotation from Malachi is likewise ascribed to Isaiah.

Barnabas has added a further quotation based on Ps. li. 17 and, according to a note in C, of the *Apocalypse of Adam* which is no longer extant. It is interesting that Irenaeus *adv. haer.* iv. 17. 2. appends the same words to the same quotation: 'Sacrificium Deo cor contribulatum; odor suavitatis Deo cor clarificans eum qui plasmavit'. (For other patristic references to Jewish sacrifice, cf. Justin *Dial.* xxii; Clem. Alex. *Paed.* iii. 12, 90. 3 ff.; Tert. *adv. Marc.* i. 20, ii. 18ff.; Aug. *Civ. dei.* x. 4 ff.)

These data do not suggest that Barnabas is quoting from a composite *written* testimony book of the kind compiled by Cyprian or Pseudo-Cyprian. Rather, it looks as if the passages from Isaiah, Jeremiah and Ps. li had been drawn together as providing suitable anti-sacrificial testimonia which each writer used in his own way. Perhaps we can visualize an oral stage and one of partial transcripts; but the quotation from Ps. li. 17 and the Apocalypse of Adam, found in both Barnabas and Irenaeus, suggests that this composite testimony was at least circulating in a written form.

It may be considered strange that these anti-sacrificial testimonia are employed at a time when sacrifice had long ceased to be offered by the Jews, the national sanctuary having been destroyed in A.D. 70 and the replica of the Temple at Leontopolis in Egypt ceasing to function in A.D. 73. But the belief in the rebuilding of the Temple and the resumption of sacrifices was a cardinal doctrine of the Tannaim (see J. Klausner, *The Messianic Idea in Israel*, pp. 513–14) and many Mishnas and Baraithas have the prayer: 'May it speedily be rebuilt in our time' (Mish. Taanith iv. 8; Tamid vii. 3; Baba Metsia 28b). Barnabas moreover was writing at a time when a belief in Hadrian's promise to rebuild the Temple was proving an attraction for certain Christians. The question of Jewish sacrifices was a live one for the Church for a period long after A.D. 70.

(b) The Sabbath: As Christianity drew apart from its Jewish cradle, and as Sunday worship became more fully established in the Church as the celebration of Christ's resurrection, it was inevitable that hostility towards the Jewish sabbath would manifest itself and that Old Testament testimonia would be found to buttress this attitude. To some extent this hostility could find a starting point in the attitude of Jesus Himself whose teaching is summed up in the impressive words: 'The Sabbath was made for man, and not man for the Sabbath: so that the Son of Man is Lord even of the Sabbath.' (Mk. ii. 27-8). One method, which many patristic writers adopted, was to collect from the Old Testament examples of broken sabbaths —such as the story of the siege of Jericho and the sabbath breaking of the Maccabees. On this see Tert. *adv. Judaeos* iv; Victorinus of Pettau *de fabrica mundi*; Gregory of Nyssa on the Sabbath; Aphrahat *Hom.* xiii; Isidore of Seville, *de cessatione Sabbathi*. Rather surprisingly there is no anti-sabbath section in Cyprian's testimonies. However this method of quoting Old Testament broken sabbaths was not adopted by the writer of Barnabas who has his own theory concerning the true sabbath rest (xv. 1-9) which he equates with the millennium—a theory which he perhaps adopted from the hellenistic-Jewish Secrets of Enoch, which represents the world's history as covering six epochs of a thousand years followed by a sabbath rest of a thousand years which is the duration of the Messianic Kingdom (xxxii. 2-xxxiii. 2). The only testimonium which the Epistle employs in the course of its argument is the familiar Isa. i. 13 in xv. 8 which the writer has already quoted in ii. 5; this particular verse is used by many anti-Jewish patristic writers; cf. Justin 1 *Apol.* xxxvii. 5-8; Iren. *adv. haer.* iv. 17. 1; Tert. *de idol.* xiv, *adv. Marc.* i. 20, ii. 18ff., *adv. Jud.* 5; Clem. Alex. *Paed.* iii. 12, 90. 3; bar Salibi *adv. Jud.* (ed. de Zwaan) iv. 8, etc. Barnabas appears to have been the first to use this particular testimonium although in the opinion of Harris (vol. II., p. 105) there is a suggestion of the employment of anti-sabbath testimonia in the Fourth Gospel where the question is raised whether a child circumcised on the eighth day breaks the sabbath (John vii. 23). It seems possible that the Isaiah testimonium may have been in use in the Church just before the time of our Epistle.

(c) Circumcision: The debate over the question of circumcision belongs to the earliest history of the Church (Gal. ii. 7; Rom. ii. 25-9; Col. ii. 11; Eph. ii. 11) and continued to occupy the attention of the later patristic writers; cf. Justin *Dial.* xii, xvi, xix, xxviii, xxix, cxiv; Tert. *adv. Jud.* iii; Cyprian *test.* i. 8; Novatian *de cib. Jud.* i; Athan. *de sabb. et circum.* 5 ff.; Cyril *Alex. c. Julian* x; Lact. *Div. inst.* iv. 17, etc. Barnabas devotes a whole chapter to the subject (Ch. ix) and I have argued [1] that he was acquainted with the scheme of the Tannaitic catechism where detailed teaching on the nature of circumcision was given to proselytes. In ix. 1-3 the writer quotes a

[1] ATR 41 (1959), pp. 177-90.

series of testimonia from Ps. xviii. 45; Isa. xxxiii. 13; Jer. iv. 4; Jer. vii. 2–3; Ps. xxxiii. 13; Isa. i. 2, 10, xl. 3; the repeated emphasis on 'hearing' is designed to lead up to the circumcision of the Christian's hearing in order that he may hear the Word and believe, series of testimonia from Ps. xviii. 45; Isa. xxxiii. 13; Jer. iv. 4; which happened most effectively in corporate worship. Barnabas then continues with a further series of testimonia based on Jer. iv. 3–4; Deut. x. 16; Jer. ix. 25–6:

'But moreover the circumcision in which they trusted has been abolished (κατήργηται). For he declared that circumcision was not of the flesh, but they erred because an evil angel was misleading them. He says to them, "Thus saith the Lord your God" (here I find a commandment), "Sow not among thorns, be circumcised to your Lord". And what does he say? "Circumcise the hardness of your heart, and stiffen not your neck". Take it again: "Behold," saith the Lord, "all the heathen are uncircumcised in the foreskin, but this people is uncircumcised in heart."' (ix. 4–5.)

These testimonies are also found in Cyprian, who heads his section on circumcision thus:

'Quod circumcisio prima carnalis evacuata est et secunda spiritalis repromissa est' (*Test.* i. 8),

followed by a quotation from Jer. iv. 3–4 with the addition 'renovate inter vos novitatem', before 'sow not among thorns'. Gregory of Nyssa has the same quotations, in his section on circumcision, and significantly with the insertion before 'sow not among thorns' of Νεώσατε ἑαυτοῖς νεώματα. Cf. also Justin *Dial.* xii.

It would seem that Cyprian and Gregory of Nyssa are quoting the same testimonia in a written form while Barnabas is more discursive and is simply using traditional material which had begun to cluster around the New Testament arguments against circumcision. He has however woven the cento of texts into his own theory, viz., that circumcision had no validity from the beginning, the Jews having misinterpreted their scriptures through their being deceived by an angel (ix. 4) who was, presumably, one of the ἄγγελοι τοῦ Σατανᾶ of xviii. 1 who were set as guides over the way of darkness.

Other testimonies are used by certain writers (not Barnabas) in support of their arguments against circumcision. In particular Christ was regarded as the New Circumciser, the spiritual Joshua, the instrument of a spiritual circumcision, for the knife was a Stone and the Stone was Christ. So Justin *Dial.* cxiv:

'Our circumcision, second in order of time to yours, and revealed later than yours is made by sharp stones, that is to say, by the words of the prophets of the chief corner-stone, the one of whom Daniel speaks as having been cut out without hands, and this circumcision rids us of all idolatry and the sum total of villainy; and with our hearts thus circumcised from all evil, we gladly face death for the Name of our Fair Stone.'

Cf. Col. ii. 11 and Cyprian i. 8:

'Item apud Jesum Naue: et dixit Dominus ad Jesum: fac tibi cultellos petrinos nimis acutos et adside et circumcide secundo filios Israel. Item Paulus ad Colossenses: Circumcisi estis circumcisione non manufacta in expoliatione carnis sed in circumcisione Christi.'

This linking up of circumcision with the Stone testimonium, one of the earliest of anti-Jewish proof texts, is to be noted.

It is possible that testimonia against sacrifice, the sabbath and circumcision were grouped together at an early stage. Certainly by the time of Gregory of Nyssa this was so, for he introduced the series of proof texts in this way: 'The Jews will all of them say, If you really worship the same God as we, why are you not circumcised, and why do you not offer animal sacrifices, nor keep sabbath, when the scriptures are emphatic on all these points?'[1]

(d) The Davidic Sonship: Barnabas, in xii. 10–11, develops a curious theory that Christ is not Son of Man-Son of David, but only Son of God.

'See again Jesus, not as son of man, but as Son of God, manifested in a type (τύπῳ) in the flesh. Since therefore they are going to say that Christ is David's son, David himself prophesies, fearing and understanding the error of the sinners, "The Lord said to my Lord, sit thou on my right hand until I make thy enemies thy footstool". And again Isaiah speaks thus, "The Lord said to Christ my Lord, whose right hand I hold, that the nations should obey before him, and I will shatter the strength of Kings". See how "David calls him Lord" and does not say Son.'

It is not to be supposed that by τύπῳ the writer meant that Jesus' incarnation had no corporeal reality, rather he has in mind Joshua's manifestation in the flesh as 'man' as a type of Christ's. Why, then, does he deny the Son of David Christology which is found in certain strata of the earlier Christian tradition? cf. Mk. x. 47 ff., xi. 10; Acts ii. 25 ff. xiii. 23; cf. *Did.* x. 6. It is possible that he may have had in mind Christians of Ebionite tendency who maintained that

[1] Tr. Harris, op. cit., Vol. II, p. 106.

Jesus could not be both scion of David and Son of God. In any case Barnabas' strong antipathy towards the Jews would have rendered a Son of David Christology unacceptable to him, as the Jews, in his time, held strongly to the Davidic descent of the Messiah (see Schürer, *G.J.V.* I, pp. 660–1).

In support of his view Barnabas quotes testimonia from Ps. cx. 1 and Isa. xlv. 1. The former was one of the fundamental proof texts of the primitive apostolic kerygma and is cited independently in the New Testament by Mark, Acts, St. Paul, Hebrews and 1 Peter (Dodd, *According to the Scriptures*, pp. 34–5). The writer may well have taken it over from the outline pattern of teaching which was known to most of the Apostolic Fathers (J. N. D. Kelly, *Early Christian Doctrines*, p. 34) and which formed, no doubt, the background of liturgy and catechesis in the Alexandrian Church. The Isaiah quotation is not found in the New Testament and does not appear to belong to the earliest testimony tradition. But it was used by Cyprian as a proof that the Jews were to be replaced by the Gentiles: 'Sic dicit Dominus Deus Christo meo domino: cujus tenui dextram, ut exaudiant eum gentes: fortitudinem regum disrumpam', etc. (*Test.* i. 21); both passages are brought together by Gregory of Nyssa: 'Whereas David says: The Lord said unto my Lord, Sit on my right hand ... Isaiah puts it more clearly, the Lord said unto my Christ Cyrus. ...'[1] Thus it appears that the testimonium from Ps. cx concerning the Lordship of Christ was enlarged, at some stage, by the addition of a testimonium from Isa. xlv. 1 although we cannot be sure that this had happened before the time of Barnabas. The substitution of 'Lord' for 'Cyrus' in support of the writer's theological purpose and the breaking up of the first quotation suggests that the two testimonia had not yet come together in written form.

(e) 'Let us make man.' In Barn. v. 5, vi. 12, the writer cites Gen. i. 26 (LXX) in support of his belief in the converse of the Father and the Son before the creation of the world—'Let us make man in our image and likeness'. The use of this testimonium belongs to early anti-Jewish argument; cf. *Dialogue of Athanasius and Zacchaeus* i; Justin *Dial.* lxii. It is even found in a late Arabic discourse in which a Christian seeks to convert a Muslim; Harris proposed to call this work *contra Muhammedanos*. This testimonium may have been selected to buttress the doctrine of Jesus' pre-existence before the time of Barnabas, for the doctrine of the Trinity, to which it was later applied, had not yet been fully developed in Egypt. (On the patristic exegesis of Gen. i. 26 see further *Studia Patristica* I, p. 420 f.).

The evidence assembled in this chapter will have shown that the

[1] Tr. Harris, Vol. I, p. 37.

use of testimonies in the Epistle of Barnabas represents a later stage than that found in the New Testament. Further proof texts are beginning to cluster round those quoted by our Lord and in the New Testament Epistles and the writer feels free to select, adapt and supplement many of the earlier testimonia. Yet always his use of testimonia is subservient to his particular theological views, which they are made to support by much intricate and forced exegesis.[1] There appears to be little to support the view that the writer is drawing on a fixed, stereotyped testimony book—a written *Corpus anti-Judaicum* —although it is possible that, by this time, certain testimonia had been grouped together in a written form. We must probably vizualise a strong oral tradition and a variety of partial transcripts of testimonia behind this Epistle. This process reached an end in the monumental compilation of Cyprian or Pseudo-Cyprian who provided headings and introductions to the proof-texts.

Additional Note: M. Prigent on Testimonies in the Epistle of Barnabas

The important work of Pierre Prigent, 'Les Testimonia dans le christianisme primitif: l'Épître de Barnabé i–xvi et ses sources', Études Bibliques (Paris 1961), came to my notice after this work had been completed. I can only offer here a summary and a few observations on Prigent's thesis.[2] Prigent unravels four groups of testimonies in Ep. Barn.:

(1) *Anti-cultic* testimonies based on straightforward quotations from the LXX; e.g., Barn. ii–iii, ix. 5, xiv. 1–3, xv. 1–2, xvi. 1–3; cf. also ix. 1–3 and xi. 2–3. Prigent believes that these testimonia came from a single collection which originated in Syria, similar in outlook to the views of St. Stephen (see chapter 6 of this book). These testimonies are not anti-Jewish *per se*.

(2) *Midrashic* testimonies in which Old Testament ritual commandments and episodes are allegorically interpreted to yield a Christian meaning; e.g., Barn. vii, viii, ix. 7–9, x, xii and xiii. Prigent believes that these are not anti-Jewish in tone but are midrashim destined for internal Christian use. Again they reflect a Syrian milieu.

[1] Testimonies later passed out of controversial use into regular Church teaching which professed to represent the apostolic tradition. A good example of this process is Irenaeus' *On the Apostolic Preaching* which is the equivalent of a Church catechism, although it is full of anti-Jewish testimonies. Subsequently the Gospels replaced the testimonies in doctrinal instruction.

[2] See the full review of this book by Dr. R. A. Kraft in JTS 13 (1962), pp. 401–8.

(3) *Messianic* testimonies which are divided into 'Christological' (v. 2, 12–14, vi. i, 2–4, 6–7, viii. 5, xii. 1, 4) and 'Universal' (xii. 10–11 and xiv. 6). These derive from a Christian use of Old Testament texts to formulate convenient summaries of the Christian faith and to attest Jesus' passion. The Christological testimonia are used to support a Docetic interpretation of Christ's Person.

(4) *Other kinds of source material*, such as references to Jewish Apocalyptic writings, Two Ways material and 'targumic' paraphrases.

We have no space here to discuss Prigent's theory in detail, and limit ourselves to the following observations:

(a) The assumption that much of the source material in Ep. Barn. originated in Syria is hazardous in view of the very strong literary connexion of the Epistle with Alexandria. An Alexandrian milieu is also much more likely in view of the contacts with Aristobulus, Pseudo-Aristeas, *Secrets of Enoch* and Philo.

(b) I think Prigent over-emphasizes the anti-cultic nature of Barnabas' testimonia and underestimates the anti-Jewish character of the Epistle. While it is true that certain Jewish circles were critical of the Jerusalem cultus it is also true that Jewish belief in the rebuilding of the Temple and restoration of the cultus was still strong in the period after A.D. 70. Moreover Jewish Christianity and non-Christian Judaism were in many areas in mortal conflict during this period. A satisfactory interpretation of this Epistle should not minimize its hostile references to the Jews. Note especially the following:

iii. 6 (note expressly ὡς ἐπήλυτοι τῷ ἐκείνων νόμῳ).
iv. 6 (note ἐκείνων καὶ ἡμῶν).
v. 11 (note ἵνα τὸ τέλειον τῶν ἁμαρτιῶν ἀνακεφαλαιώσῃ . . . .).
viii. 7
x. 3–5
xiii. 1 (note οὗτος ὁ λαός contrasted with ὁ πρῶτος).
xiii. 6
xiv. 1 (note διὰ τὰς ἁμαρτίας αὐτῶν); cf. xiv. 4.
xv. 6
xvi. 1–2 (against the Temple).

In view of the above I cannot see why it is misleading to describe Barnabas as 'anti-Jewish'. It is true that he uses anti-cultic and other Jewish material but he adapts and modifies it to serve his immediate practical and theological purpose.

(c) Prigent's assertion that the 'Christological' testimonia in Barn. v were used to support a Docetic interpretation of Christ's Person is very doubtful. It is noticeable that the Epistle shows no trace of the Gnostic under-valuing of Jesus' humanity (Barnabas never says that He only *seemed* to come in the flesh but that He was manifested to suffer and endure—which is quite another thing). Furthermore the Epistle is equally free from an adoptionist christology. I believe that the repeated references to Jesus' coming in the flesh leave no doubt that the writer is firmly rooted in the New Testament tradition as to the reality of Christ's body.

M. Prigent's work is a very valuable contribution to the study of the testimony tradition of the Early Church and will repay careful study, although it will provoke disagreement at some points.

X

HADRIAN AND CHRISTIANITY

Hadrian, who was Roman Emperor from A.D. 117–38, was a ruler of genius who has left his mark on world history as a great statesman and administrator, as the inaugurator of the classic age of Roman jurisprudence and as an unparalleled example of a man of restless energy, curiosity and intellectual enthusiasm. Only in his dealings with the Jews did he falter. The precise reason for this is obscure. Was Hadrian at last goaded on by the astonishing spectacle of a minority group carrying on practices which offended against his idea of civilized behaviour? Or did he see in Judaism a fanatical nationalistic movement intent on destroying the *Pax Romana* and undermining his idea of Imperial Unity? The latter appears more probable, to judge from the element of direct provocation in the assault which he launched against the Jews which culminated, after much bloodshed, in the destruction of Jerusalem and the Temple and the building of Aelia Capitolina in its place.

If such was Hadrian's attitude towards the Jews how would he regard Christianity, which had stemmed from a Jewish cradle? This question is not simply one of evaluating the evidence which derives from Hadrian's reign but involves the wider question of the relationship of the early Church to the Roman Empire.

The Early Church and the Roman Government

The relations between the Church and the Empire were at first friendly in spite of the fact that Jesus had been put to death at the behest of a Roman Governor. Christianity, in the eyes of the State, was a Jewish sect during the apostolic age and as such entitled to the protection then granted to that religion. The early missionaries of the Church were much indebted to this protection and St. Paul could regard Rome as acting as a restraint to the power of lawlessness in the Universe.[1] Recent study [2] has shown that teaching on the duty of Christian obedience to the State was present in the earliest catechetical forms underlying the New Testament Epistles. Thus both Romans and 1 Peter are emphatic as to the divine origin and sanction of the civil

---

[1] Cf. 2 Thess. ii. 6–7. A. N. Sherwin-White, in his magisterial Sarum Lectures, *Roman Society and Roman Law in the New Testament*, accepts the basic historicity of the N.T. evidence on this question. See especially pp. 186–92.

[2] Selwyn, op. cit., pp. 426–9. The relevant passages are Rom. xiii. 1–7; 1 Pet. ii. 13–17; 1 Tim. ii. 1–3; Tit. iii. 1–3, 8.

power ('the powers that be are ordained of God') and as to its function in restraining and punishing crime—although St. Paul develops both points at greater length than St. Peter and in characteristically Pauline phraseology. Romans and 1 Peter also agree on the positive function of the State in encouraging well-doing— teaching which is also implied in 1 Tim. ii. 2 and Tit. iii. 1, 8. It follows that Christians owe the State an inward loyalty and not only external submission. St. Peter goes further in stating that one purpose of civic obedience is that society should be favourably impressed with the new religion—a thought which frequently occurs in the Epistle and which derived from the *verbum Christi* Mt. v. 14–16.[1] But it is worth noting that this early catechetical teaching which underlies the New Testament Epistles connects civic obedience with the universalistic element in Christianity: Christians are to 'honour *all* men', 'render to *all* their dues', show meekness 'towards *all* men', offer prayers 'for *all* men'.[2]

How then was it that Christianity came to incur the hostility of the State, if, as a religion, it was well disposed towards the Governing Power? The reason was that the Roman Government knew little or nothing of the content of Christian theological and ethical teaching. It was only concerned with the question of loyalty and legality and once Christianity drew apart from its Jewish cradle and ceased to be a sect of an authorized national religion it automatically sank to the position of an unlawful cult (*religio non licita*). This was perceived only gradually; Titus however in 70 A.D. was definitely aware that Christians were not Jews, and earlier the outbreak under Nero must have shown the Romans that Christians were members of a new religion. Thus the Church, especially in the last decades of the first century, was seen to be an alien body within the Roman world having its own laws and customs and claiming a higher sanction than mere State recognition. This was the ultimate cause of persecution whatever forms it subsequently took; Christians were outsiders —a disintegrating force which was obnoxious to the law.

There were many grounds of complaint against the Christians. In the first place they formed societies not recognized by law (*hetaeriae, collegia illicita*), and of such societies the Empire was always jealous. Next, these societies practised a new and unlawful worship (*religio nova et illicita*), for Jesus of Nazareth was neither a national deity nor

[1] Selwyn, op. cit., pp. 97ff., 428.
[2] In the New Testament only the Apocalypse adopts a hostile attitude towards the Roman Power; cf. Rev. xvii. 1–6. This attack stands almost alone in early literature. Even 1 Clement, which likewise derived from a time of persecution, in its great liturgical prayer enjoins obedience to the Ruling Power; cf. 1 Clem. lx. This Epistle, however, contains evidence that some Christians were persecuted. See Chapter 2.

recognized by public authority; and they were also to a large extent secret societies which were suspected of magic (*religio malefica*) for which the punishment of burning was prescribed by the *Lex Cornelia* which the Emperors never abolished. Worse than this, they refused to take part in recognized ceremonies of the State or to worship its gods. Hence there arose the double charge of atheism and treason. Atheism, in the early Christian centuries, meant a denial of the State deities rather than denial of any belief in God or a supernatural end for man. And the real State deity of any moment was the Caesar.[1] Christians might on occasions be asked to worship the gods but far more commonly they were brought before an image of the Emperor and commanded to offer worship. They came before the court as suspected persons and the simplest test was to ask them to offer sacrifice, incense or swear the oath by Caesar's genius. If they refused, they were guilty of treason (*majestas*, in the form of *impietas circa principes*), and had committed their crime in open court—hence they could be imprisoned or sent for execution without further ado.

This was the full process, used in the main for Roman citizens, and it still left considerable discretion to the local magistrate. He might encourage accusations; he might refuse to receive them; or he might nullify the usual test of loyalty by allowing the accused to swear by Caesar's safety—an oath which members of the Church were usually willing to take. The magistrate's discretion was even more free in the case of *cognitio*, or summary jurisdiction. The Christians were a society without legal standing and its members might be punished like other disturbers of the peace. The only question then was whether the accused were Christians; if they confessed that they were they might be executed or tortured to extract a renunciation.

It is obvious that the Christians were very much at the mercy of the local Governor, who might be hostile and provoke the cry '*Christianos ad leonem!*' Opportunities for paying off private scores also easily arose for this was an age in which the informer flourished as freely as in the modern totalitarian state (cf. Eus.*E.H.* iv. 26. 5). Roman law allowed the successful *delator* to claim part of the property of the condemned—an incentive to this type of action. Economic and personal causes would also provide motives for denunciation; Tertullian specifies among the accusers of Christians such people as panders, pimps, astrologers and wizards (*Apol.* xliii). Trade jealousy also no doubt played a part, for those who derived their livelihood from soothsaying and the manufacture of idols were unlikely to

---

[1] The figure of the Emperor took on a terrible form to his blasphemers; cf. Tert. *Apol.* xxviii: 'men forswear themselves more willingly by all the gods than by Caesar's genius'.

make no reply to their denunciation by Christians. But there is no evidence that the pagan priests were earnest persecutors or *delatores*. They were more concerned with the dignity of their office than with the honour of the state deities and took no active part in bringing the Christians to the courts.[1] It is necessary to emphasize the sporadic and local nature of many of the persecutions of Christians in the early Empire. There was no general persecution instituted and carried through by the State; not until those under Decius, Diocletian and Valerian was this the case. Local persecutions of Christians would however break out in one Province which were often unknown to the next. It would therefore be unsafe to assume that the extant records represent the sum total of local actions against the Church. Thus no Christian writer, not even Melito of Sardis, appears to have known anything of the persecution of Christians in Bithynia in A.D. 112 alluded to in the famous Pliny-Trajan correspondence. Another factor is that the Church kept no systematic records of its persecutors.

The Pliny-Trajan [2] correspondence reveals a development in the technique used against Christians who were being brought before the Younger Pliny, Governor of Bithynia. Without going into particular charges he simply asked them if they were Christians and sent for execution those who persistently avowed it—while reserving Roman citizens for trial at Rome. Pliny has no doubt that whatever the Christians believed, obstinacy and unbending perversity deserved punishment ('Neque enim dubitabam, qualecumque esset quod faterentur pertinaciam certe et inflexibilem obstinationem debere puniri'). Difficulties arose when anonymous accusations were made on an unsigned paper implicating many people. Some of these people cleared themselves by prayer to the gods, worship before Trajan's statue and by cursing Christ—a thing which no real Christian would do ('Qui....praeterea male dicerent Christo, quorum nihil posse cogi dicuntur qui sunt re vera Christiani, dimittendos esse putavi'). Others admitted the offence but said that they had ceased to be Christians some three years ago, some a good many years, and some as many as twenty years ago; now they were quite ready to worship in the prescribed State form. Pliny, from an examination of two deaconesses by torture, concluded that Christianity was but a perverse and arrogant superstition ('Nihil aliud inveni quam superstitionem pravam immodicam.') Thus the Governor came to consult Trajan in view of the danger to public order and the fact that 'the contagion of that superstition has penetrated not the cities only, but the villages and country' ('Neque civitates tantum sed vicos etiam

[1] *E.R.E.*, Vol. IX, p. 744.
[2] Pliny *Ep*. x. 96, 97.

atque agros superstitionis istius contagio pervagata est'). Was not a milder policy worth trying in view of the numbers implicated?

Trajan's reply is sagacious and expressed with commendable brevity: 'You have followed, my dear Secundus, the process you should have done in examining the cases of those who were accused to you as Christians, for indeed nothing can be laid down as a general law involving something like a definite rule of action. They are not to be sought out; but if they are accused and convicted, they must be punished—yet on this condition, that whoso denies himself to be a Christian, and makes the fact plain by his action, that is, by worshipping our gods, shall obtain pardon on his repentance, however suspicious his past conduct may be. Papers, however, which are presented unsigned ought not to be admitted in any charge, for they are a very bad example and unworthy of our time.'[1]

The Emperor regards Christianity as a crime but Christians are not to be harried or noticed until some accuser appears in court. Trajan's chief desire, however, is to lay down the procedure for the pardoning of apostates of past years who were often in danger from the activity of *delatores*. But the Christian also receives some measure of protection—especially from the anonymous accusation which is not now to be admitted. The informer must come forward publicly and prove his case—something from which a coward would shrink. Tertullian sums up the relationship of Church and Empire in Trajan's reign when he says that the Emperor partly frustrated the persecution.[2]

Hadrian and the Church

Hadrian carried on the policy of his soldier predecessor. The tolerant Emperor had not the zeal of a persecutor nor the fear which so often is the mother of barbarism. As one who had been initiated into the Eleusinian mysteries; who had affected Stoicism; who had posed as the patron of Epictetus; who had maintained the traditional Roman ritual—it is unlikely that he would be much perplexed by Christian doctrinal beliefs. As with Trajan it was simply a question of loyalty to the state and the preservation of public order. If the

---

[1] Actum quem debuisti, mi Secunde, in excutiendis causis eorum qui Christiani ad te delati fuerant secutus es. Neque enim in universum aliquid quod quasi certam formam habeat constitui potest. Conquirendi non sunt: si deferantur et arguantur, puniendi sunt, ita tamen ut qui negaverit se Christianum esse idque re ipsa manifestum fecerit, id est supplicando diis nostris, quamvis suspectus in praeteritum, veniam ex paenitentia impetret. Sine auctore vero propositi libelli in nullo crimine locum habere debent. Nam et pessimi exempli nec nostri saeculi est. (*Ep.* x. 97).

[2] *Apol.* v: quas Traianus ex parte frustratus est vetando inquiri Christianorum.

Christians were willing to fit into Hadrian's idea of Imperial Unity and to behave as good citizens then all well and good; they could continue to live in freedom. But Hadrian bestowed no legality on Christianity as such. The 'Name' remained a crime which was punishable in the courts.

Hadrian was however more emphatic than Trajan in warning accusers that false evidence laid against Christians would be visited by severe penalties; there was to be no sacrifice of law to popular prejudice. This is the purport of Hadrian's rescript to Minicius Fundanus, which is undoubtedly genuine. It has the clarity and conciseness of a master of jurisprudence and the mark of the statesman who could deal in an objective spirit with what was, to him, a minor matter. Some Christian scholars have described Hadrian's language, in the rescript, as sarcastic and studiously vague.[1] The reader must judge for himself; suffice it to say that Hadrian was a lawyer, and sarcasm and vagueness were not his particular vices.

Quintus Licinius Silvanus Granianus Quadronius Proculus, Governor of Asia, wrote to Hadrian early in his reign asking for instructions concerning the treatment of accusations made against Christians. In reply Hadrian sent this rescript to his successor, Caius Minicius Fundanus, who had meanwhile become Governor instead of Silvanus:

'I have received the letter addressed to me by your predecessor Serenius [2] Granianus, a most illustrious man; and this communication I am unwilling to pass over in silence, lest innocent persons be disturbed and occasion be given to the informers to practise villany. Accordingly, if the inhabitants of your province will so far sustain this petition of theirs as to accuse the Christians in some court of law, I do not prohibit them from doing so. But I will not suffer them to make use of mere entreaties and outcries. For it is far more just, if anyone desires to make an accusation, that you give judgement upon it. If, therefore, anyone makes the accusation, and furnishes proof that the said men do anything contrary to the laws, you shall punish them in proportion to the offences. And this, by Hercules, you shall give special heed to, that if any man, through mere calumny, bring an accusation against any of these persons, you shall award to him more severe punishments in proportion to his wickedness.' [3]

The genuineness of this rescript has been challenged by a number

[1] W. Ramsay, *The Church in the Roman Empire*; J. B. Lightfoot, *Apostolic Fathers* II, Vol. I, p. 478.
[2] This appears to be a mistake for Silvanus.
[3] *Eus. E.H.* iv. 9; cf. Justin 1 *Apol.* lxviii.

of German scholars.[1] But the external evidence in its favour is very strong indeed: Justin Martyr's *First Apology*, which quotes the rescript, is to be dated *c.* A.D. 150, only 25 years or so later than the original and it is also mentioned by Melito of Sardis *c.* A.D. 165. It is true that Eus.*E.H.* iv. 10 states that Justin appended a copy in Latin (τὴν 'Ρωμαϊκὴν ἀντιγραφήν) and that he (Eusebius) translated it into Greek—while the present text of Justin has Eusebius' Greek version. A later scribe has no doubt substituted this for the original Latin. Is then the Latin text of Rufinus the original or did Rufinus re-translate from Eusebius' Greek version? The former is by no means improbable. Rufinus knew Ulpian's collection of the Imperial Ordinances relating to the Christians and he cannot have been unacquainted with Justin's *Apologies*, as he lived in the West. Moreover the Latin version has a juristic tone which is unlike Rufinus' own hand.

The language of the rescript is perfectly clear and its effect must have been wholly favourable to the Christians. No longer, at least in Asia Minor, could they be falsely accused by the hated *delator*. Law, not prejudice or mob violence, was to be the Roman basis of dealing with them. Accusers of the Christians must from now on bring a charge against them in legal form which was to be the subject of a legal enquiry. Many would now shrink from the light accusation based on hearsay. Even to accuse Christians of the 'Name' would not be too easy, as the burden of proof lay directly on the accuser. The Church had good reason to regard Hadrian with favour and later apologists, such as Melito of Sardis, made a cautious use of the rescript.

If such was Hadrian's attitude towards Christianity it is highly improbable that he would have set in motion any general persecution of Christians. His desire for peace within the confines of the Roman world was against such a policy. Bishop Lightfoot, after an examination of all the available evidence for a Hadrianic persecution, carried through with his usual thoroughness, concludes that it melts away under critical examination.[2] Eusebius knows of no such persecution. Even the martyrdom of Telesphorus, Bishop of Rome, which Irenaeus places late in Hadrian's reign, is ascribed to his successor Antoninus Pius.[3] Eusebius also quotes Melito's mention of the favourable attitude of Hadrian towards the Christians as shown in the rescript to Fundanus.[4]

[1] Lightfoot, op. cit., Vol. I, pp. 477–8, for details.
[2] Op. cit., Vol. I, pp. 507 ff.
[3] Iren. iii. 3. 4: μετὰ δὲ τοῦτον [Σύστον] Τελεσφόρος ὃς καὶ ἐνδόξως ἐμαρτύρησεν. In the Liberian catalogue his death is assigned to A.D. 138.
[4] Eus. *E.H.* iv. 26.

It was St. Jerome who ascribed a very severe persecution to Hadrian's reign, apparently through his wrong identification of Quadratus the Apologist with Quadratus the Bishop under whom the persecution occurred which was fatal to Publius (*de vir. ill.* 19; *Ep.* 70). St. Jerome's authority reigned supreme in the Western Church and from him there spread the belief in a Hadrianic persecution, as is shown by the fact that the legends of martyrdom under this Emperor are mainly confined to Italy and the West; Eusebius and later Greek writers have no knowledge of such a persecution. These legends are for the most part quite grotesque and fantastic. Symphorosa and her seven sons were cruelly sacrificed by Hadrian upon the inauguration of his Tibur Villa [1]; St. Thalelaeus and his companions, again seven in number, perished at Aegae for the faith [2]; St. Dionysius the Areopagite was tortured at Athens by order of the Emperor [3]; Alexander Bishop of Rome perished with others [4]; and so on.

At the most occasional local persecutions may have occurred during Hadrian's reign. But the evidence is decisive against any general persecution initiated by the Emperor. The Church had good reason to consolidate its position during his reign for, in contrast to the Jews, it was largely unmolested. Hadrian, who stamped his genius upon the Roman world, was too great a man to descend to the vice of religious intolerance—that besetting sin of smaller men.

The Age of the Apologists

The reign of Hadrian coincides not only with the age of the Apostolic Fathers, but also with the appearance of the first Christian Apologetic writings. Christianity was at first expressed in its catechesis and liturgy in thought forms derived from the Old Testament. But by the early decades of the second century a new type of convert, who had received training in Greek thought, was entering the Church and a need was felt for a statement of the Faith in terms of contemporary thought. Gnosticism, in one of its aspects, was an attempt to do this on the basis of an Oriental movement of thought which had widespread ramifications in the second century. The Greek Apologists sought rather to present the case for Christianity to the Roman Emperors, and to the educated world of which they were the

---

[1] Given in the *Passio Symphorosae* (Ruinart, *Act. Mart. Sinc.*, p. 70). The framework of the story is common to several other stories of martyrdom and is not specifically Christian.
[2] See F. C. Conybeare, *Monuments of Early Christianity*, pp. 239–55.
[3] *Martyrologium Vetus Romanum*, p. 170 (Migne P. G. cxxiii).
[4] *Acts of Alexander*.

patrons, through the medium of a philosophical literature based on Greek models. Their approach was similar to that already undertaken by Jewish Hellenism in seeking to bridge the gap between the Greek world and Judaism. There was nothing 'apologetic' about their work in the modern sense of the word. Apologia [1] meant the case for the defence—especially when presented in the law court. Socrates' speech made at his trial was an apologia and may well have been the model for the first Christian apologies which were significantly made at Athens—the traditional home of philosophy.

The earliest of these Christian Apologists appeared in the reign of Hadrian, according to Eusebius,[2] and actually presented their case to the Emperor. No doubt, the more educated members of the Church felt that at least they had a chance of a favourable hearing from one who was 'curiositatum omnium explorator'.[3] The names of these Apologists were Quadratus and Aristides, but it now appears likely that Eusebius was misinformed about Aristides who may have presented his Apology to Antoninus Pius sometime before the year A.D. 147 when Marcus Aurelius became joint Emperor.[4] There is however no reason to doubt his information concerning Quadratus' Apology which may be dated A.D. 124-5 when Hadrian was in Athens. Unfortunately the text of this work has not survived and our sole information depends upon a passage quoted in Eusebius:

'But the works of our Saviour remained permanent, for they were genuine; that is to say, those who were healed, and those who rose from the dead. They were not only seen when they were healed or raised; they remained permanently—and not only while the Saviour was dwelling (on earth) but also after his departure—they lived on for a considerable time, and some of them survived even into our own times.' [5]

[1] Antiphon v. 7; Thuc. vi. 29; Eupator 357 and many other references in Liddell and Scott. P. Carrington, *The Early Christian Church*, Vol. II, pp. 94-5.
[2] *E.H.* iv. 3.
[3] Tert. *Apol.* v.
[4] For Aristides see Eus.*E.H.* iv. 3 and Chron. ad. a. 2140; Jer. *de vir. ill.* 20. In 1878 part of the *Apology* was published in an Armenian translation and in 1891 a Syriac translation was edited by J. R. Harris, *Camb. Text and Studies* I (1). The Armenian fragments are given in G. B. Pitra, *Analecta Sacra* IV (1883), pp. 6-10 and 282-6. The original Greek, somewhat expanded, is also to be found in the apologetic *Lives of Barlaam and Josaphat*. The brevity of Eusebius' reference to Aristides, compared with that to Quadratus, is to be noted and suggests that he knew little about this Apologist.
[5] Eus.*E.H.* iv. 3: Τοῦ δὲ Σωτῆρος ἡμῶν τὰ ἔργα ἀεὶ παρῆν. Ἀληθῆ γὰρ ἦν· οἱ θεραπευθέντες, οἱ ἀναστάντες ἐκ νεκρῶν, οἳ οὐκ ὤφθησαν μόνον

Several points are of interest in this short extract: the statement that some of those healed by Jesus survived into the time of Quadratus is quite possible if the Apologist is referring to his own boyhood or early years. It is likely that eyewitnesses of our Lord's Ministry *did* survive until late in the first century and perhaps later. The expression Τοῦ δὲ Σωτῆρος ἡμῶν is also to be noted and may suggest that Quadratus was concerned to present Jesus as Σωτήρ, in contrast to the many 'healers' or 'saviours' of the Graeco-Roman world.[1] Eusebius further describes his apology as θεοσεβεία, which looks as if it was a refutation of atheism and a defence of Christianity as a monotheistic worship.

St. Jerome identifies the apologist with Quadratus, Bishop of Athens (*de vir ill.* 19; *Ep.* 70). On chronological grounds this identification is doubtful, as it is unlikely that anyone who had known the subjects of Jesus' miracles would be alive as late as A.D. 170. There was also confusion with another Quadratus whom a writer against the Montanists states had a prophetic gift and whose behaviour contrasted favourably with that of the Montanist prophetesses.[2] Since the author whom Eusebius quotes wrote in Asia Minor it seems that it was there that this other Quadratus enjoyed his reputation.

How Hadrian responded to Quadratus' defence of Christianity is not known. No doubt, as with so many other matters small and great, he gave it his undivided attention. But it was simply one among many religious apologies which had been propounded to him.

The Letter to Servianus

Christians are mentioned in one other letter purporting to have been written by Hadrian to his aged brother-in-law Lucius Julius Ursus Servianus *c.* A.D. 134 when Servianus had become consul for the third time. This relative in earlier times had been jealous of Hadrian, but subsequently friendlier relations set in—at least until A.D. 136 when Servianus was put to death. The letter is a shrewd assessment of the Egyptian character:

θεραπευόμενοι, καὶ ἀνιστάμενοι, ἀλλὰ καὶ ἀεὶ παρόντες· οὐδὲ ἐπιδημοῦντος μόνον τοῦ Σωτῆρος, ἀλλὰ καὶ ἀπαλλαγέντος, ἦσαν ἐπὶ χρόνον ἱκανὸν, ὥστε καὶ εἰς τοὺς ἡμετέρους χρόνους τινὲς αὐτῶν ἀφίκοντο. The *Apology* of Quadratus survived as late as the 6th century; several passages are quoted in the controversy between the monk Andrew and one Eusebius (Photius Cod. 162). Rendel Harris suggested that borrowed matter in the *Passion* or *Martyrdom* of Saint Catherine of Alexandria might be part of Quadratus' *Apology*. This however must be regarded as uncertain.

[1] Carrington, op. cit., p. 22, makes this suggestion.
[2] Eus. *E.H.* v. 17; cf. iii. 37.

'So you praise Egypt, my very dear Servianus! I know the land from top to bottom, a fickle, tricky land, blown about by every wind of rumour. In it the worshippers of Serapis are Christians, and those who call themselves Bishops of Christ pay their vows to Serapis. There is no ruler of a Jewish synagogue there, no Samaritan, no Christian presbyter, who is not an astrologer, a soothsayer, a quack. Whenever the patriarch himself comes to Egypt he is made to worship Serapis by some and Christ by others. The men are a most seditious, addle-pated, riotous crew. The town is rich, prosperous, productive. There is not an idle person in it. Some are glass makers, others paper manufacturers, others linen weavers. Everyone seems to have some trade and is supposed to have one. The gouty are busy; the blind are energetic; not even hands crippled by gout keep the victim from an active life. They all of them have one and the same God, Money. Christians adore him, Jews worship him, all the Gentiles give him adoration. It is a pity that the town has not got better morals. For its productivity certainly makes it deserve the reputation which its very size gives it, that of the first town in Egypt. I have made the town every possible concession. I restored its old privileges to it, and I gave them new ones so bountifully that while I was actually staying there they paid me thanks! No sooner was my back turned than they began saying many things against my son Verus—and what they have said against Antinous I think you know. My one wish for them is that they may have to eat their own fowls. How they fatten these I blush to repeat. I am sending you some multicoloured drinking cups, which the priest of the temple presented to me; consecrated they are specially to you and my sister. Please use them for holiday feasts. But be careful that our Friend Africanus does not indulge too freely with them.'[1]

Vopiscus prefaces the letter thus: 'Sunt Christiani, Samaritae, et quibus praesentia semper tempora cum enormi libertate displiceant. Ac ne quis mihi Aegyptiorum irascatur et meum esse credat quod in litteras rettuli, Hadriani epistolam ponam ex libris Phlegontis liberti ejus proditam, ex qua penitus Aegyptiorum vita detegitur.' This may indicate that the letter was published in Phlegon's name—as was Hadrian's autobiography.

The genuineness of the letter has been usually accepted by Christian scholars, but challenged by a number of Roman historians.[2]

[1] Vopiscus, *Vita Saturnini* 8.
[2] B. W. Henderson, *The Life and Principate of the Emperor Hadrian*, p. 229, regards the letter as a forgery. 'The tone of the letter can hardly recommend it as one of Imperial authorship. Would Hadrian concern himself with

The latter argue that Hadrian describes Verus as his son (*filium meum*) although Verus was not adopted by the Emperor until A.D. 136. This difficulty is however not insuperable, as long before A.D. 136 Hadrian had taken steps to bring this about (cf. Spartianus Helius 3).

The letter has several interesting features. The Emperor is well aware of the eclecticism of second century Egypt with its underworld of astrology, soothsaying and quackery; all religions were to him the same—to be sampled if a man so desired. Yet Hadrian knows the difference between Christianity and Judaism; he is aware that the Christians have Bishops and presbyters although he has no high regard for the office. In any event he might be expected to know something about ecclesiastical organization from his interrogation of the Apologist Quadratus. But who is the patriarch mentioned in the letter? This is most probably the Jewish Patriarch of Tiberias, in view of the fact that he is described as coming to Egypt and there being subject both to Egyptian and Christian propaganda (an interesting insight into proselyte tendencies at work). The references to Alexandria betray the Emperor's shrewdness. Hadrian appreciates the prosperity and industry of Alexandria but he has no illusions about the moral state of the city with its seditious and gossiping groups.[1]

THE EMERGENCE OF CHRISTIAN GNOSTICISM

The reign of Hadrian saw the rise of distinct Gnostic schools of thought within the Church. Gnosticism is treated by Irenaeus, Tertullian and Hippolytus as a Christian heresy which had been brought about by the adulteration of apostolic doctrine with pagan philosophy, astrology and the tenets of the Greek Mystery Religions[2] —Simon Magus[3] being the founder of the system. Gnosticism drew upon Jewish, pagan and oriental sources and brought certain characteristic ideas to the solution of the problem of evil and of the nature of man and his destiny.

The most typically Christian types of Gnosticism were distinguished by eminent teachers, who founded Gnostic schools within the bosom of the Church. These teachers had at first no wish to

Christian Bishops and presbyters, with patriarchs of doubtful provenance and Samaritans unspecified?' (op. cit., p. 231).) But why not if the Emperor was 'Curiositatum omnium explorator'?

---

[1] According to Dio lxix. 8. 1a, Hadrian on another occasion had to write a letter remonstrating with the Alexandrians for squabbling among themselves.

[2] Iren. *adv. haer.* ii. 14; Tert. *de praescr.* vii. 30; Hippol. *Ref. praef.* 8.

[3] Acts viii; cf. Iren. *adv. haer.* i. 23, 2; i. 27, 4.

withdraw from communion with their fellow Christians, and they sought to find in the Gospel, as re-interpreted by them, the key to life; their one wish was for intellectual freedom so that they might develop their speculations. The first of the heads of these schools whose name has come down was Saturninus or Saturnilus, a Syrian, who taught at Antioch during Hadrian's reign.[1] He appears to have believed that matter was evil and that God was unknowable. God however had created the angels and seven of these angels created the world and man. The God of the Jews was only one of the angels who kept men under his control; the work of Christ was to abolish his power and to lead men back to the truth. Basilides and Valentinus, the great Egyptian Gnostic teachers, may also have begun to teach during Hadrian's reign.

The sins of Gnosticism have often been laboured. Certainly its triumph would have meant the overthrow of Christianity as a historical religion based upon an incarnation of the Divine Word within the historical process. But its more positive achievements have frequently been forgotten. The great achievement of Gnosticism was to stimulate interest in Christianity not only as a way of salvation but as the way of knowledge in the widest sense of that word. Moreover it did much to introduce studies, literature and art into the Christian Church and to challenge other thinkers to show that Christianity was the fullest and widest truth which had been apprehended, although dimly, by the pre-Christian religions and philosophies. The doctrine of the Divine Logos, ceaselessly at work in the Universe, as worked out by the great Christian Platonists of Alexandria, was the answer to the challenge of Gnosticism.

We do not know if Hadrian ever came into direct contact with Christian Gnostic teachers. To be sure he encouraged speculation and himself dabbled in occultism and eastern thought. One who had been willing to hear the *Apology* of Quadratus would have been equally willing to listen to an exposition of the Christian Gnostic position, for its eclecticism [2] would have appealed to him. But whether, as a statesman and practical man of action, the Emperor could have stomached the Gnostic attitude to matter and the material world is another question.

The evidence given in this chapter has shown that Hadrian was

[1] Iren. *adv. haer.* i. 22; Hipp. *Philosoph.* vii. 28; Ps.-Tert. *Praescr.* iii; Epiph. *adv. haer.* 23; Eus.*E.H.* iv. 7.
[2] For the eclecticism of Hadrian see Lampridius in *Alex. Sever.* 43 who says that the Emperor erected temples without statues, which were intended to have been dedicated to Christ. But he was restrained by oracles which warned him that the religion of the Empire would be perverted.

not as hostile to the Christians as he became towards the Jews in his later years because Christianity was not so fanatical and was not intent on opposing the Emperor's idea of unity within the Roman world. Christians, on the whole, wanted to be good citizens and to obey, in all things lawful, the ruling power. Hadrian's reign was therefore favourable to the growth of the Christian Church. The popular cry *Christianos ad leones* was hushed and no organized persecution took place. The appearance of an apologetic literature was a sign that Christians were now prepared to appeal with confidence to the intellectual judgement of mankind. But the Emperor's wide tolerance, which was favourable to the growth of the seed of the Gospel, also favoured the growth of Gnostic schools of thought which were later to present such a challenge to orthodox theologians.

XI

HERMAS, THE CHURCH AND JUDAISM

In the latter half of the second century there circulated in the Church a book of visions and allegories purporting to be written by one Hermas, a slave, which was known as *The Shepherd*, after the angel of repentance who appears in the book. The work was widely accepted as inspired and it was read in public worship in many Churches. Irenaeus (*adv. haer.* iv. 20) quotes it with the comment 'Well said the Scripture', a fact taken notice of by Eusebius (*E.H.* v. 8). It seems likely that in the time of Irenaeus it was read and was well known in the Gallican Churches, as otherwise he would have named the source of his quotation. Clement of Alexandria gives about ten quotations from the book, always with an acceptance of the divine character of the revelations vouchsafed to Hermas but without any note as to who Hermas was. The great scholar Origen frequently quotes the book which he regards as very useful and divinely inspired (*in Rom.* xvi. 4). Yet he carefully separates his quotations from those from the Canonical Scriptures and often adds a clause giving the reader permission to reject *The Shepherd* if he is so disposed. Eusebius states that the book, although rejected by some, has been publicly used in churches, that certain eminent writers had used it, and that some judged it suitable for those in need of elementary instruction in the faith (*E.H.* iii. 3). Athanasius classes *The Shepherd* with some of the deutero-canonical books of the Old Testament and with the 'Teaching of the Apostles' as not canonical, yet useful for catechetical instruction. The work is also found in the Codex Sinaiticus following the Epistle of Barnabas and is clearly there regarded as an appendix to the New Testament. In the West the Muratorian fragment on the Canon states that the book had been written during the episcopate of Pius (*c.* A.D. 140–50) by Hermas, a brother of that Bishop, and that it is of 'very recent date'. The fragment concludes that the book ought to be read, but not to be used publicly, in Church among the prophetical or apostolic writings. This is high recognition of the value attributed to it by this writer and may suggest that in some places the use of the book had been such as to cause it to be set on a level with the canonical scriptures. Tertullian, in his earliest days, is a further witness to the importance assigned to *The Shepherd*. In *de oratione* he disputes the practice of sitting down immediately after prayer for which he knows no reason than that Hermas is said to have sat on the bed on ending prayer. A book which could influence the liturgical practices of churches must have enjoyed high recognition at the time. In his Montanist days Tertullian seems to have turned against the book but his later view does not invalidate his earlier references.

The accord given to *The Shepherd* in early times may seem to the modern reader somewhat fulsome. An age which delights in statistics and returns, which calculates diocesan quotas on the basis of the number of Easter communicants, which exalts parochial and diocesan 'efficiency', may well become bored with the allusiveness of Hermas of whom so little is known. The fact is, however, that vivid imagination and graphic descriptions of mysterious experiences were not decried in the early Church and indeed were regarded as the hallmark of inspiration. These were of more importance than a correct pedigree in Crockford's Clerical Directory. It may well be that the early Church was correct in its estimate of *The Shepherd*, for how would Bunyan's *Pilgrim's Progress*, Dante's *Divina Commedia* and the visions of St. Teresa and St. Catherine of Siena have appeared to the hard-pressed modern ecclesiastic who had not read them before? It may be doubted whether recent psychological advances have done much to elucidate the mystery of the visionary faculty in early Christianity. But whatever is the correct interpretation of the strange mental states of certain early Christians, a sure test is the life which they lived and the sentiments which they expressed. Hermas passes this test with flying colours. His strong moral earnestness and didactic purpose is apparent throughout the book. He had been freed from slavery, and had become the property of one Rhoda in Rome (*Vis.* i. 1), had gained his freedom, and had prospered in business (iii. 6). Disaster had however come upon him and he had lost his wealth and so had become useful and profitable unto life (*Vis.* iii. 6). The strong moral character of Hermas' teaching is apparent in his call to repentance addressed to Christians among whom the memory of persecution is still fresh (*Vis.* iii. 2, 5; *Sim.* ix. 28) and over whom hangs the shadow of another great period of testing (*Vis.* ii. 2, iv. 2). The theme of the whole work is the need for repentance and amendment of life. This note is sounded in the first vision, with its emphasis on the sinfulness of sins of thought, to the last Parable where the greatness of the Shepherd, the supernatural angel, to whom is given authority over repentance in the whole world (*Sim.* x. 1), is ordered to be declared to man. This is not the work of 'pottering mediocrity' (B. H. Streeter) but of a genuine if simple Christian mind seeking to understand and use the visions vouchsafed to it.

What was Hermas' position in the Roman Church? Was he an accredited prophet or teacher or merely an earnest visionary who wrote a work of allegorical fiction as a vehicle for teaching moral

HERMAS, THE CHURCH AND JUDAISM

truths? The evidence given above is decisive that the Church in the latter part of the second century regarded him as an inspired writer whose visions were real. Furthermore the book itself contains directions to one Clement (Clement of Rome?) to send it to 'cities abroad', i.e., other Churches (*Vis.* ii. 4). We need not doubt that this was carried out and stamped *The Shepherd* as an authoritative prophetic work. This seems to me the only satisfactory explanation of the high regard in which it was held, second only to the Canonical Scriptures, in distant Christian communities, and the place which it occupied in public reading in the context of Christian Worship.

Indications that Hermas became an accredited Christian prophet are not hard to find. In *Vis.* iii. 8 he is directed to go after three days and speak in the hearing of all the saints the words which he had heard in his vision. Elsewhere we are given an insight as to how this was carried out. In *Mand.* xi. 9 we are told that if a meeting of righteous men, i.e., the Christian assembly, makes intercession for an inspired man 'then the angel of the prophetic spirit rests on him and fills the man, and the man, being filled with the Holy Spirit, speaks to the congregation as the Lord wills'. The fact that the Roman Church accepted *The Shepherd* as an inspired work surely indicates that Hermas eventually held the position of a recognized prophet, much as Quadratus and Ammia of Philadelphia did elsewhere, and that he delivered in public worship the message which he believed was vouchsafed to him.

However the earlier parts of *The Shepherd* suggest that Hermas' claim to be a prophet was not easily admitted. In *Vis.* iii. 1 there appears a most interesting reflection of his struggles to obtain public recognition. In the corner of the field where he was to meet the white-haired lady he saw an ivory couch with a linen cushion and fine linen cover over it. This is evidently the seat on which the presiding elders of the Church sat, but at first no person is in sight. Hermas trembles, his hair stands on end and he is stricken with panic; however a time of prayer and confession of sins restores him. It seems very probable that this is a reflection of his own feelings when first allowed to deliver one of his visions to the Roman Church.

The ancient lady, the Church, now appears and tells Hermas to sit on the seat. He replies that the elders should sit down first. She then repeats the request. Hermas continues:

> 'Yet when I wished to sit on the right hand she would not let me, but signed to me with her hand to sit on the left. When therefore I thought about this, and was grieved because she did not let me sit on the right hand, she said to me: "Are you sorry, Hermas? The seat on the right is for others, who have already been found

well-pleasing to God and have suffered for the Name. But you fall far short of sitting with them. But remain in your simplicity as you are doing, and you shall sit with them, and so shall all who do their deeds and bear what they also bore. . . . But both (i.e., martyrs and ordinary Christians), whether they sit on the right or left, have the same gifts, and the same promises, only the former sit on the right and have somewhat of glory. And you are desirous of sitting on the right hand with them, but your failings are many."' (*Vis*. iii. 1–2.)

Behind this vision we sense a certain reluctance in recognizing Hermas' prophetic gift. The Roman Church, as is the case with many readers today, must have sensed the strangeness of his visions. The odd-man-out is not easily accepted in any age or generation! The composition of the work may have taken thirty to forty years and towards the end of Hermas' life, and as the second century wore on, the public exercise of prophetic powers seems to have waned. Such at least we may infer from the advent of Montanism with its challenge to the Church to become the abode of the Spirit. The controversy that ensued caused the Church to insist strongly on the distinction between the inspiration of the writers of the Canonical Scriptures and that of holy men of later times—a view held by the writer of the Muratorian fragment. But this was not the case in the earlier part of Hermas' ministry when the accredited, inspired prophet was accepted in the Christian communities.

Some further indications of the position of prophets in the Church are provided by *The Shepherd* and are significant for the understanding of Hermas' own position. *Mand*. xi. 1 reads:

'He showed me men sitting on a bench (*subsellium*), and another man sitting on a chair (*cathedra*), and he said to me, "Do you see the men sitting on the bench?" "Yes sir," said I; "I see them." "They," said he, "are faithful, and he who is sitting on the chair is a false prophet, who is corrupting the understanding of the servants of God. He corrupts the understanding of the double-minded, not of the faithful."'

The prophet, although in this case a false one, is given a seat of honour, the chair of teaching, a *cathedra*, while his hearers sit before him on a *subsellium*. This interpretation is confirmed by *Vis*. i. 2. 2, 4.1, in which the Church, the ancient Lady, when she reads her book, sits on a *cathedra*—clearly the chair of teaching. We thus infer that in the Roman Church besides presbyters there were prophets who taught or prophesied from recognized seats of honour —'teaching' chairs—and that on occasions certain of the false prophets, which plagued the early Church, usurped this chair of honour and sought to use it for their own ends. The only way of judging true from false was pragmatical—'test the man who has the divine spirit by his life'. (*Mand.* xi. 7). We are reminded of a similar situation mentioned in *Didache* xi. There was a fluidity of Church life and order in the second century, even in Rome where law was exalted, which is often forgotten in our desire to read our own tidy ecclesiastical systems into the evidence for this early period. Yet underlying this diversity was a deep fundamental unity of men and women who were 'in Christ'.

What was the relationship of Hermas to the heresies which arose in the early second century within the Church? According to Irenaeus (*adv. haer.* iii. 4), Valentinus and Cerdo came to Rome in the episcopate of Hyginus, i.e., c. A.D. 135, and there propagated their systems. The discovery of the Gospel of Truth, if correctly assigned to Valentinus, has shown that Gnosticism in its earlier stages was 'more Christian' and 'less Gnostic' than had formerly been believed. It was firmly soteriological and placed the Redemption wrought by Christ at the centre of its system. Only later, with the advent of Gnostic schools of thought, did the more characteristic teaching appear, and it is this later brand which is so strongly condemned by the Fathers. We must not assume that Valentinus had already evolved his system of 'aeons' as early as A.D. 135. The evidence from *The Shepherd* of Hermas, such as it is, tends to support this view. The author's language concerning the pre-existence of the Church (*Vis.* ii. 4), which finds an exact parallel in 2 Clement xiv, does not suggest that it was based on the Gnostic aeon *Ecclesia*, which would have brought discredit on the idea in Christian circles. Rather it appears to derive from Eph. i. 22-3 and possibly from a background in Judaism (cf. Qumran Manual of Discipline ii. 25, xi. 7-8; Thanksgiving Pss. iii. 21, vi. 14, xi. 11-12). The only references in *The Shepherd* which appear to refer to Gnostic or Docetic teaching are *Sim.* v. 7, where the tendency to divide flesh and spirit and to regard the acts of the flesh as unimportant, is combated; and *Sim.* ix. 22 which refers to false teachers within the bosom of the Church who are 'believers, but slow to learn and presumptuous, and pleasing themselves, wishing to know everything, and yet they know nothing at all. Because of this presumption of theirs understanding has departed from them, and senseless folly has entered into them, and they praise themselves for having understanding and they wish to be teachers in spite of their folly.' Yet even for these 'repentance is waiting, for they were not wicked, but rather foolish and without understanding'. Hermas is combating false speculation on the part of accredited teachers of the Church. There is however no indication whatsoever that he has any knowledge of Gnosticism in its more developed forms—we should have expected him to have referred to such if he had known it. For this reason I should not place the completion of his book later than c. A.D. 135. Most probably it was composed over a period of 30–40 years, the earliest parts dating from the end of the first century.

This dating is also relevant to the question of Montanist affiliation. It has often been noted that the leading ideas of Montanism and *The Shepherd* have an affinity. In both the difficulty was felt that the Church, which was ideally composed of holy men, in fact included many unworthy people who had sinned wilfully after receiving baptism 'for the remission of sins'. The question faced by both was whether it was possible to renew such repentance. *The Shepherd* and Montanism eagerly awaited our Lord's second coming and both sought knowledge of God's ways through visions and revelations given to 'inspired' people. The fact that they dealt with similar problems and questions is however no proof of affiliation and the answers given by Hermas are quite independent of Montanism and bear the marks of an earlier period. We have already noted that in Hermas' day the Church was willing to accept prophetic utterances 'in the spirit' as genuinely inspired and worthy of a hearing in public worship. This was not the case with Montanism which quickly drew upon itself the hostility of the Catholic Bishops. Moreover the Montanists refused restoration to grave offenders while Hermas offered complete forgiveness, once, for the worst of sins; they refused second marriages as a religious duty while Hermas allowed these, although it was a counsel of perfection to abstain from them. The Montanists added to the fasts of the Church; Hermas did not make fasting a matter of obligation, insisting more on the spirit in which it was observed. In these and other respects Hermas is less rigorous than the Montanists and the special teaching of Montanism, such as the 'Age of the Paraclete', is unknown to him. His book reflects a fluidity in doctrine and practice appropriate to a time before the Church had to grapple seriously with the great heresies.

It has been contended that *The Shepherd* in its angelology has contacts with that form of Jewish Christianity known as Ebionism. It is true that Hermas speaks of six chief angels but there is no indication that he regards the Son of God as a seventh, so making up the Ebionite number of seven angels (*Sim.* ix).

The number seven is nowhere used in his work—rather he speaks of twelve angels, six principal and six secondary ones. Hermas' Christology, while adoptionist in parts and reflecting early Roman speculation on the Person of Christ, is thoroughly Christian. The Son of God is older than all creation; was a fellow counsellor with the Father in the creation; is the rock on which the Church is built; and is the only name by which any can enter the Kingdom of God (*Sim.* ix. 12). Such is his firm background of Christian teaching.

*   *   *

The question of the relationship of *The Shepherd* to Judaism presents difficult problems to the investigator. In a work consisting of visions and which abounds in allusive references and allegories we should not expect, and indeed do not find, any direct quotations from the Old Testament. The only explicit quotation in the whole book is from the lost apocryphal book of Eldad and Modat (*Vis.* ii. 3) which is classed among the apocrypha in the Athanasian Synopsis and in the *Stichometry* of Nicephorus, but is not now extant. In his disuse of the Old Testament Hermas differs from his near contemporaries, Clement of Rome and the writer of Barnabas, whose Epistles are steeped in the language of the LXX and reflect a Jewish background. It seems probable that Clement, Bishop of Rome, came from Jewish stock and that the author of Barnabas was a converted Rabbi or Magid who brought into the Church the exegetical methods, and particularly the Rabbinical Midrashim, of the synagogue. *The Shepherd* reflects a different background. Hermas is not an exegete concerned to demonstrate the fulfilment of the Old Testament in the New Testament but a Christian prophet who, knowing the 'freedom of the spirit', was concerned to grapple with fundamental moral problems which were troubling the Roman Church—in particular the question of post-baptismal sin and the danger of close contact with pagan social influences. Hermas is not interested in Judaism as such. The Jewish nation and its privileges are never mentioned; neither is there anything about the distinction between Jew and Gentile—indeed an uninitiated reader of *The Shepherd* would not discover that the Jewish nation had ever existed. Michael is the guardian angel, not of the Jews, but of the Church. The twelve tribes refer not to the tribes of Israel, nor to the Apostles, but to the division of the human race into twelve nations (*Sim.* ix. 17). Hermas recognizes no ceremonial washings, as in Judaism, and his work is singularly free from formalism and rigorism. Christian baptism alone is the rite which is essential but this had no antecedent in Jewish circumcision. Such then is the comparative neglect of Jewish institutions and traditions.

Caution is however needed before we conclude that Hermas is anti-Jewish. The contacts, short of direct quotation, which the book shows with the Epistle of James, one of the most 'Jewish' writings in the New Testament, have been frequently noticed.[1] Moreover the argument from silence in regard to Jewish sources is always a precarious one and the more so in the case of a Christian prophet possessed of the visionary faculty. Hermas was dealing with practical problems of Church life [2], rather than with doctrinal niceties, and so the question of the fulfilment of the Old Testament in the coming of Christ did not come within his purview.

There are, I believe, indications in *The Shepherd* that Hermas was acquainted with Jewish teaching and traditions not found in the New Testament or early Christian literature—an interesting indication of the persistence of Jewish influence in the Church of the late first and early second centuries. Most of this teaching occurs in the *Mandates* and in the first five *Similitudes* which follow, which in their present form, appear as a Christianized version of the Old Testament moral code. In this part of Hermas' work very few personal or family references or precise indications of time or place occur, in comparison with *Vis*. i–iv. The writer is now drawing on a body of earlier teaching which had come down from the Jewish origins of the Church. We shall select just a few examples of this Jewish background.

The Emphasis on Truth

In *Mand*. iii. 1–2 the Shepherd says to Hermas:

'Love truth: and let all truth proceed from your mouth, that the spirit which God has made to dwell in this flesh may be found true by all men, and the Lord who dwells in you shall thus be glorified, for the Lord is true in every word and with him there is no lie. They therefore who lie set the Lord at nought, and become defrauders of the Lord, not restoring to him the deposit which they received. For they received from him a spirit free from lies. If they return this as a lying spirit, they have defiled the commandment of the Lord and have robbed him.'

Hermas is convicted by this revelation and weeps because he has 'never yet in his life spoken a true word'—a note of false humility. He is then told that he ought to have walked in truth as God's servant, that an evil conscience ought not to dwell with the spirit of truth; from henceforth he is to keep the whole truth that he may obtain life for himself.

---

[1] Whole sections are framed with a recollection of St. James' Epistle: e.g. *Vis*. iii. 9; *Mand*. ii, ix, xi; *Sim*. v. 4. Cf. also *Mand*. xii. 5, 6 = James iv. 7, 12; *Sim*. viii. 6 = James ii. 7.

[2] The best type of visionary and mystic is often an eminently practical person, e.g. Evelyn Underhill.

This teaching is different from that found in the Fourth Gospel where 'the truth' is the Christian revelation brought by and revealed in Jesus (Jn. i. 17, xiv. 6). For St. John there is no truth or love of truth apart from the Incarnate Son. In the *Mandates*, on the other hand, there is no mention of our Lord. Neither is loving and speaking the truth mentioned in the Old Testament decalogue although it is implied in the negative command not to bear false witness against one's neighbour. Moreover in the early Christian lists of virtues and vices found in the 'Two Ways' in *Did*. i–v and Barn. xviii–xx there is no mention of 'truth' among the precepts there listed which appear to be based on earlier Jewish Christian or Jewish catechetical teaching. However in Jewish tradition there are many examples of the 'truth' being identified directly with the *Torah* (the law) engraven on the heart [1] and in the Qumran Manual of Discipline iii. 13–iv. 26, which appears to be a sermon accompanying the reading of the *Torah* by the priests of the sect, we have a close parallel to this section of *The Shepherd*. We are told that God appointed Two Spirits—the spirits of truth and error. The origin of truth lies in the Abode of Light and that of error in the realm of darkness. These Two Spirits struggle for possession of the heart of man; 'an abomination to truth are deeds of error, and an abomination to error are all ways of truth. And contentious jealousy is on all their judgements, for they do not walk together'. While Hermas' theology does not have the dualistic emphasis of the Qumran sect there is nevertheless a correspondence between the earlier Jewish teaching and his idea of the 'truth' as being due to the activity of the spirit of truth within the human heart. There is an inwardness and a mystical side to Hermas' teaching which is similar to that found at Qumran; it is different from the more external and legalistic form which Jewish and Jewish Christian teaching later took in the 'Two Ways'. This we will now consider.

The Two Angels and the Two Ways or Paths

The metaphor of two ways of life, or two paths, which men can choose to follow, is a familiar one in classical literature where it can be traced in the 'antitheses' of Heraclitus, in Hesiod, Theognis and Xenophon; in the Old Testament it is found in Deut. xi. 26 ff., xxx. 15–19; Jer. xxi. 8; and in Ps. i. This metaphor was taken up by Our Lord in his famous saying recorded in Mt. vii. 13–14, 'Enter ye in by the narrow gate: for wide is the gate, and broad is the way, that leadeth to destruction, and many be they that enter in thereby.

---

[1] In Samaritan 'the Verity' (*Qushtah*) is a common term for the Law and in Mandaean thought Truth (*Kushta*) is virtually mystic revelation. See T. H. Gaster, *The Scriptures of the Dead Sea Sect*, p. 305.

For narrow is the gate, and straitened the way, that leadeth unto life, and few be they that find it.' In this teaching the emphasis is on the outward following of the straight and narrow *path*, the way of life or light, and the avoidance of the opposite path. There is a similar emphasis in *Mand.* vi. 2: 'For that which is righteous has a straight path, but that which is unrighteous a crooked path. But do you walk in the straight path, but leave the crooked path alone.' This could easily be taken as another version of the familiar *verba Christi*; cf. also John xi. 9–10. But in *Mand.* vi. 2. 1, ff. Hermas introduces the conception of two angels with man, one of righteousness, one of wickedness, who dwell in men's hearts causing good and evil dispositions. In reply to the Angel of Repentance Hermas says:

'How then, sir, said I, shall I know their workings, because both angels dwell with me? Listen, said he, and understand them. The Angel of righteousness is delicate and modest and meek and gentle. When, then, he comes into your heart he at once speaks with you of righteousness, of purity, or reverence, of self-control, of every righteous deed, and of all glorious virtues. When all these things come into your heart, know that the angel of righteousness is with you.'

Then follows a list of the dispositions caused by the presence of the Angel of Wickedness; ill temper (was this one of Hermas' failings —he often mentions it?), bitterness, desire of many deeds, overeating and drinking, desire for women, covetousness, haughtiness and pride. Hermas is then commanded 'to follow the angel of righteousness, but to keep away from the angel of wickedness'. (*Mand.* vi. 2. 9.)

This conception of the Two Angels or Impulses, one good, one evil, (also found in *Mand.* xii. 1) finds an exact parallel in the Rabbinic *yetzer ha-tob* and *yetzer ha-ra* mentioned in many Jewish writings (e.g., Ecclus. xv. 11–14, IV Ezra iii. 21, iv. 30 ff.; Test. Asher i. 6). The general view among the Rabbis was that the sphere where the struggle for mastery between good and evil impulses occurred was the heart, which stood for the volitional and intellectual elements in man. It was a man's will and mind which the evil impulse attacked, urging him to all kinds of sin. The chief means of protection against this impulse was the study of the *Torah*. Thus 'In the school of R. Ishmael it was taught: If this abomination meets you, drag it to the House of Study; if it is hard as stone it will be crushed; if it is hard as iron, it will be broken in pieces'. (B. Kidd. 30b.) There can be little doubt that behind the 'Two Angels' and 'Two Desires' of Hermas is much earlier Jewish teaching. The discovery of the Dead Sea Scrolls has confirmed this for, as we have already mentioned, in

Manual of Discipline iii. 13–iv. 26 Two Spirits are described as struggling for possession of men's hearts and the lists of virtues and vices (the latter perhaps based on the *Vidui* of the Day of Atonement) associated with the Two Spirits bear a general resemblance to Hermas' lists—indeed almost all the virtues and vices he mentions can be paralleled at Qumran.

A further confirmation of Hermas' Jewish background is provided by his frequent use of the word 'double-mindedness' in connexion with that disunity of the heart which renders a man vulnerable to the assaults of temptation. (*Vis.* ii. 2. 4; iii. 7. 1; *Mand.* x. 1. 2, 2. 4). It is double-mindedness which causes men to forsake the true way and those who do so are following evil desires. Behind Hermas' use of this word lies the familiar Rabbinic teaching of the two *yetzarim* or impulses already mentioned.

What is interesting is the presence of Jewish traditions and ways of thought in the Church of Rome in the late first and early second centuries. Judaism had a far greater influence on the developing thought of the early Church than is often realized—even on writers who show no great interest in Judaism. As Père Daniélou has said, 'much of the theology of the early Church came out of a late Jewish environment'.

The Emphasis on Jewish Monotheism and the Fear of God

Mand. i. 1–2 reads:

'First of all believe that God is one, "who made all things and perfected them, and made all things to be out of that which was not", and contains all things, and is himself alone uncontained. Believe then in him, and fear him, and in your fear be continent. Keep these things, and you shall cast away from yourself all wickedness, and shall put on every virtue of righteousness, and shall live to God, if you keep his commandment.'

It is significant that in this introductory Mandate there is no command to love God, no mention of the Trinity, as might be expected in a Christian work which nowhere directly quotes the Old Testament, but rather a free expansion of the Decalogue's 'Thou shalt have none other Gods but Me'. The mention of the creation *ex nihilo* appears to be based on 2 Macc. vii. 28 and Wisd. i. 14.

The command to believe and fear the One God is characteristically Jewish and is reiterated throughout the *Mandates*. Indeed a whole Mandate (vii) is devoted to this commandment . . . 'the fear of the Lord is mighty and great and glorious'. Hermas even states that people with 'might' or 'power' gain the fear of the Lord (*Mand.* vii. 2). Nowhere does love or meekness balance fear as in the New Testament writings. In this Hermas is at one with the Old Testament and Jewish tradition (cf. Ps. cxi. 10; Ecclus. xl. 26; *Pirqe Aboth* iii. 13).

Life

The Shepherd many times states that those who keep the commandments will 'live unto God'—a theme constantly reiterated throughout the work. Indeed almost every Mandate ends with this phrase. There is nothing in the book to connect this 'living with God' with the work of Christ as in the Johannine literature. Hermas never states that this life is the gift of God mediated through Jesus Christ. It would seem that he is here drawing on a Jewish background of thought. Thus Prov. viii. 35 says of the Divine Wisdom: 'Whoso findeth me findeth life, and shall obtain favour of the Lord'. In Judaism the *Torah* was the supreme means of life for men; so Ecclus. xvii. 11: 'He added unto them knowledge, and gave them a law of life for a heritage.' 'The more a man studies and obeys the commands of the *Torah* the more life he has' (saying ascribed to Hillel). 'As oil is life for the world, so also are words of *Torah* life for the world' (*Deut. Rabba* vii. 3). It is true that the idea of life is also found in Hellenistic religions and philosophical thought—indeed a fundamental principle of Gnostic thought is that only the bestowal of knowledge can give life. But in Hellenistic thought life is not obtained through the keeping of God's commandments, as is constantly stated by Hermas. It therefore seems probable that his emphasis on 'life' and 'living unto God' comes from his familiarity with Jewish ways of thought.

The Holy Spirit represented by Virgins

Hermas, as a Christian prophet, emphasizes the work of the Holy Spirit. Nevertheless there are indications of Jewish influence at work in the way he depicts the Third Person of the Trinity. The Hebrew for Spirit (*ruach*) being feminine, the Spirit was sometimes represented symbolically as a woman. Hermas goes further and resolves the one woman into seven in *Vis.* iii. and into twelve Virgins in *Sim.* ix. These by their plurality represent the distributions of the Holy Ghost although their oneness and significance are carefully indicated by the expression, 'clothed in the Holy Spirit of these Virgins' (*Sim.* ix. 24. 2).

*   *   *

Hermas presents something of an enigma to the student of the early Church. Many scholars openly describe him as dull, pious, stupid and vague—a perfect example of mediocrity. So W. J. Wilson can write: 'If such men as Hermas had become the real leaders of Christianity, if such books as his had made up the New Testament, the Church could hardly have survived. For the intellectual quality of its leadership has been one large secret of Christianity's success.'[1] This is to underestimate Hermas' achievements. He is in close contact with the Christian life as it was being lived by ordinary Church members in the Church of Rome and gives us a valuable insight into what people were thinking and the way they were behaving. No sadness or difficulty can quench his incurable optimism. There can be little doubt that his power of vivid narration and description, his moral earnestness and sincerity, his power of perseverance through trials which would have crushed a lesser man, ensured that his name would not be forgotten and that his literary work would gain a wide popularity among the rank and file of the Church. Hermas is no theologian and what theology there is in his book is confused. We cannot visualize him pondering the Epistle to the Romans or finding solace in the thought of a Tertullian or a Cyprian. He was essentially a visionary and prophet who sought to express, sometimes in quaint language, what he had 'seen'. These visions were real to him—the very stuff of inspiration—and he copied them down in a state of intense exaltation, although before his work reached its present literary form his visions passed through a stage of conscious reflection. During this time Hermas also drew upon much Jewish traditional teaching, known in the Hellenistic synagogues, which had come down in the tradition of the Roman Church. He must not be judged too harshly or by ecclesiastical standards of a later age. It was not only the powerful and lucid thinkers, the great doctors, the masters of ecclesiastical organization, who shaped the history and thought of the early Church. It was also men of the type of Hermas, who had seen visions and dreamed dreams, who powerfully influenced the current of Christian life. Diversity of gifts, rather than a colourless uniformity, often within the one Christian community, was the rule rather than the exception in those early days.

[1] HTR 20 (1927), p. 35.

XII

THE ENIGMA OF THE EPISTLE TO DIOGNETUS

The *Epistula ad Diognetum* is one of the most enigmatic writings which have come down from Christian antiquity. No one has yet succeeded in opening the lock which will reveal the origin of a work which, on the grounds of style and thought, has been accorded such high praise by Classical and Christian scholars. Much labour has been expended on this 'pearl of the patristic age' without decisive result. Our concern is to consider afresh the question of the integrity of the Epistle, to see if some progress can be made, and then to offer some remarks on authorship and date which are closely connected with the first problem.

The Problem of Chs. xi–xii

Cod. Argent. 9 (the Strassburg MS) shows a lacuna at the close of Ch. x (after ὅταν ἐκεῖνο τὸ πῦρ ἐπιγνῷς) and has a marginal note 'here the copy had a break'. There was a gap of half a line in this MS, fifteen letter spaces in the Tübingen transcript, and in the latter the line was completed, after the break, by the first two words of Ch. xi. It is a profitless task to fill the gap although speculation has not been wanting on the part of those advocating the integrity of the Epistle or a change of authorship at this point. The apparent incongruity of Chs. xi–xii with the rest of the Epistle, first noted by Stephanus, has been widely accepted and indeed some editors only print Chs. i–x in their editions.[1] The case for the separation of Chs. xi–xii from i–x rests on these considerations:

(A) Chs. i–x are addressed to an earnest seeker after the truth (undoubtedly a pagan) whose enquiries are answered point by point. In Chs. xi–xii there is no suggestion of this earnest pagan; on the contrary these chapters deal with the blessings of friendship with the Logos, as embodied in the Church, and have in view catechumens,—'those who are becoming disciples of the truth' (xi. 1). The strong emphasis on the Church, on γνῶσις and on mysticism is not evident in Chs. i–x.

(B) There is a difference in the attitude adopted towards Judaism. In Chs. i–x the Jewish Sabbath, circumcision, fasts, festivals,

[1] So Wilamowitz-Moellendorff (3rd edn. 1906); Geffcken (1942); Blakeney (1943).

dietary laws and sacrifices are ridiculed and rejected,[1] as in the Epistle of Barnabas, and no appeal is made to any fulfilment of Old Testament prophecy; whereas in xi. 6 the Law and the Prophets are placed on the same level as the Gospels and the tradition of the Apostles.

(3) Chs. i–x, while showing reminiscences of the New Testament, have no direct citations; xii. 5 exactly quotes 1 Cor. viii. 1 which is ascribed to 'the Apostle'.

(4) Chs. xi–xii give the impression that they are a portion of a homily with vestiges of metrical form, while Chs. i–x are a tract in epistolary form exhibiting a high literary skill addressed to an educated pagan but probably intended for a wider circle.

(5) Differences of vocabulary and style exist between the two parts of the Epistle, e.g., particles, plentiful in i–x, are rather limited in Chs. xi–xii. Thus τε καί, γε, δή, ἄν do not appear and ὡς only once. Chs. xi–xii use the prepositions and conjunctions ἄνευ, διό, εἶτα, μετά which are not found in i–x. Some favourite words of the author in i–x, such as ἴδιος, λοιπός, θεοσέβεια do not appear in xi–xii.[2]

Armed with these facts scholars have not been slow to argue for differences of authorship. Bunsen [3] was the first to assign the authorship of Chs. xi–xii to Hippolytus and he has been followed by many later writers. The late Dom Connolly argued forcibly for the view that Chs. xi–xii are the lost ending of Hippolytus' *Philosophumena* [4]; H. G. Meecham held that the author of these chapters belonged to a school of thought represented by Melito and Hippolytus.[5]

In all these attempts to solve the enigma of *ad Diognetum* it would appear that insufficient attention has been paid to a simple fact which, after so much expenditure of effort, proved to be the correct solution of another patristic puzzle, viz., Polycarp's Epistle to the Philippians. Harrison [6] showed that that Epistle comprised two distinct works by Polycarp belonging to different periods in his life and *presupposing different situations*. Chs. xiii–xiv of Polyc. *ad Phil.* was a covering letter to a collection of the Ignatian Epistles, written while Ignatius was still alive, while Chs. i–xii was a later letter

[1] See especially iii. 5, iv. 1–6.
[2] H. G. Meecham, *The Epistle to Diognetus*, pp. 65–66.
[3] *Hippolytus and His Age*, I, p. 414 ff.
[4] JTS 37, pp. 2–15.
[5] Op. cit., p. 67.
[6] *Polycarp's Two Epistles to the Philippians* (1936). This theory has been widely accepted; see Chapter 4 of this book.

written to the Philippians after Ignatius' death, dealing, at their request, with certain problems which had arisen in their community. The two letters, originally distinct, had become fused together in the course of MS transmission.

Let us now take another look at *ad Diognetum* with this in mind. To test our theory we will consider the case for the separation of the two parts of the Epistle enumerated above:

(1) This hypothesis accounts satisfactorily for this objection. Chs. i–x are a tract with educated pagan objections to Christianity in mind, i.e., the writer had both an apologetic and a propagandist purpose, viz., to commend the Christian faith and to assert its distinctiveness and newness relative to older faiths and religious practices. Chs. xi–xii, on the other hand, are clearly addressed *to Christians*. The writer alludes obliquely to the fact that he is also a 'teacher of the heathen' (xi. 1a) but his concern is with catechumens of an advanced stage: 'I administer worthily that which has been handed down to those who are becoming disciples of the truth' (xi. 1b). The writer also has in view full disciples (πιστοί) who receive revelation from the Logos (xi. 2); these apparently are the ἅγιοι of xi. 4–5. xi. 5 suggests that these chapters are a homily, or part of a homily, belonging to a Feast of the Church. But we cannot be sure that the reference to 'the eternal one, who today is accounted a Son' (xi. 5) is alluding to the Feast of the Nativity, as in early times this had not been separated from other Christian Festivals. In the pre-Nicene period there was only one feast, the Pascha,[1] which in liturgy and theology fused together the historical 'moments' of the Incarnation, Passion, Resurrection and Ascension. That Chs. xi–xii of *ad Diognetum* is a homily belonging to the Paschal Vigil is suggested by the liturgical close in xii. 9, 'Salvation is set forth, and apostles are given understanding, and the Passover of the Lord advances, and the seasons [2] are brought together, and are harmonized with the world, and the Word teaches the saints and rejoices, and through it the Father is glorified; to whom be glory forever. Amen.' This would then link up with xi. 6, 'Then is the fear of the Law sung, and the grace of the Prophets known, the faith of the Gospels is established, and the tradition of apostles is guarded, and the grace of the Church exults.'

[1] F. L. Cross, *1 Peter: A Paschal Liturgy* (1954).
[2] Reading καιροί with Sylburg; but if κηροί is read (Otto) then the reference is to wax tapers used on Easter Day in connexion with the Paschal Candle. Cf. the homily ascribed to Cyril of Jerusalem on the Feast of Hypapante; Migne P.G. 33. 1187.

The differences in milieu and audience addressed in Chs. i–x and xi–xii also accounts for the difference in subject matter in the two sections. We should hardly expect the writer to refer to the beauty and order of the life of the Church or to the Apostles in an apology addressed to an educated pagan enquirer who had had no experience of the Church. It would be equally nonsensical for a Christian today in addressing scientists to extol institutional Christianity without first preparing the way by seeking some common ground.

The emphasis which the writer places on γνῶσις in Chs. xi–xii is accounted for by the needs of catechumens and members of the Christian community gathered together for the Paschal Feast. γνῶσις was the catchword of Gnosticism, then rearing its head in the Christian communities. Christians needed to know that true knowledge and true life go together (xii. 4)—a thoroughly Johannine idea. The writer has grasped the truth of the *verba Christi* 'by their fruits ye shall know them' (Mt. vii. 20). It is quite unnecessary to argue for the separate authorship of Chs. i–x and xi–xii because xi–xii emphasize the subjective, mystical side of γνῶσις, coupled with the idea of the Church as the home of grace, instruction and worship, while i–x deal more with the moral and spiritual elevation brought into the world by Christianity. Both were addressed to different audiences possibly at different times.

(2) It is true that the attitude towards Judaism in Chs. i–x is deprecatory. But it is no different from that found in the Epistle of Barnabas and the Apology of Aristides. There was a theological strain in the early Church which did not see in Judaism a *praeparatio evangelica* for the Gospel but rather a religion which had been wholly superseded by the coming of Christianity into the world. Thus the peculiar practices of Judaism were not those appropriate to Old Testament times but a sign that the Jews had been misled by an evil angel (cf. Barn. ix. 4). It is however worth noting that the writer to Diognetus does acknowledge the monotheistic faith of the Jews (ii. 2)—it was their method of worship and their religious practices which he believed to be ridiculous and unworthy of defending (iv. 1) in an apology addressed to the educated pagan world. In a tract such as this it would have been inappropriate to have quoted Old Testament texts in support of his argument *adversus Judaeos* because his readers would not have known the LXX. In this the writer differs from the author of the Epistle of Barnabas who is addressing a *Christian* community of mixed racial com-

position [1] in which the LXX would have been quite familiar. It was natural for him to buttress his arguments *adversus Judaeos* with texts from their own scriptures.

Chs. xi–xii of *ad Diognetum*, on the other hand, comprised a homily which the same writer addressed to catechumens (who were perhaps on the verge of their baptisms) as well as to instructed Christians who were assembled for the Pascha which culminated in the Paschal Vigil, Baptisms and Easter Eucharist. It was natural, on this occasion, to refer to the Law, the Prophets, the Gospels and the tradition of the Apostles (xi. 6), for lections from these would be read on this solemn yet joyous occasion. There is no suggestion in xi. 6 that the writer is advocating progressive revelation while denying this in Chs. i–x. Rather he is referring to Christian Worship, the *raison d'être* of the Pascha, while he gives his views concerning Judaism, in the light of the 'newness' of the Christian Faith, in Chs. i–x.

(3) This objection is easily dealt with. No author would directly cite New Testament books unless his readers had some point of contact with them. In Chs. i–x reminiscences of the New Testament appear without exact quotations because the author cannot assume that his readers know the New Testament or are familiar with its leading ideas. In xii. 5, however, in a homily expressly intended for Christians, the author can quote 1 Corinthians and refer to 'the apostle' knowing full well that he will be understood. A further point is that Chs. i–x may date from a time before the New Testament Canon had come into existence and the New Testament writings had circulated widely.

(4) We have dealt with this objection above.

(5) The differences of vocabulary and style between the two sections of the Epistle are largely to be accounted for by differences of subject matter and audience addressed. The argument as to the absence of favourite words in Chs. xi–xii is particularly precarious. Dom Andriessen, in his remarkable studies, states that 'a difference of style is out of the question. Considering the richness of ideas, the percentage of new words occurring in the epilogue is extremely low.' [2] As with the comparative study of the New Testament Epistles, no sure conclusion can be drawn from the very slight differences in style and vocabulary between Chs. i–x and xi–xii.

---

[1] This may be inferred from Barn. iii. 6 where the variant readings ἐπήλυτοι ℵ, προσήλυτοι C, proselytae L all mean proselytes.

[2] See especially VC 1, p. 136.

Having queried some of the long-standing objections to unity of authorship the reader will wish to know what positive indications there are that the same hand is to be discerned in Chs. i–x and xi–xii. In two separate works addressed to different audiences we should not necessarily expect close correspondence; nevertheless the following points seem to me significant:

(a) the conception of the Logos is the same in both sections of the Epistle although the title itself is only used in Chs. xi–xii. In both the Logos appears as the correlative to Reason in man. Cf. vii. 2: ἀλλ' αὐτὸς ἀληθῶς ὁ παντοκράτωρ καὶ παντοκτίστης καὶ ἀόρατος θεός, αὐτὸς ἀπ' οὐρανῶν τὴν ἀλήθειαν καὶ τὸν λόγον τὸν ἅγιον καὶ ἀπερινόητον ἀνθρώποις ἐνίδρυσε καὶ ἐγκατεστήριξε ταῖς καρδίαις αὐτῶν, with xii. 7, ἤτω σοὶ καρδία γνῶσις, ζωὴ δὲ λόγος ἀληθής, χωρούμενος. However, it is in the homily addressed to Christians (Chs. xi–xii) that the author has most to say about the Logos. In noble language he extols the blessings brought by the Word; 'He was from the beginning, and appeared new, and was proved to be old, and is ever young, as He is born in the hearts of the saints' (xi. 4).

It is to be noted that neither section of the Epistle has anything to say about the Holy Spirit—a sure indication of a second century date. In this the author is in line with the other second century apologists [1] who either ignore the Spirit or ascribe to the Son the functions of the Spirit.

(b) Both Chs. i–x and xi–xii of *ad Diognetum* are indebted directly or indirectly to the Johannine theology. The most striking example in Chs. i–x is vi. 3: καὶ Χριστιανοὶ ἐν κόσμῳ οἰκοῦσιν οὐκ εἰσὶ δὲ ἐκ τοῦ κόσμου; cf. John. xvii. 11: καὶ αὐτοὶ ἐν τῷ κόσμῳ εἰσίν, 14: οὐκ εἰσὶν ἐκ τοῦ κόσμου.
Cf. also vi. 5 with Jn. xv. 19, xvii. 14
      vii. 4–5 with Jn. iii. 17, xii. 47
      ix. 1 with Jn. iii. 5
      x. 2 with Jn. ii. 16, 1 Jn. iv. 9
      x. 3 with 1 Jn. i. 4, iv. 19.
The same indebtedness is found in Chs. xi–xii. Thus xi. 2, οἷς ἐφανέρωσεν ὁ λόγος φανείς has a Johannine ring. Cf. also xi. 4 with 1 Jn. i. 1, xii. 9 with Jn. xiii. 31, xiv. 13.

Although the degree of literary dependence is not clear there is little doubt that the writer was familiar with the theological ideas of both the Fourth Gospel and 1 John.[2] No indication of place of

[1] See especially Theophilus *ad Autol.* ii. 10. Cf. the remarks of Meecham, op. cit., pp. 50–51.
[2] J. N. Sanders. *The Fourth Gospel in the Early Church* (1943), p. 19.

composition can however be inferred from this as the tenets of the Johannine theology were widely known in the second century, e.g., at Ephesus, Antioch and Alexandria.

(c) The term πίστις is used in Chs. i–x and xi–xii with the same connotation, i.e., belief in the divine revelation as a basis of true knowledge (vii. 6, x. 1). This is a more formalized belief than the Pauline idea of justification, as the object of faith, God or Christ, is not specified. In Chs. xi–xii πίστις is similarly used. Thus in xi. 2 the knowledge of the mysteries of the Father comes to the disciples who are πιστοί.[2] In xi. 5–6 the term πίστις becomes even more objective and is virtually equated with a system of belief.

There would therefore appear to be no insuperable objections to regarding Chs. i–x and xi–xii of *ad Diognetum* as coming from the same writer. The first letter is an apologetic and propagandist tract addressed to the pagan, and perhaps the Stoic, world with a definite enquirer in mind; Chs. xi–xii is a homily, or part of a homily, addressed to catechumens and Christians at the Paschal Vigil. The fact that two separate works by the same author were fused together, perhaps with a connecting link now lost, should cause no surprise to students of MS transmission. We have already cited the example of Polycarp's Epistle to the Philippians and others come readily to mind. Many scholars believe that 2 Corinthians is composite, an earlier and shorter letter (Chs. x–xiii) having been joined to a later one (Chs. i–ix); moreover there is a strong case for believing that 2 Timothy contains earlier notes of genuine Pauline material. Another instance of fusion is provided by Tertullian's *de præscriptione haereticorum* where Chs. 1–44 and the first two sentences of Ch. 45 belong to a different document from the rest of the work. Many examples of MS fusion are found in the papyri; e.g., P. Tebtunis 705 contains a letter from one Theogenes to Apollonius enclosing a copy of a letter written by Theogenes to Tothoës; P. Berol 13989 [2] contains four private letters written continuously.

DATE AND AUTHORSHIP

We now pass briefly to the vexed question of date and authorship. Almost every conceivable name and date has been canvassed for *ad Diognetum*. Marcion (Bunsen and Buonaiuti), Clement of Rome (Baratier), Apollos (Gallandi), Aristides (Kihn), Apelles (Dräseke), Lucian (Chapman), Ambrosius (Birks), Hippolytus (Con-

[1] This is well brought out by Meecham, op. cit., p. 52.
[2] G. Manteuffel, *Epistulae Privatae Ineditae* (1927), pp. 214ff.

nolly), Theophilus of Antioch (Ogara), Quadratus (Dorner and Andriessen), Pantaenus (Marrou) have all had their supporters. Similarly dates ranging from the first to the eighth and ninth centuries have been suggested, some supported by fantastic arguments. The most learned and exhaustive recent study of the problem is that of Dom P. Andriessen in a series of articles [1] purporting to show that *ad Diognetum* is the lost Apology of Quadratus which he presented to the Emperor Hadrian (Eus.*E.H.* iv. 3), who is the Diognetus mentioned in Ch. i. This theory, in spite of the immense thoroughness of the author's work, goes beyond the evidence—too much has to be inferred from the one fragment of Quadratus' Apology which has survived. In fact we have no means of determining the length of the break in the MS in Diogn. vii. 6–7; neither is it certain that Quadratus, the first Christian Apologist, was the same person as the Bishop of Athens—and an Athenian milieu is essential for Andriessen's theory. The Eleusinian influence allegedly present in the Epistle seems particularly far-fetched. We must confess that the author of this Epistle, like the Diognetus to whom it is addressed, and the place where he wrote, are likely to elude identification unless further MS discoveries are made. However we can be sure that the author was a Christian of cultured mind, with a Classical training, who was possessed of a considerable literary skill and style. It is not for nothing that *ad Diognetum* has been ranked 'among the finest remains of Christian Antiquity' (Neander); 'after Scripture the finest monument we know of sound Christian feeling, noble courage, and manly eloquence' (Bunsen); 'the noblest of early Christian writings' (Lightfoot); 'one of the most brilliant things ever written by Christians in the Greek Language' (Norden). It is also certain that the author belonged to a Church in close contact with cultured pagan enquirers, yet which had a strong worshipping life of its own. He was of sufficient importance in this Christian community to compose a homily for the Paschal celebration.

As to the Epistle's date I believe that we are on more solid ground. There is however no sure internal evidence, as the references to persecution are vague in character. Nevertheless more general considerations may not be without value. The writer's attitude towards Judaism in Chs. i–x is more extreme than that found in the New Testament and other second century Apologists. Yet it finds an exact parallel in the Epistle of Barnabas and, like that tract, appears to reflect the outlook of the period when the Church and synagogue had come into irreconcilable conflict, i.e., A.D. 70–135. In this period, and especially after A.D. 100, Jewish Christians were

[1] RTAM 13 (1946), pp. 5–39, 125–49, 237–60; 14 (1947), pp. 121–56; VC 1, pp. 129–36.

expelled from the synagogues and were not allowed to observe the practices of their ancestral faith. In particular the promulgation of the *Birkhathha-Minim* hardened the opposition between the two groups. Moreover there is no indication in Diogn. i–x that a sacred Canon of New Testament writings had yet been established or that these possessed any special authority. Recent discoveries from Nag Hammadi [1] have shown that the New Testament Canon was beginning to come into existence by *c*. A.D. 140 and I should therefore date Chs. i–x of this Epistle not later than *c*. A.D. 130. On the other hand the use of the Johannine theology indicates that it should not be placed much before this. Some further considerations support this date. The Christology of Chs. i–x is more simple and undeveloped that that of Justin or Origen. The lack of reference to the Holy Spirit is noticeable, as is the absence of asceticism and sacerdotalism. The Epistle dates from a time when a lively faith in Christ's presence (παρουσία) [2] existed in the Church. In accord with this, Christianity is spoken of as a recent, new thing; Christians are a new class; Jesus has been 'now' set forth (Chs. i, ii, ix).

The date of the author's Paschal homily is more difficult to determine. I incline to think that it is slightly later than Chs. i–x. Nevertheless the Church is still in its first stage (xii. 9); revelation is still a present fact and knowledge of the Logos is personal and profound (xi. 5). The writer's antipathy to Judaism is pushed into the background as he discourses to Christians gathered together for the supreme festival of the Christian year. He would have his hearers become sharers with him of the love of revealed things (xi. 8). A date *c*. A.D. 140 would not be out of keeping for this homily.[3] In any event the Epistle can hardly be later than the age of Justin Martyr.

[1] E.g. *The Gospel of Truth.*
[2] vii. 6, 9.
[3] The parallels cited by Connolly, JTS 37, pp. 4–12, and Campbell Bonner, *A Homily on the Passion by Melito, Bishop of Sardis* (1940), pp. 60–62, with Hippolytus and Melito seem too slight to warrant any certainty in the matter. H. I. Marrou's view, in his excellent edition in the *Sources Chrétiennes* series, p. 259, that the Epistle dates from *c*. A.D. 200 also appears to be precluded by the above evidence.

INDEX

I CLEMENT

i. 1	9, 12
i. 3	37
i–vii	12
iv–vi	10–11, 12
vi. 4–vii. 1	15
vii. 1	11, 12
xxi. 8	36
xxxvii. 1–3	16
xlvii. 6	11
lix–lxi. 3	16
lx	138
lx. 4–lxi. 2	17, 18

II CLEMENT

ii. 3	125
xiii	99
xiv	155

IGNATIUS

ad. Eph.

iv. 1	22
iv. 2	22
x. 1–3	22
xii. 2	28, 31, 38
xvii. 1	22
xviii. 2	3, 75, 81
xix. 1	26
xx. 2	28

ad Magn.

iii. 1	38
viii. 1	23, 24, 25
viii. 2	26
viii–xi	23
ix. 1	23
x. 3	22, 23, 26
xi	23
xi. 1	24

ad Trall.

viii. 1–2	24
ix. 1–2	3, 75
xi. 1	22, 24
xi. 1–2	22

ad Rom.

Inscr.	27
iii. 3	22

iv. 3	28, 31
v. 1	19, 28

ad Phil.

i. 2	22
ii. 2	3
iii. 1	24, 27
vi. 1	22, 25
vii. 2	3
viii. 1	24
viii. 2	25

ad Smyrn.

i. 1–2	3, 75
i.–vii	34
iii. 2	3
vi. 2	24
vii. 1	28
ix. 1	24

POLYCARP

ad Phil.

i. 1	33
i–xii	31–39, 166
ii. 1	3, 73
ii. 3	3
iii. 1	34
iii. 2	38
iv	34
iv. 2	36
v	34
v. 3	37
vi	34
vi. 3	2
vii	33, 35, 38
vii. 1	34
vii. 2	3
viii	34
ix	32
ix. 2	32
x. 2	37
xi	34
xi. 1–2	37
xi. 3	31
xii. 1	2
xiii	31–33, 38
xiii. 2	38
xiii–xiv	35, 37, 166
xiv	31, 33

Martyr. Polyc.

ix	14
x	22
xiii	39

DIDACHE

i. 1	84
i. 3	102
i. 3b–ii. 1	102–5
i. 5	102, 105
i–iv	103, 104, 158
i–v	82, 93
i–vi	93
ii. 4	102
iii. 3	104
iii. 7–8	102
iv. 8	103
iv. 9	36
v	104
v. 1	96
vi	104
viii	102
viii. 2	100
ix. 5	100
x. 3	103
x. 6	131
xi	155
xi. 2	100
xi. 4	100
xi. 8	100
xi. 11	104
xiii. 3	102
xv. 4	100
xvi. 1	100
xvi. 6	102
xvi. 7	100

EPISTLE OF BARNABAS

i	33
i. 1–5	54
i. 4	84
i. 5	50, 90
i. 6	79
i. 7	50, 91
i. 8	54
i–iv	70

INDEX

i–xvii	47, 93	vi. 12	132	xiv. 1	134
ii. 3	70	vi. 13	77	xiv. 1–3	133
ii. 3–4	50, 90	vi. 14	77, 80, 83	xiv. 1–4	79, 126
ii. 4–8	67	vi. 16	84	xiv. 1–9	79
ii. 4–10	54, 127	vi. 17	77, 83	xiv. 3	48
ii. 5	129	vii	133	xiv. 4	54
ii. 6	83	vii. 1–11	47	xiv. 4–5	66
ii. 8	68	vii. 2	74, 82	xiv. 5	66
ii. 9	83	vii. 8	47	xiv. 5–7	80
ii. 10	68, 83	vii. 9	69	xiv. 5–8	79
ii–iii	133	vii. 11	75	xiv. 6	84, 134
iii. 1–6	54	viii	133	xv. 1–2	133
iii. 6	126, 134, 169	vii. 1–2	47	xv. 1–9	47, 129
iv	48	viii. 1–7	46	xv. 4	47
iv. 1–2	89	viii. 5	47, 134	xv. 5	67
iv. 3	71	viii. 7	134	xv. 6	134
iv. 4–5	63	ix	129	xv. 8	78, 129
iv. 6	54, 134	ix. 1–3	129, 133	xv. 8–9	88
iv. 7	54	ix. 4	54, 130, 168	xv. 9	78, 82
iv. 7–8	65, 69, 79, 126	ix. 4–5	130	xvi. 1	64, 65
iv. 8	48	ix. 5	133	xvi. 1–2	54, 64, 134
iv. 9	47, 54, 70	ix. 7–9	133	xvi. 1–3	133
iv. 11	50, 90	ix. 8	46–8, 50, 91	xvi. 2	64, 92
iv. 14	2, 3	ix. 9	47	xvi. 3–4	49, 63, 88
v	134	x	70, 133	xvi. 4	63
v. 2	134	x. 3–5	134	xvi. 5	54
v. 3	79, 90	x. 5	89	xvi. 6	70
v. 3–4	49, 87	x. 10	47	xvi. 6–10	62
v. 4	50, 90	x. 11	79	xvi. 7	64
v. 5	69, 132	xi	80	xvi. 8	80, 81
v. 5–6	3	xi. 1–7	80	xvi. 9	48
v. 6–7	76, 82	xi. 1–11	46, 80	xvi. 10	50, 90
v. 7	54, 90	xi. 2	83	xvii. 7	84
v. 10	47	xi. 2–3	133	xvii. 8	84
v. 11	66, 69, 134	xi. 8	81, 83	xvii. 9–10	69
v. 14	77, 120	xi. 11	79–81	xviii. 1	48, 50, 84, 90, 130
v. 12–14	134	xii	133		
v–xvi	70	xii. 1	134	xviii. 1–2	94
vi. 1	134	xii. 1–11	47, 69	xviii–xx	47, 70, 82, 93, 159
vi. 1–11	46	xii. 2–9	79		
vi. 2	76	xii. 4	134	xix. 1	50, 90
vi. 2–3	77, 120	xii. 10–11	131, 134	xix. 2	79, 89, 103
vi. 2–4	76, 115, 117, 120–2, 134	xiii	127, 133	xix. 2–7a	94
		xiii. 1	54, 90, 125, 134	xix. 5	82
vi. 3	76	xiii. 1–6	122	xix. 6	89
vi. 4	77	xiii. 1–7	47	xix. 7	82
vi. 6–7	134	xiii. 2	126	xix. 7b	95
vi. 7	69, 74, 75	xiii. 2–3	127	xix. 8	90
vi. 8	47, 77, 83	xiii. 4	126	xix. 9	95
vi. 8–17	79	xiii. 4–5	127	xix. 10	82, 103
vi. 9	50, 83, 91	xiii. 5	126	xx. 1	47, 96
vi. 10	70, 77, 83	xiii. 6	126, 134	xxi	70
vi. 11	70, 80, 83	xiii. 7	50, 91	xxi. 5	70

INDEX

xxi. 5-9	54	EPISTLE TO	
xxi. 9	79	DIOGNETUS	

SHEPHERD OF HERMAS

Vis.
i. 1	152
i. 2.2	154
i. 4.1	154
i-iv	158
ii. 2	152
ii. 2.4	161
ii. 3	157
ii. 4	153, 155
ii. 4.3	9
iii	162
iii. 1	153
iii. 1-2	154
iii. 2.5	152
iii. 6	152
iii. 7.1	161
iii. 8	153
iii. 9	158
iv. 2	152

Mand.
i. 1-2	161
ii	158
iii. 1-2	158
vi. 2	160
vi. 2.1	160
vi. 2.9	160
vii	161
vii. 2	162
ix	158
x. 1.2	161
x. 2.4	161
xi	158
xi. 1	154
xi. 7	155
xi. 9	153
xii. 5.6	158

Sim.
v. 4	158
v. 7	155
viii. 6	158
ix	156, 162
ix. 12	157
ix. 16.4-6	80
ix. 17	157
ix. 22	155
ix. 24.2	162
ix. 28	152
x. 1	152

EPISTLE TO DIOGNETUS

i	172, 173
i-x	165-73
ii	173
ii. 2	168
iii. 5	166
iv. 1	168
iv. 1-6	166
vi. 3	170
vi. 5	170
vii. 2	170
vii. 4-5	170
vii. 6	171
vii. 6-7	172
ix	173
ix. 1	170
x	165
x. 1	171
x. 2	170
x. 3	170
xi	165
xi. 1	165, 167
xi. 2	167, 170, 171
xi. 4	170
xi. 4-5	167
xi. 5	167, 173
xi. 5-6	171
xi. 6	166, 167, 169
xi. 8	173
xi-xii	165-171
xii. 4	168
xii. 5	166, 169
xii. 7	170
xii. 9	73, 167, 173

PAPIAS

Fr.
i. 4	1
xiii. 2	1

177